THE
THREAT

Revealing

the Secret Alien

Agenda

DAVID M. JACOBS, PH.D.

A Fireside Book
Published by Simon & Schuster

FIRESIDE
Rockefeller Center
1230 Avenue of the Americas
New York, NY 10020

First Fireside Edition 1999

FIRESIDE and colophon are registered
trademarks of Simon & Schuster Inc.

Manufactured in the United States of America

3   5   7   9   10   8   6   4   2

The Library of Congress has cataloged the
Simon & Schuster edition as follows:
Jacobs, David Michael.
The threat: the secret alien agenda /
David M. Jacobs.
p.   cm.
Includes index.
1. Human-alien encounters—United States.
2. Alien abduction—United States.
I. Title.
BF2050.J33   1998
001.942—dc21   97-27040   CIP
ISBN 978-0-684-84813-6
ISBN 0-684-84813-9 (Pbk)

To Evan and Alexander

Contents

The Threat

1

Recognizing
the Signal

In the 1996 blockbuster motion picture *Independence Day,* hostile aliens come to Earth hell-bent on death and destruction. Resourceful humans band together, defeat the common enemy, and save Earth. This Hollywood scenario is not new—it has dominated screen versions of alien contact since 1951 with the release of *The Thing,* in which a single alien wreaks havoc on a group of humans.

A more peaceful version of alien contact has also become a cultural staple. From 1951 and *The Day the Earth Stood Still* to 1977 and *Close Encounters of the Third Kind,* benign aliens have come to Earth to help humans. In this scenario, the aliens offer world leaders, scientists, and media representatives their assistance and cooperation. There is mutual respect: The humans expect to learn from the aliens' technological advancement, and the aliens expect to help the humans live in peace and cooperatively build a better world.

Still another vision of alien intervention in human life is the idea that they are coming to save specially chosen individuals from a rapidly approaching cataclysm. Cult groups who believe this have existed since the early 1950s.[1] Members of the Heaven's Gate cult in 1997 were so convinced that a UFO would save them from the apocalypse and carry them to a higher physical and spiritual realm that thirty-nine members committed suicide to facilitate their rescue and transportation.

A careful examination of the UFO abduction phenomenon shows us that contact has, in fact, occurred—but it bears no relationship to these scenarios. There has been no public meeting, no involvement of leadership, no press coverage. There has, as yet, been no assistance, no cooperation, no war, no death, and no apocalypse. The contact has been on the aliens' terms—and in secret.

I never imagined such a scenario in 1966 when I first started to study the UFO phenomenon. Nor did I imagine that I would spend so many years of my adult life involved with the subject. I never imagined that I would have to tell my children not to talk about my research at their school because they could be unmercifully teased. I never dreamed that my wife would learn not to mention my interests at her workplace because her employer might think she was married to a madman, and that could hurt her career. When I talk about the subject to my colleagues in the academic community, I know they think that my intellectual abilities are seriously impaired. I find myself intertwined with a subject that I have learned to dislike and even to fear.

I am first and foremost a professor of history specializing in twentieth-century America. I think, read, and teach about the past, but the study of the UFO phenomenon has thrust me into speculation about the future. The study of history proves that predicting events is an extremely unreliable and usually futile task. Yet, ironically, I now find myself in the uncomfortable position of trying to divine the future.

My research began in one of the leading bastions of historical inquiry—the Department of History at the University of Wisconsin, where I was a graduate student. My major professor was the legendary Merle Curti, who founded the field of intellectual history. When Curti retired, I studied under Paul Conkin, who applied stringent analytical procedures and evidentiary criteria to every research topic. I immersed myself in the study of UFOs and received my Ph.D. under Conkin's direction. My doctoral dissertation focused on the controversy over unidentified flying objects in America from the perspective of intellectual, social, and military history. In researching this topic, I spent weeks at Maxwell Air Force Base and the Library of Congress, reading government documents about UFOs. I traveled the country to interview some of the most important civilian and military UFO researchers. In 1975, Indiana University Press published an expanded version of my dissertation as *The UFO Controversy in America*.[2]

My early research concentrated on sightings of UFOs. My working hypothesis was that if careful analysis of the sightings showed that UFOs were extraterrestrial, it would be the most important scientific discovery of all time. On the other hand, if analysis concluded that the objects were simply misidentification of conventional phenomena and the products of overwrought human imagination, the phenomenon would be relegated to the history of popular culture. It was one or the other. To conceive of UFOs as representing a potential alien takeover was to be either impossibly prescient or foolish. I was neither.

Thus, I joined the other researchers whose objective it was to determine if witnesses were sighting anomalous, artificially constructed, and intelligently controlled vehicles. We scrutinized photos, motion picture footage, radar traces, soil samples, and other residue purportedly generated by UFOs. Collectively we amassed hundreds of thousands of sighting reports from around the world. We worked out a methodology to determine if witnesses were credible. I became a field investigator for the now defunct Aerial Phenomena Research Organization, interviewing puzzled witnesses, knocking on doors searching for others, and publishing the results of my investigations in UFO journals.

By the early 1970s, the UFO research community had collected so many sighting reports that we found ourselves with an uncomfortably huge database. We knew the time of a UFO sighting, its duration, movements, color changes, and number of witnesses, as well as the object's effects upon the environment, automobiles, electrical equipment, animals, and humans. Each of these reports were carefully investigated and documented; in many cases, there were multiple witnesses to lend credence to the evidence. The leading UFO researcher of his time, J. Allen Hynek, called this enormous body of information and reports an "embarrassment of riches."

Of course, there were internal debates over specific cases and fierce arguments with debunkers, but these could not discredit the legitimacy of the phenomenon. By the late 1970s, the evidence for UFOs as a truly anomalous phenomenon was so massive that I, along with most UFO researchers, could no longer deny that witnesses were seeing something extraordinary and probably not from Earth.

As part of our research, we of course thought about the ramifications of contact between humans and alien species. We theorized about how such contact might affect religion, government institutions, and the place of humans in the universe, but we devoted little thought to whether direct contact was already taking place, or whether the UFO occupants had hostile intentions. There seemed to be little reason to think along those lines. The UFOs behaved as if they wanted to keep their distance from us. They avoided contact on a formal level. They were not making mass landings. They would fly about for a few seconds or minutes and then vanish. Their apparent "shyness" suggested neutrality, or at least nonhostility, toward humans.

Nevertheless, curiosity and questions about the motivation of the aliens remained just beneath the surface of UFO research. But because there was so little information, most researchers did not spend a lot of time in useless speculation. And the more we learned about the occupants of UFOs, the more difficult it was to understand their motivation. The UFO and occupant reports that began to increase in number in the 1960s and 1970s were truly bizarre. The objects chased cars, disappeared in midair, and left marks on people; they operated in secret for no apparent reason. Witnesses sometimes said that they saw UFO "occupants" outside the UFOs. Occasionally they reported coming across humanoids (the word "alien" being too dramatic and fringy) near a landed UFO who would paralyze the hapless humans and then inspect them. The humanoids were also seen "repairing" a UFO or digging in the ground; sometimes they appeared to be looking over the terrain, or collecting plants. Some of the occupants' activity was consistent with the hypothesis that they were curious about earthly flora and fauna. At other times they engaged in more baffling behavior. For example, they would pay no attention to a witness, or they would suddenly appear holding a small box in front of a witness and then disappear.

The accounts of these activities were a challenge to researchers who tried to make sense of them. Our mindset was not, however, that the humanoids had any hostile intentions—in fact, they appeared to be examining, surveying, and gaining knowledge.

When abductions were first reported, as in 1961 with the Barney and Betty Hill case, they seemed to fit into the hypothesis that the aliens were primarily curious. Yet, although Barney and Betty Hill were not typical of the notorious 1950s "contactee" charlatans who tried to make money off their tall tales, one could never be sure whether they had invented their story.

As other abduction reports surfaced, UFO researchers were suspicious about the possibility of fabrication. It was easy for me to be skeptical. Most abductees had little to present in the way of evidence for the reality of their experiences. Unlike some UFO sighters, they had no photos, no radar traces, no movies, and usually no other witnesses. Their accounts were hypnotically retrieved, which was an obvious impediment to believability.

Because of the extreme nature of the abductees' claims, I stood on the sidelines while our knowledge about the phenomenon began to mount. The Barney and Betty Hill case was typical. They encountered the now "standard" gray aliens who communicated telepathically, gave the Hills an "examination," and seemed interested in human reproduction. Afterward, the Hills experienced a form of amnesia, and their memories of the incident had to be recovered with the use of hypnosis. The Hill case was serialized in a major weekly magazine, was the subject of a best-selling book, and became the best-known abduction case in history.[3]

There was an even earlier abduction, which happened to Antonio Villas Boas in Brazil in 1957. Villas Boas, who was home for vacation from college, was abducted while riding a tractor on his father's ranch. He was made to have sexual intercourse with a strange but almost-human-looking female. This case was too embarrassing and bizarre for researchers to take seriously, and it was not published until 1966, the same year the public learned about the Hills.

Only a few other cases came to light during the mid-1960s and early 1970s. One was the Pascagoula case of 1973, in which two men said they were abducted as they fished on the banks of the Pascagoula River in Mississippi. During the abduction, aliens "floated" them into an object and a football-shaped machine was passed over their bodies as if it were examining them. The two men seemed traumatized by the event, and one did not talk about it in public for many years.

Another case occurred in 1975. Travis Walton was abducted and physically missing from his normal environment for five days. Moments before his abduction, six witnesses had seen Walton knocked over by a ball of light emanating from a UFO. The witnesses fled in panic, and when they returned a short time later, Walton was gone.

I read about these abductions and was not impressed. Debunkers had stated (incorrectly) that Walton had wanted to be abducted, making the entire event suspicious. Furthermore, the Pascagoula aliens did not match the descriptions given by other abductees. In 1976, I confidently, and erroneously, told J. Allen Hynek that I thought the highly publicized Pascagoula and Travis Walton cases were most probably hoaxes because they did not seem to fit our knowledge of the phenomenon. Besides, they just did not *feel* right. I thought the chances that these cases were hoaxes far outweighed the chances that the claimants were actually kidnapped by aliens from another planet.

In 1976, I interviewed Betty Hill, who told me something that had been kept out of public accounts—the beings had taken a sperm sample from Barney. I found this fascinating. It not only reinforced the rising number of accounts of alien interest in reproduction, but if the Hills' story had been psychologically generated, why concoct something with the express intention of not telling it to anyone? In my mind, the abduction mystery was deepening and becoming more complex. However, I still concentrated on the sightings paradigm in which I had become fairly expert. Sightings, although still considered illegitimate by the general public, were safe and comfortable. The growing number of credible witnesses, radar contacts, photos, films, and physical effects gave us a solid evidentiary base on which to rely. Abductions, in spite of my interest, still lacked the evidence that I required for believability.

I was skeptical of veteran UFO researcher Ray Fowler's 1979 study of abductee Betty Andreasson. The case demonstrated that the aliens could mentally control people from a distance: They "switched off"—rendered unconscious or immobile—people who were in Andreasson's house while they abducted her and her daughter. This case also illustrated a physical manipulation of matter that, according to other reports, the aliens routinely performed. They came directly through the wall of the house to accomplish the abduction. And, during the abduction, Betty Andreasson saw puzzling and inexplicable images of strange places and bizarre animals. But I remained doubtful and believed that the images she saw, and perhaps the entire abduction, were generated from her mind.[4]

By 1980, most of the abduction accounts were beginning to display patterns of similarity: paralysis, physical examinations, telepathy, amnesia, and little gray beings with large black eyes. Many of these reports told of a continued alien interest in human reproduction. I had read some of the abduction literature, but I was not persuaded to give up my focus on sightings. The abductees could be lying, or they could have serious psychological problems.

Then, in 1981 Budd Hopkins published *Missing Time,* a study in which he examined seven abductees and found that a person could be taken many times during the course of his or her life and might have "screen memories" that masked other abduction events. Hopkins discovered telltale scars on abductees, which they incurred during the abduction, and his work confirmed the beings' interest in reproduction. His book gave UFO researchers the first systematic comparison of abductee experiences and showed that the phenomenon could be studied on a society-wide basis.[5]

A year later, in 1982, Tracey Tormé, a mutual friend of Budd Hopkins's and mine, brought the two of us together. I visited Hopkins at his vacation home on Cape Cod and learned more about what he was doing. I noted how cautious and conservative he was. He had been developing patterns in his research that were hard to ignore. The abductees he worked with were serious, sober people genuinely concerned about what had happened to them. I became intrigued.

After my meetings with Hopkins, I called Hynek and told him that I thought Hopkins was on to something important. Hynek warned me to stay away from the abduction cases because they were eccentric and led us off the main path of sighting analysis. I disagreed and told him that I thought Hopkins's research seemed solid. Hynek reiterated his warning, trying to steer me back to the "correct" course of research. Abduction reports were too bizarre for him; he could not subject them to the kind of scientific analysis that he could use for sighting reports.

Although I had adopted a stance similar to Hynek's for over fifteen years, this time I had to follow the evidence. I had begun to understand that if abductions were actually happening, they could be the key to the UFO mystery because they allowed us to enter inside the UFOs. They gave us knowledge that examining the outsides of the objects had never provided. I decided that I would begin to study these cases myself so that I could carefully weigh the evidence. To do this research, I would have to learn hypnosis.

I conducted my first hypnotic regression in August 1986. By 1992 I had conducted more than three hundred hypnotic regressions and had discovered that analyzing abductee accounts was not easy. Asking the right questions and separating reality from fantasy was difficult and even treacherous; false memories and confabulation could lead researchers and abductees into a never-never land of wishful thinking and fantasy.

In 1992, I published the first segment of my research results as *Secret Life: Firsthand Accounts of UFO Abductions*. In it I delineated the structure of a typical abduction and the variety of mental procedures performed on abductees. I also described a multiplicity of hitherto unknown physical and reproductive procedures and was able to re-create minute-by-minute a typical abduction experience from beginning to end.[6]

From my research, I could add to Hopkins's findings on the aliens' reproductive procedures of ova harvesting and fetal extraction. We both found that the aliens required abductees to interact physically with odd-looking babies and toddlers, whom the abductees generally said resembled a combination of human and alien—hybrids. By uncovering these elements of the abduction phenomenon, Hopkins discovered one of the central aspects of why the beings are here.[7] Having analyzed my own research on the aliens' reproductive procedures, I knew when they were taking eggs or sperm. I could identify when a fetus was extracted or implanted in an abductee. To all appearances, the aliens were engaged in some sort of breeding program. But the ultimate reasons for their physical and reproductive procedures remained a mystery.

The mental procedures were even more baffling. Aliens almost always stared into an abductee's eyes at a distance of a few inches or less and seemed thereby to elicit love, fear, and anger. Some of these "Mindscan" procedures could provoke intense sexual arousal in both men and women. By staring into people's eyes, the beings could cause them to see prearranged scenarios and "movies" in their minds. At that time I had no idea how and why this took place. Now I think I understand why.

I was also puzzled about why abductees were subjected to strange *staging* and *testing* procedures in which they acted out a scenario with aliens or found that they could operate complex devices or perform tasks they do not remember having learned. These procedures seemed unrelated to the breeding program.

The aliens themselves were enigmatic. I did not know whether they ate or slept, or had any kind of life outside the abduction context. The same was true of the hybrid babies, toddlers, adolescents, and adults; their lives were a mystery. One thing was certain—the aliens were engaging in a tremendous number of abductions. A national poll by the Roper Organization in 1991 revealed the possibility of an abduction program far more extensive than we had ever imagined.

Our continuing UFO research raised many other questions. For example, abduction researcher Karla Turner reported in 1993 that some abductees claimed the American military was abducting them in cooperation with the aliens.[8] In 1994 Harvard professor John Mack discussed what was apparently an alien interest in the earth's environment.[9] Abductees increasingly claimed that hybrid adults were involved with their abductions. Budd Hopkins found that aliens were pairing young abductees for long-term relationships.[10] To complicate matters, although the abduction phenomenon was traumatic for most abductees, many found spiritual enlightenment and an expansion of their consciousness.

As if these issues were not complex enough, until recently I did not have even provisional answers to the most important questions: What is the purpose of the breeding program? What constitutes alien authority and society? Why are they operating in secrecy? What is the magnitude of the abduction program? What is the purpose of hybridization? For the first twenty years of my research, I thought that we would never have the answers to the fundamental questions of alien motivation and intentions. All that has changed now. In the past ten years, I have gathered information that I feel certain answers these questions satisfactorily.

In my most recent research, I have uncovered information that allows UFO researchers to solve the UFO mystery—at least the questions that will have the greatest impact upon us. I have put many pieces of the puzzle together. I have focused the picture, and I do not like what I see. For the first time in over thirty years of researching the UFO phenomenon, I am frightened of it. Understanding has not led to a feeling of contribution or accomplishment. Rather, it has led to profound apprehension for the future. The abduction phenomenon is far more ominous than I had thought. Optimism is not the appropriate response to the evidence, all of which strongly suggests that the alien agenda is primarily beneficial for them and not for us. I know why the aliens are here—and what the human consequences will be if their mission is successful.

"I Know This Sounds Crazy, But..."

It is the abductees themselves who have the answers to questions about alien intentions. But it is not easy for them to speak about their abduction experiences. They have learned to remain silent. As a child, for example, an abductee may have told her mother and father about the little "people" in her room who came through the closed windows and took her away. Her parents probably reassured her that this was only a dream, and the child's insistence that it was real—"I was *awake!*"—did no good. Eventually the abductee stopped telling her parents.

In school, she may have confided in a friend and talked about seeing ghosts, perhaps aliens, in her bedroom. The friend may have held the secret for a short time, but it was not long before all the other children knew and the teasing grew mean and merciless. The abductee learned to tell no one else.

As an adult, she probably kept quiet about her experiences. If she told anyone, it was within a protective, humorous context that allowed her to have a good-natured laugh—usually accompanied by the vocalized "woo-WOO-woo" of 1950s science fiction theremin music. But she secretly wished someone would say, "You know, that happened to me, too!"

When she married, she did not tell her husband about her experiences and continued to keep them secret. She did not want him to think she was crazy, and she knew he would not accept the reality of the story and be supportive. Thus, most abductees learn over the course of their lives that the best method of protecting themselves against ridicule and further victimization is to tell no one. They live their lives harboring their secrets and hiding their fears.

Contacting an abduction researcher like me is an act of bravery. People who suspect that something unusual is happening to them begin their letters with plaintive phrases: "I know this sounds crazy, but . . ." or "I know you'll laugh when you read this," or "I've written this letter a hundred times in my mind." They desperately want someone to believe them, but they know they are telling an inherently unbelievable story and opening themselves up to more ridicule. Most abductees come to me with the basic question, "What has been happening to me?" Some have a specific triggering incident that has propelled them to contact me: "In 1979 my boyfriend and I saw a UFO close up and it swooped down low toward us. All I remember was running, and then we found ourselves in our car and it was six hours later. I have thought about this incident every day of my life since then."

During the subsequent hypnotic sessions with me, the abductees recall events that can be profoundly disturbing, bizarre, and frightening. When asked if they would undergo hypnosis and relive their experiences if they had a choice to do so all over again, they are often ambivalent. While most say yes and some are uncertain, a few say no—they would rather not know what has been happening to them. They all realize that they have traded one set of problems for another. They have been freed from constantly wondering about what has been happening to them, but now that they know, they are scared. Most acknowledge that becoming aware of their plight transforms them psychologically. They feel more integrated, less confused about their situation, and emotionally stronger. They also feel frightened and powerless in the face of unwelcome sudden physical intrusions into their lives.

I approach abductees individually in search of some new and perhaps revealing information about the phenomenon, although nearly all contribute confirmatory information. For example, in over 700 abduction investigations I have conducted using hypnosis, I have been told of egg-taking procedures almost 150 times, physical examinations about 400 times, Mindscan (staring) procedures about 375 times, and baby and toddler contact 180 times. Some experiences I have heard only occasionally. If I hear anything only once, and I am not yet certain of the thoroughness and veracity of the person who is telling it to me, I withhold a conclusion pending confirmation from other abductees.

Virtually everything I will describe in later chapters has been confirmed many times over. I have interviewed abductees from North and South America, Europe, Africa, and Asia. I have used transcripts of the hypnotic sessions I have conducted with over thirty of the 110 individuals in my population. They come from all walks of life, cutting across ethnic, racial, educational, cultural, economic, political, and geographical boundaries. Brief descriptions of a few of these brave people indicate the broad human dimension of the abduction phenomenon.

Allison Reed was twenty-eight when she called me in June of 1993. She and her husband operated a successful home-based business. She reached me while my family and I were on vacation on Long Beach Island, New Jersey. She was worried about odd things that had been happening to her throughout her life. She had learned to cope with them silently, but now her eight-year-old son and five-year-old daughter had been telling her of strange and frightening things happening to them, too. She grew increasingly alarmed as her children's descriptions of their experiences seemed to be confirmed by physical marks on their bodies.

When her children independently drew pictures of what was happening to them, Allison decided to act. First she came across amateur UFO buffs who were convinced that the government was covering up a UFO crash on the East Coast. Eventually she found me. I do not work with children because we do not understand the effect that knowledge of an abduction experience might have on their psychological development. But I agreed to look into Allison's strange experiences. When Allison found that she, too, was involved with abductions, she became fiercely determined to find out as much as possible in order to do something to stop this threat to herself and her family. The accounts she gave in her regression sessions were as precise as any I have ever heard. We uncovered abductions that ranged from neutral and procedural to traumatic and even physically harmful. It was not until we had had sixteen sessions together that she told me about an event that had happened to her, her husband, and her ten-month-old baby in 1986. The event took place over a five-day period. Together we examined it in meticulous detail over the next eight sessions.

Allison has become resigned to being involved in the abduction phenomenon. She has tried to prevent the abductions by using a video camera, which is trained on her all night, but with only limited success. She, like all abductees, has sought to find a psychological accommodation with the abductions so that she can get on with her life without having to think continually about what is happening to her and her family.

I first saw *Christine Kennedy* in 1992. A woman of twenty-nine with three children, she had had a lifetime of unusual experiences, "dreams," and episodes. As a young girl, she had used alcohol to block out her "night terrors." She had been in recovery and sober for a number of years before she saw me, and she continued to go to recovery meetings. Christine often woke up with bruises on her body. When she was six years old, she woke up and "knew" about sexual intercourse. She had seen UFOs; she had seen beings in her room. When she was pregnant with her first child, she remembered arguing with someone that the baby was "hers" and not "theirs." She had read an article about me in *OMNI* magazine and sought me out.

Like Allison, Christine resisted her abductors. She never surrendered to what was happening to her and tried to fight back as best she could whenever she could. She eventually used video and magnetic equipment in her room to try to detect the presence of aliens and to try (vainly) to deter them from taking her and her children. She hates the beings and has tried but failed to protect herself from them.[1]

Pam Martin has led an even more unusual life. She was born in 1944 and lived for a few years in an orphanage. She grew up in New Jersey living a marginal and nonconformist existence for many years. An eighth-grade dropout, she was basically self-taught with talent in both writing and art. As a young woman, she worked as a "taxi dancer," a waitress, a truck driver, and later a home health-care worker.

As a result of her UFO experiences, Pam had come to believe over the years that she was leading a "charmed" life with "guardian angels" helping her overcome life's difficulties. She became a devoted member of a "New Age" ministry. After one particularly vivid abduction experience, she decided that aliens were actually wonderful beings visiting her from the Pleiades constellation. She felt certain that she had been given "powers" that enabled her to manipulate time and reality to her benefit. For example, when she drove somewhere, she would sometimes arrive there much earlier than she should have.

I have had over thirty sessions with Pam, and during that time she has come to have a less romantic idea about what has been happening to her. She was initially disappointed that what she remembered under hypnosis were not the pleasant experiences she had imagined, but she now accepts the reality of what has been happening to her. She realizes that neither guardian angels nor the Pleiades have anything to do with her experiences, and that she cannot manipulate time and reality. Now she wants to be able to confront the beings without fear and force them to answer questions about their activities. Her husband has been supportive and feels that he also might be an abductee, although he does not want to look into his experiences.

Claudia Negrón was born in Puerto Rico in 1941 and came to the mainland when she was six years old. She raised two children as a single mother after her divorce in the mid-1970s. At the age of thirty-two, she began college. She has graduated and now works as an executive secretary. Fascinated by the UFO phenomenon as an adult, she joined a local UFO group. She has had a lifetime filled with abductions and has become sensitized to their occurrence. When the particulars of her abductions were revealed under hypnosis, she wanted to learn as much as possible about them. Yet she is ambivalent. As much as she feels intensely curious about the phenomenon, she wants it to stop.

Susan Steiner was born in New York in 1950, graduated college, and began her career as a photography technician at a New York studio. She married in 1987 and has since begun her own marketing consulting business. At first, Susan was extremely skeptical about what was happening to her. Like many abductees, she had developed alternative explanations for her lifelong experiences, but she had a major triggering event in 1985 that eventually propelled her to seek me out. She and a friend were on a camping trip and saw a UFO close up. A period of fear and confusion followed, and when it was over she could not account for several hours of missing time. She thought about that incident continually for years before finally coming to me for hypnosis. She has decided that her husband would not be supportive if she told him she is an abductee.

Terry Matthews wrote to me about her unusual experiences in October 1994. She was born in a small town in Pennsylvania and grew up in an upper-middle-class family with an abusive father. She assumed that her lifetime of unusual dreams and experiences was in some way related to her father's actions. This was seemingly confirmed by a therapist who, during hypnosis, uncovered "repressed memories" of abuse, both emotional and sexual. She became convinced that she had been sexually abused and underwent years of therapy for it. Always emotionally "grounded," she angrily broke off with one therapist when he began to introduce ideas about her "past lives." Even though she is a very religious person, it was difficult for Terry to associate her unusual experiences that seemed unconnected to her father with religious visitations. She found an outlet for her inner turmoil in creative writing, and when I met her she was seeking a publisher for her novels.

As the daughter of a clergyman, *Michelle Peters* thought that some of her experiences were religious in nature. Like Terry, she copes with her memories by writing about them and is the author of an unpublished novel. Possessed of a charming, self-deprecating sense of humor, she never felt victimized by the phenomenon. Like Pam Martin, she had a strong sense that she was being visited by a "guardian angel." She thought that the visitations had stopped when she married at age twenty in 1982. But when she was thirty-two, she woke up in the middle of the night to see bright blue lights coming into her house from the outside. She tried to wake her husband but could not. She walked into the living room and looked out the window, but the light was too bright to make out details. The next thing she knew, she was awake the next morning feeling sick; her nightgown was off, and her robe was on backward. This frightening event compelled her to find the origin of her experiences.

Reshma Kamal was born in India and moved with her family to Minneapolis when she was a young girl. She eventually married a man from India and proudly maintains a traditional Indian household. When she realized as a teenager that bizarre things were happening to her, she embarked on a quest to discover their origin. Her mother took her back to India, thinking that traditional healers might rid her of these experiences, but Reshma found their attitude infuriatingly naive. The village doctor and other friends of the family decided that she was fabricating these experiences to attract attention to herself because she wanted to get married. Years later, Reshma's desire to understand her experiences grew stronger as she realized that they were also happening to her five children. She consciously remembered many details and, through the years, kept a detailed journal. Her husband is extremely supportive of her and their children's plight but, as with other abductees, the family has felt powerless to stop it.

I met *Kathleen Morrison* when she sat in on my "UFOs and American Society" course at Temple University. She had returned to college after a long absence to receive her doctorate. As the course material turned toward the abduction phenomenon, she became uncomfortable and could no longer attend my class. She told me that a few years earlier she gone to a play that contained a scene in which an actor seemed to be floating in air. The scene triggered vague memories that caused her to panic, and she became so frightened that she had to escape to the lobby. There she hung on to a banister to steady herself while hyperventilating with raw fear. We eventually had twenty-six sessions together, during which she learned the reason for her fear response as she became aware of the many alien intrusions into her life. Despite her marriage of twenty years, she has not told her husband, fearing that the sexual aspects of the abductions would be too difficult for him to handle.

Jack Thernstrom was a graduate student studying for his Ph.D. in physics at an Ivy League university. He came to me to examine puzzling events in his life, some of which he had at first interpreted to be of a religious nature. He also had confusing and disturbing memories of being in the basement and seeing a small being "coming out of a radio," of "snakes" following him, and of being "molested" in the woods. His hypnotic sessions were difficult. He would clench his teeth, tighten his muscles, and literally shake violently with anxiety during each session. After ten sessions he suddenly felt strongly that he should not be telling me about his experiences because it was a violation of some sort. He discontinued hypnosis, although he still comes to my support group meetings.

Both Budd Hopkins and I have worked with *Kay Summers*. She is thirty-one, lives in the Midwest, and has had perhaps more hypnosis sessions than anyone else. She has experienced the full range of abduction procedures, but hers have been more violent than most. Although she has often suffered a series of physical injuries in her abductions, including, upon two occasions, broken bones, her resolve in the face of adversity is extraordinary. She insists on leading a normal life and refuses to give in to the depression that she often feels. Her parents are hostile to the reality of the phenomenon and give her no support, and she has not told the man with whom she lives for fear of alienating him. Because of her predicament, Kay leads an emotionally isolated existence—except for talking to Hopkins and me. She is totally resigned to her lot, and in her more depressed moments she tells me that she wishes the beings would kill her so that she can be free of them once and for all. I do all I can to lift her spirits and channel her depression into more productive areas of resistance. I must admit, however, that depression is a frequent and predictable response to the phenomenon.

All the abductees in this study are united by the desire to understand what has been happening to them. They share the common bond of being involved with a phenomenon that at first they could not understand, then could not believe, and now cannot control.

They are all determined to gain intellectual and emotional mastery over their experiences.

As they have recounted their abductions, they have often described neutral or sometimes even enjoyable experiences. By far, however, the most prevalent type is disturbing and traumatic. I can only listen and encourage them to cope. My responsibility is to be as honest and knowledgeable as possible; amateur—and misleading—speculation can be found anywhere. I help them understand both what has been happening to them and how they can get on with their lives in the face of it. This is all I can do. I know that the only way to help them permanently would be to stop the abductions, and this I cannot do.

During the process of remembering their experiences, many abductees realize their special situation. They are on the front lines of investigating this monumentally important phenomenon. They are the "scouts" who come back and report what they have seen and experienced. As "participant/observers," they have the most important role of all. They bring researchers like me the pieces of the puzzle so that we can put them together. They are not just the victims of abductions, they are also the heroes, without whose accounts we would have no meaningful insight whatsoever into the UFO phenomenon.[2]

3

Shadows of
the Mind

I have received thousands of calls and letters from people who have memories of unusual experiences that have been greatly disturbing to them. They have searched for years in vain to discover the origin of these memories. They think that I might be able to help them. Of course, a person's experiencing unusual events does not necessarily mean he or she is an abductee. I have designed a screening process to eliminate those people who are not serious about their quest (they might merely be on a lark), those who are not emotionally prepared to look into their experiences, and those who have not had, in my estimation, experiences suggesting that they are abductees.

First, I purposely put them through a series of tasks. I require them to fill out a questionnaire about the experiences that propelled them to come forward, and about others that they might not have realized could be part of the abduction phenomenon (for example, "Have you ever seen a ghost?"). I ask them to send the completed questionnaire to me and then to call back. I analyze the questionnaire and decide if their experiences are significant enough to warrant further investigation with hypnosis. When I talk with them again, I try to persuade them not to look into what could be a Pandora's Box. I give them a strong and frank warning about the dangers of going forward with hypnosis and uncovering an abduction event: They might become depressed, they might have sleep disturbances, they might feel emotionally isolated, and so forth. In effect, they could easily be trading one set of problems for another. I urge them to talk over their decision with their loved ones and call me back later. I then send them a pamphlet that reiterates my warnings so that they can make as informed a decision as possible.

About 30 percent of the people who contact me decide not to undergo hypnosis at this point. This is the right decision for them no matter what their reasons. If they do decide to go forward with the process, I give them another verbal warning about the potential dangers and, if they are still willing, we make an appointment for a session. By the time they arrive for their first hypnosis regression, I have typically already spent several hours talking to them, and they are aware of the problems that might result from their regressions. They are also aware that what they remember, if anything, may not necessarily be accurate or even true.

When they finally arrive at my home, we climb the stairs to my third-floor office and talk for an hour or two before we begin hypnosis. We agree about which event in their lives we want to investigate during this session. It might be, for example, a period of missing time, or an incident in which they awoke and found little men standing around their bed. They then lie down on my daycouch and close their eyes, and I begin a simple relaxation induction that allows them to concentrate and focus. At their first session, they are often puzzled because they are not in some "dreamland" or because they feel quite normal. They find that they can argue with me, get up and go to the bathroom, and be completely in control.

I never know what is going to come out of a hypnosis session. If the subject recalls an abduction event—and there are "false alarms," when it seems that an abduction might have taken place but it did not—I begin a series of cautious questions, usually in a conversational style, that organically spring from what they are saying. Some abductees recount their experiences with detachment, as though they were looking back at the past from a present-day standpoint, others relive their memories as if they were the age at which the event took place. Some are calm about what is happening to them, others are so frightened it becomes difficult for them to continue, although I gently help them through the experience. Some remember the events haltingly, as the memories come in spurts and starts. Others have trouble describing their experiences because the memories rush back in a flood. Nearly all abductees recall their experiences with a combination of astonishment, surprise, and familiarity. When they are finished, they remember what happened to them, and we talk about their account for an hour or so. When the abductee leaves my office about five hours have passed.[1]

Even with all my warnings and the preliminary discussions before the first session, about 25 percent stop at this point—usually they are too frightened to go on. For those who continue with me, I conduct as many hypnosis sessions with them as I can. They desperately want to understand what has happened to them and how it has influenced their lives. I have conducted as many as thirty-three sessions with one individual, although the average for all the 110 abductees with whom I have worked is six. I usually do not go over the same event twice.

My style of questioning is not interrogatory. I engage in a give-and-take with the abductee after I am sure that they cannot and will not be led, even inadvertently. I force them to think carefully about the events. I try to give them perspective and the ability to analyze as they remember. Above all, I try to "normalize" them so they can extricate themselves from the unconscious emotional grip the phenomenon often has had them in throughout their lives. I try to give them the strength to untangle themselves from the abductions' psychological effects so that they can get on with their lives without having to constantly think about their situation. I like to get them to the point where they no longer feel the necessity to seek out a hypnotist to understand what has been happening to them.

Hypnosis is easy. As long as a person wants to be hypnotized, anybody can do it. Asking the right questions in the right way, at the right time, and interpreting the answers is where the trouble comes in. The correct dynamic between hypnotist and abductee depends on the amount of knowledge the hypnotist has acquired about the abduction phenomenon, the experience he or she has with hypnosis, and the preconceptions the hypnotist brings to the session. In addition, the hypnotist must help the abductee cope with the sometimes traumatic memories by intervening therapeutically during the session to provide context and reassurance. Thus, a competent hypnotist/researcher must have a professional knowledge of hypnosis, a thorough knowledge of the abduction phenomenon, a familiarity with confabulation and false memories, and skill in therapy. Unfortunately, there are few individuals with those qualifications.

All competent researchers quickly learn that memory is unreliable. It is not unusual for a person to remember details of a "normal" traumatic event inaccurately. Researchers have shown that they can make people remember something that never happened. A casual, but calculated, discussion of an event with a person can instill "memories" in him that have no basis in reality. Through the passage of time, memory also degrades, events blend into one another, and fantasy intrudes upon reality.

I was extremely fortunate to have encountered unreliable memory the very first time I conducted a hypnotic regression session. Melissa Bucknell, a twenty-seven-year-old real estate management employee, and I agreed before the session to investigate an incident that had occurred when she was six years old. She began by describing playing in a field with a friend of hers. She bent over to look at a butterfly, froze in that position, and then found herself being lifted into a hovering UFO. Strange-looking beings removed her clothes and placed her on a table. They conducted a physical examination and, to her embarrassment, did a gynecological procedure as well.

After the examination, a more human-looking alien, whom she called Sanda, led her into a hallway where she met a small alien. Melissa was required to touch the small alien's head and immediately felt love, warmth, and affection emanating from him. Sanda then took her into another room in which a council of several aliens sat around a table. The aliens discussed how bright, strong, and good Melissa was and said she would have the same traits as an adult. After that she was led down a hallway, her clothes were put back on, and she was taken to the field where she had been before.

Later that evening, I listened to the audiotape that I had made of the session. To my horror, I discovered that Melissa had spoken too softly to be picked up by my tape recorder's condenser microphone. The tape had almost nothing on it. I continued to work with Melissa, and three months after our first session, I suggested that we revisit our initial abduction regression, explaining that I had had a problem with the tape recorder.

This time Melissa was less sure about what had happened. She described floating up into the UFO. She remembered the gynecological portion of her examination, which she once again was embarrassed to relate. She talked about how the beings lifted her up off the table, redressed her, and took her back to the field. But to my surprise, she did not relate the hallway encounter with the small gray alien, during which she was required to touch his head and feel his love. The meeting in which the aliens sat around a table and discussed her development was also absent from her new account.

I was perplexed. The first time Melissa had told me about the small alien with great conviction and emotion. Now when I asked her about the encounter, she was not sure that it had ever happened. I then questioned her about the council meeting with the aliens. Melissa thought for a second and said that perhaps this had happened to another abductee with whom she had been friends. She was pretty sure that it had not happened to her.

This experience taught me an invaluable lesson because I realized that, in all sincerity and honesty, abductees might sometimes remember things that were not true. I resolved to work out a strict methodology to ensure vigilance about false memories. As my research progressed and an abductee reported something I had never heard before, I would wait for confirmation by another abductee unaware of the testimony. I carefully questioned every inconsistency, gap, or logical leap. I worked for a complete chronology and tried to obtain a second-by-second recounting of each abduction event, with no skips, no gaps, and no omissions.

I never received, nor did I ever hear of, another report of an abductee who had been required to touch an alien's head and receive loving emotions. I have heard a few reports of aliens sitting behind a "desk" and talking to the abductee, but the circumstances were quite different from Melissa's account. Also, Melissa would never, in our more than thirty abduction sessions, recall a similar event. All this suggested that she might have unconsciously absorbed a memory fragment from her abductee friend and been confused about other details.

Melissa had done me a tremendous favor. She had taught me the dangers of hypnotically recalled testimony. It was a lesson I was grateful to learn, and one that all abduction hypnotists and researchers have to learn.

Normal Event Memory

Normal memory is not well understood. Neurologists know that the human brain registers events and gives them a "priority" code. For example, remembering a crime you witnessed receives a higher priority than remembering who passed you on the street. The brain then organizes the material according to its sensory impact. It first places the visual, auditory, olfactory, and tactile component parts in short-term memory and then, if these are important enough, it stores them in the myriad neurological sites that constitute long-term memory.

The brain has a retrieval system to recall memory in a variety of ways: by thinking about the event; by allowing another event to trigger recall; or by allowing a sight, sound, smell, or touch to facilitate recall. Memory may also reside in one's consciousness without a triggering mechanism, such as difficult-to-forget traumatic events.

Memory is not stored linearly. It is stored in a "relational" database, where various bits of memory are placed in various neurological "slots." The date and time of an event are stored in one slot, location in another, sounds associated with the event in another, color and smells in yet other slots, feelings in another, and so on. Each of these memory fragments can be forgotten. Each can decay and become distorted. Sometimes a person recalls a memory fragment that only makes sense if the person unconsciously creates a scenario, even if it is a fictional scenario, to incorporate it.[2]

Given the complexities of memory, it is to be expected that many critics of the abduction phenomenon argue that abductions are only tricks that the mind plays on people. They point to false memory syndrome, to screen memories, and to media "contamination" to explain abduction accounts. They also attack the use of hypnosis in recalling events on the grounds that it, too, can elicit false memories. Are their objections valid?

False Memory Syndrome

Critics of the abduction phenomenon charge that abductees, often with the encouragement of researchers, unknowingly concoct abduction fantasies. That people can have false memories is beyond doubt. Given certain circumstances, they can, for example, invent complex accounts of sexual and physical abuse. The False Memory Syndrome Foundation in Philadelphia is filled with members who have been unfairly accused of sexual abuse.

False memories of abuse occur when people remember events, usually as children, that did not happen. Nevertheless, the details the victims relate can be extraordinary. They relive their experiences with the emotional impact of real events. Some remember Satanic cults that terrorized them and even killed babies in human sacrifice rituals. When the "victims" are confronted with facts (investigators have not found dead babies; no babies were reported missing at the time and place of the ritual abuse cases), they angrily provide explanations—such as that the mothers themselves were Satanists who gave up their babies for sacrificial purposes and did not report them missing. People can convey false memories with such conviction and sincerity that they have fooled many investigators. Uncovering false memories of sexual abuse can also lead to major emotional upheavals in people's lives. Families are torn apart, siblings are estranged, lawsuits are instituted, innocent people are unjustly accused and even jailed.

Uncovering false memories is usually facilitated by a therapist who is convinced that a client has been sexually abused (or whatever abuse the false memory recounts), even though the client has no memory of it. Through insistent persuasion, the therapist inculcates the idea into his client that all his emotional problems stem from the repression of the memory of some earlier trauma. The therapist might tell the client that if he thinks hard enough, he will remember the traumatic event. Healing can only begin, the therapist says, after the memories begin to flow. Not remembering the trauma means that the victim is in denial, and denial becomes further "proof" of the abuse. Caught in this loop, the victim of an earnest but misguided therapist finds it difficult to break out. Eventually, as in the widely publicized case of Paul Ingram and his daughters, the subject "remembers" the abuse.[3]

There are expert investigators of false memory syndrome, who have had extensive experience with allegations of sexual abuse and are able to detect false memories. However, they have begun to extend their expertise to areas in which, unfortunately, they are not expert. The abduction phenomenon has become an irresistible target.

For example, psychologist and hypnosis specialist Michael Yapko writes, in *Suggestions of Abuse,* that the abduction phenomenon is simply a matter of "the phenomenon of human suggestibility," which causes him "irritation and disbelief."[4] Psychologist and memory expert Elizabeth Loftus, in her book *The Myth of Repressed Memory,* treats abductions as a form of irrationality engaged in by otherwise "sane and intelligent" people.[5] She cites psychologist Michael Nash's assertions that he "successfully treated" a man who claimed that he had a sperm sample taken from him during an abduction. Using hypnosis and other therapeutic techniques, Nash calmed the man and helped him return to his normal routine, but, Nash laments, "He walked out of my office as utterly convinced that he had been abducted as when he had walked in." Loftus agrees with Nash that the power of this man's false memories enabled him to continue to believe his ridiculous story.[6]

Loftus and Nash, along with other critics, are incorrect. Neither they nor any other critics have ever presented evidence that abduction accounts are the products of false memory syndrome (or, for that matter, of any causative factor other than what the abductees have experienced). The reason they have not presented this evidence is that they do not understand the abduction phenomenon. If they did, they would realize that abduction accounts differ from false memory syndrome in five significant areas.

1. In contrast to victims of false memory syndrome, abductees do not recount only childhood experiences. They do, of course, recall abduction events during childhood, because the abduction phenomenon begins in childhood, but they also recall abduction events as adults. In fact, many abduction accounts, unlike false memory accounts, are of very recent events. Of the last 450 abductions that I have investigated, nearly 30 percent happened within the previous thirty days and over 50 percent had occurred within the past year. I have also investigated abduction events that were reported to me only a few hours, or even a few minutes, after they took place.[7]

In 1991, for example, Jason Howard, a schoolteacher, was on his way to my house for an abductee support group meeting. He put on his shoes, which he keeps by the front door. It is the last thing he always does before he leaves his house. Suddenly it was four hours later and Jason was on his bed in his bedroom upstairs. He called me immediately, explaining that he vaguely remembered putting on his shoes and then lying on the couch. When I conducted a hypnotic session on this event, Jason remembered putting on one shoe and then feeling an irresistible urge to lie on the couch. He recalled that small beings appeared in his living room and floated him directly up through the ceiling into a waiting UFO. A series of procedures followed, including sperm sampling and mental envisioning sequences. The aliens returned him to his house, but instead of putting him on the couch, where he was at the beginning of the abduction, they put him on his bed in his upstairs bedroom. When he came to consciousness, he realized that something had happened, and he called me. The immediate reporting of this event does not fit the description of false memory syndrome.

2. In contrast to victims of false memory syndrome, abductees have indirect corroboration of events. For example, I was on the phone with Kay Summers, whose abduction experiences began while we were talking. She described a roaring noise sometimes associated with the beginning of an abduction, and I could hear this noise over the phone. Hypnosis later revealed that soon after she

hung up the phone, she was abducted. False memories do not take shape simultaneously with the occurrence of actual events during which a researcher is an indirect corroborator.

3. In contrast to victims of false memory syndrome, abductees often remember events without the aid of a therapist. They can remember events that happened to them at specific times in their lives. They have always known that the event happened, and they do not need a therapist to reinforce their memories.

4. In contrast to victims of false memory syndrome, abductees are *physically missing* during the event. The abductee is not where he is supposed to be; people who search for him cannot find him. The abductee is usually aware that there is a gap of two or three hours that neither he nor anyone else can account for. Such physical corroboration does not exist in false memory.

5. In contrast to victims of false memory syndrome, abductees can provide independent confirmation of the abduction. Approximately 20 percent of abductions include two or more people who see each other during the abduction event. They sometimes independently report this to the investigator.

In addition, it is important to note that unlike victims of false memory syndrome, abductees do not usually experience disintegration of their personal lives *after* they become aware of their situation. In fact, in many ways the opposite takes place. When abductees undergo competent hypnosis and understand the nature of their memories, they often begin to take intellectual and emotional control over these memories. They feel more confident as they realize that their supposedly inappropriate thoughts and fears over the years (for example, fear of going into the bedroom at night, thoughts about lying on a table in a strange room surrounded by creatures, being unduly frightened of physicians) were appropriate reactions to a powerful, but unknown, stimulus. By remembering the events, abductees seize control of the fears that have plagued them for years and get their lives back in order, even though they know that the abduction phenomenon will not cease. Knowledge of the abduction phenomenon helps them to lead more "integrated" lives, rather than having the powerfully disintegrating effects so common with victims of false memory syndrome.

Screen Memories of Sexual Abuse

Before false memory syndrome came to prominence, therapists assumed that abduction accounts were due to repressed memories of sexual abuse in childhood. They postulated that because the abuse was so traumatic, the victim unconsciously transposed the abuse into an abduction account. To cope with the terror, the person lived with the more "acceptable" trauma of being kidnapped by aliens.

There is no evidence for this explanation. There are no instances on record of an abduction account being a "screen memory" of sexual abuse. In fact, the opposite is true. There is a great deal of evidence that people "remember" being sexually abused when in reality they were victimized by the abduction phenomenon.

Jack Thernstrom remembers walking with his sister in a wooded area behind their house when he was twelve. On the walk Jack met a man wearing "dark glasses" who sexually abused him. He was unclear about the details, but he remembered having his clothes taken off and his genitals exposed. He was unclear about what happened to his sister, but he thought that perhaps she had run away. He never told anybody about the event, and he lived for the next eighteen years with the traumatic memory that he had been subjected to sexual abuse by a stranger. When Jack recounted the episode during hypnotic regression, the man with dark glasses turned out to be an alien, and the incident was a routine abduction event in which Jack underwent a physical examination. He had not been sexually abused. Jack had formed a "memory" of bits and pieces of the event so that, horrible as it might have been, an account of sexual abuse made sense to him.[8]

In another case, "Julie" recalled an event that occurred when she was ten years old. She was at home in the basement bar with her father and three neighbors. She remembered her father holding her hands above her head while the neighbors sexually assaulted her. In hypnotic regression the woman revealed that this had been an abduction event, which began when she was in the basement bar with her father and his friends. The father and two of the neighbors were placed in an immobile and semiconscious state ("switched off") during the event. The aliens took her and one neighbor, Mr. Sylvester, out of the basement and into a UFO. During the abduction event, she was made to visualize scenes of sexual contact between a man and a woman (she thought that perhaps the man was Mr. Sylvester). When the episode was over, the aliens returned her and the neighbor to the bar. She had not been sexually violated on that occasion. Mr. Sylvester, whom she despised for years after, turned out to be as much a victim as she was.[9]

Obviously, not all sexual abuse cases are abduction events. An abductee remembered that she had been sexually assaulted when she was thirteen. She did not remember how she got downstairs into her teenage assailant's basement bedroom, and she was confused about other details. Suspecting that this could be a screen memory for an abduction, we reviewed it under hypnosis. She remembered the boy, how she got downstairs, what happened in the basement, and what happened afterward. She had no memories of seeing aliens, being transported out of the house, or being on board a UFO. She had been sexually assaulted and not abducted.

Media Contamination

Star Trek has, in essence, become part of American consciousness. Millions of people have seen these fictional accounts of humans and aliens, just as many people have seen reports of abductions on television or have read books about them. Society has been so imbued with stories about alien abductions that it is difficult for most people to escape them. A "pure" abduction account is increasingly difficult to obtain.

The problem of media influence on UFO and abduction reports has long plagued UFO researchers. Over the years, investigators have learned to judge each UFO sighting on its own merits, and they have developed a methodology to "separate the signal from the noise." The credibility of the witness, the quality of the information, and the corroborating accounts of other witnesses have all become criteria in evaluating the validity of the report. Researchers now apply this process to abduction reports.

Does media contamination present a significant problem for abduction research? No. Although it does occur from time to time, in fact, most abductees are extremely sensitive to the dangers of cultural influences. When they examine their memories with me, they are acutely conscious of the possibility that they might have "picked up" an incident and incorporated it into their own account. In the first few sessions of hypnosis, self-censorship is so heavy that it becomes a problem. People do not want to say things that make them seem crazy, and they do not want to parrot something back to the researcher that they picked up in society. They will tell me during hypnosis when they think they might have mixed in something from the culture. They are so worried about this contamination that very often I have to tell them to verbalize their memories and not censor themselves.

When abductees tell me what they remember, their accounts usually have a richness of detail that could not have come from media contamination. The mass media disseminate very little solid information about abductions. That abductees remember and describe specific aspects of procedures—details that scores of abductees have described but that have never been published—is extraordinary and strongly militates against cultural influences.

A good example of the lack of media contamination is Whitley Strieber's highly controversial book *Communion,* published in 1987. It was on *The New York Times* best-seller list for thirty-two weeks and in the number-one position for almost five months. Strieber recounts details of his experiences that do not match what most abductees say. He tells about being transported to a dirty anteroom where he sat on a bench amid the clutter. This highly evocative passage in his book was both dramatic and frightening. If media contamination were a problem, I would expect some abductees with whom I have worked and who have read *Communion* to describe a similar situation. That has not occurred. Not one of them has ever said that he sat in a room that was dirty or littered with clothes. Similarly, Strieber's movie, *Communion,* watched by millions of people, had a scene of dancing, fat, blue aliens. Neither I nor my colleagues have ever had a similar report. Despite the apparent paucity of any evidence of media contamination, all researchers must nevertheless be vigilant about it. We may not recognize contamination if the person incorporates it smoothly into his account and it becomes part of his "memories."

Consciously Recalled Events

If abduction accounts are not part of an overall syndrome of subtle and insidious influences on the person's brain, the critics of the phenomenon say that abductees should be able to consciously remember their experiences and to provide investigators with accurate information. In fact, abductees do consciously remember abductions—sometimes fragments, sometimes long sequences, and on some occasions even entire events. Often these accounts are accurate and detailed and closely match those recovered under hypnosis. However, just as often the consciously recalled memories are grossly inaccurate, with distorted details of actual events and "concrete" memories of events that did not take place. Consciously recalled memories can be an amalgam of fragments of an abduction re-created into a logical sequence that does not reflect reality.

An excellent example is the case of Marian Maguire, a woman in her sixties with two grown daughters, who woke up one morning in 1992 and consciously recalled an instance in which she was with her daughter during an abduction years before. She remembered holding hands with her daughter and, along with other people, being "plugged into" a special apparatus on a wall. This is all she consciously recalled, but she was certain that this event happened exactly as she remembered.

I had not heard about abductees being plugged into a wall before. A few weeks later Marian and I explored this event with hypnosis. During the hypnotic regression, Marian found it difficult to remember walking up to the wall, being plugged into it, and becoming unplugged. The more I probed, the less sure she became about what had happened. She realized that the wall contained small black squares. And as she looked at them, I asked her to tell me what she saw beneath them. I expected her to say the wall or the floor. Instead, she said, "Funny hands." The hands were attached to wrists, the wrists to arms, and so on. She then realized that she was staring into an alien's black eyes. She had not been plugged into a wall. She was standing in a room with her daughters and a being came up to her and stared into her eyes. Over time, the black eyes in her mind had transmuted into an "encasing" on a "wall," and her inability to avoid them transformed into being "attached" to them. During hypnosis, the encasing transmuted to "squares." Although there was a real basis for Marian's memory, the details that she consciously recalled had not happened.

Another example is that of Janet Morgan, a single mother with two children, who consciously remembered a bizarre abduction experience. As she was lying on a table, she saw small beings struggling to bring a live alligator into the room. They put the animal on the floor next to her table, turned the reptile on its back, and then took a knife and slit its underside from top to bottom. The unfortunate alligator groaned and looked at Janet in shock. This traumatic memory threw her into a deep and long-lasting depression. At first she did not want to recall the event hypnotically because she was afraid it would bring back details that would deepen her depression. After being continually despondent over this incident for almost a year, Janet bravely decided to confront the memory and try to gain emotional control over it.

In hypnosis, Janet's memory turned out to be part of a complex abduction event in which aliens performed many different procedures upon her. They conducted an examination, took an egg from her, forced her to immerse herself in a pool of liquid, and conducted a Mindscan that elicited profound fear. Then Janet found herself alone in a room, lying on a table, filled with fear and trepidation. The aliens entered from a doorway on Janet's left, pulling the heavy alligator with them, which they placed on the floor next to Janet's table. Staring at it, she began to realize that the animal did not actually look like an alligator; she did not see an alligator's head or legs. In fact, it was a man in a green sleeping bag. When the aliens unzipped the sleeping bag from top to bottom, the man looked up at Janet and groaned. There had been no alligator. The aliens had not slit its belly.[10]

Some of the most common consciously recalled memories are of the first or last few seconds of an abduction when the person is still in a normal environment. Abductees often remember waking up and seeing figures standing by their beds. But instead of remembering aliens, they recall deceased relatives and friends or religious figures. For example, Lily Martinson, a real estate agent, recalled the following incident when she was vacationing with her mother in the Virgin Islands in 1987. Asleep in the hotel room, she woke up to see her deceased brother standing at the foot of her bed; she clearly remembered what he looked like and found this memory comforting and reassuring. When we examined this memory under hypnosis, however, Lily's description of her brother was of a person without clothes, small, thin, no hair, and large eyes. It was not her brother. Although she was disappointed that she had not seen her brother, she was satisfied that she now knew the truth.[11]

Indeed, the aliens have created, perhaps unwittingly, a unique obstacle to learning the truth about abduction events. It is the problem of "instilled memories"—images aliens purposely place in the abductee's mind. During visualization procedures, the aliens might show an abductee a multitude of images: atomic explosions, meteorites striking Earth, the world cracking in half, environmental degradation, ecological disaster, dead people bathed in blood strewn about the landscape, and survivors begging the abductee for help. Or the aliens might show abductees images of Jesus, Mary, or other religious figures. These images have the effect of being so vivid that abductees think the events "really happened" or they "really saw" the religious figure. This can be a problem, especially when the investigator is not familiar with visualization procedures and fails to identify instilled memories. Thus, Betty Andreasson in Ray Fowler's pioneering book, *The Andreasson Affair*, relates a situation in which she "saw" a phoenixlike bird rising from the ashes. It was "real" to her and she reported it as an actual occurrence.[12] I have had people remember figures that looked like Abraham Lincoln wearing a stovepipe hat, men wearing fedoras, angels, devils, and so forth.

Memories Recalled During Hypnosis

The reliability of memory recalled during hypnosis rests not with the subject but with the hypnotist. Improperly used, hypnosis can lead to confusion, confabulation, channeling, and false memories. Unfortunately, there is a great deal of improper use of hypnosis in abduction research. And when abduction events are recovered by a researcher who has little experience or training in proper hypnotic techniques, both the subject and the hypnotist can easily be led to believe that things that did not occur during the abduction actually happened.[13]

Leading the Witness

Skeptics of the abduction phenomenon often accuse researchers who use hypnosis of "leading" people into believing that they have been abducted. Critics say that cultural or psychological factors impel the person to seek out a hypnotist who has an emotional or intellectual stake in that person's actually being an abductee. The subject comes to the hypnotist and a dynamic is set up to talk about abductions. And through subtle cues and direct questioning, the hypnotist pressures the subject into "remembering" an entirely invented abduction account.

"Leading" is a serious problem in abduction research, but not in the way critics contend. When inexperienced or naive hypnotists listen to an abductee's story, they often do not recognize dissociative fantasies, confabulation and false memories, or alien-instilled memories.[14] The result is that the subject leads the naive hypnotist into believing an abduction scenario that did not, in fact, occur.

This type of reverse leading is best exemplified by a hypothetical situation. Suppose an abductee comes to me to talk about his alleged abduction experiences, and under hypnosis he tells me that while on board a UFO, he sat on the floor with the aliens and played a board game that was almost exactly like Monopoly, but the street names were really strange. If I then ask him about the street names, I am in danger of reverse leading. In my more than eleven years of investigating abductions, I have never heard of anyone playing board games and I must be sure that the event happened as described before I delve into it.

Because I know that people will sometimes confabulate, especially in the first few hypnotic sessions, I would immediately suspect in this case that confabulation was at work—although I must always remember that it is possible that the aliens *did* play Monopoly with the abductee. I would probe further to determine whether this event happened. I would look for contradictions or inconsistencies by going over the incident from different temporal perspectives, asking questions that move the abductee forward in time and then back again. I would ask the abductee to describe the sequence of events on a second-by-second basis, searching for slight disjunctures in the account. I would ask whether the aliens were standing or sitting, precisely where they were looking, and exactly what they were looking at. In other words, I would search for the alien visualization procedures that might have instilled this image in the abductee's mind, making him think he had played this game when he had not. If the abductee were inconsistent in his answers, I would regard the incident with skepticism. If he held to his story, at the very least, I would put it in the "pending" file, waiting for another abductee to confirm the same experience independently.

In contrast to the methodology I have just outlined, the naive hypnotist, unaware that he is being led, listens to the Monopoly story and asks, "What were some of the street names?" This question subtly conveys acceptance by the hypnotist, which serves to reinforce the confabulated material as "real" for the abductee. Adding such validation impels the abductee to further confabulation. An unconscious and mild form of dissociation takes place, and the abductee begins to "remember" more events that he is just imagining. (This mental state is akin to "channeling," whereby a person in a self-altered state of consciousness believes that he is receiving communication from an unseen spirit or entity who answers questions or imparts wisdom.) The abductee has unconsciously led the hypnotist and the hypnotist has reciprocated by unwittingly validating the abductee. The two join in mutual confirmation, manufacturing an account that might have a grain of truth but is more fantasy than not.

Mutual Confirmational Fantasies

Doing abduction research is exceptionally difficult—not only because of the nature of the material and how it is recovered, but because the rewards for this work are usually nonexistent. Instead, ridicule and scorn supply the main "honors." I believe that anyone who puts his or her reputation on the line and ventures into this treacherous area deserves the plaudits of all who value the search for the truth. In spite of this, even the most prominent researchers sometimes fall into investigatory traps such as mutual confirmational fantasies.

John Mack, professor of psychiatry at Harvard University and an abduction researcher, provides a good example of mutual confirmational fantasies. A nationally known social critic and Pulitzer Prize winner, Mack became fascinated with the abduction phenomenon in 1990 when he attended a lecture by Budd Hopkins. Mack quickly recognized that the abduction phenomenon was not mentally generated and therefore had an external reality. He bravely undertook a full-scale examination of the phenomenon, to the detriment of his career at Harvard and to the scorn of his colleagues.

In Mack's 1994 book, *Abduction,* he relates a hypnosis session he conducted with "Catherine," in which aliens allegedly showed her images on a screen of a deer, moss, deserts, and other "nature things." Then she saw Egyptian tomb paintings and felt certain that she was watching herself in a former life.

> Then they showed her a picture of tomb paintings with paint flaking off. "But then it switched to me painting it." But in that incarnation she was a man and as she watched this scene [she said] "This makes sense to me . . . this is not a trick. This is useful information. This is not them, pulling a bunch of shit like everything

else." Catherine now felt that her insistence upon a more reciprocal exchange of information had been affirmed.

I then asked Catherine to tell me more about this image of herself as a painter in the tomb of an Egyptian pyramid. In response
to my question she provided a great deal of information . . . about
the man and his methods and his environment. What was striking
was the fact that . . . she was not having a fantasy *about* the
painter. Instead, she was [him] and could "see things from totally
his point of view instead of from one watching it."[15]

Catherine went on to "remember" many details of Egyptian
painting and life. And, later in the session, she told Mack that an
alien had asked her if she understood the meaning of the Egyptian
scene. She then realized that "'everything's connected,' canyons,
deserts, and forests. 'One cannot exist without the other and they
were showing me in a former life to show that I was connected with
that, and I was connected to all these other things.'" Catherine also
appreciated that she was connected to the aliens. Resisting them
only meant that she was struggling against herself, and therefore
there was no reason to fight.

Mack not only accepts the validity of this "dialogue" but embraces Catherine's interpretations of it as well. Rather than treating
the entire episode with extreme caution and skepticism, he does not
question her acceptance of a previous life, her sense of connectedness, her sense that a previous request for reciprocal information
was answered affirmatively, and her decision not to resist.

Catherine also told Mack that "they were trying to get me over
fear, and that's why they were trying to scare me so badly, because
I would eventually get sick of it and get over it and go on to more
important things." Once again Mack accepts the conversation at
face value and asks her "to explain further how scaring her so badly
would get her beyond fear." This is a question that calls for information that is not within the scope of her testimony. Catherine duly
told Mack details of how this worked.[16]

Catherine's narrative contained a past life, "dialogue," alien attempts to help the abductee, an environmental message, and personal growth. For the skilled abduction hypnotist, every aspect of

this narrative should be suspect. Catherine could have easily slipped into a dissociative state in which she regarded internal fantasies as external events happening to her.

If the Egyptian past life imagery happened at all, it might have taken place during an *imaging* sequence and that automatically means that an instilled mental procedure was in process. Sometimes abductees combine imaging procedures, dreams, and fantasies for memories of external reality. Their interpretation of these "memories" is often more dependent upon their personal belief system than on the actual occurrences. Unless properly versed in the problems that these mental procedures can create, the hypnotist can easily fall into the trap of accepting fantasies and confused thinking as reality. Mack displays no skepticism about this story. He admires her "straightforward articulation" of the narrative.

There are other abduction hypnotists who, like John Mack, fall prey to methodological errors. As part of a series of thirteen hypnotic regressions with abductees, clinical psychologist Edith Fiore presents a lengthy transcript of an extraterrestrial event in her 1989 book, *Encounters*. Fiore believes that the act of relating the information—real or imaginary—has therapeutic value, and she is therefore more interested in what the abductees think has happened to them than in what actually occurred.

She describes the hypnotic regression of Dan, who "remembered" being a member of an alien military attack force and destroying enemies on other planets, visiting the planets "Deneb" and "Markel," having drinks with the captain, and other details of a remarkably Earthlike daily life. One day Dan found himself standing in the Cascade Mountains gazing at the trees. It was peaceful and beautiful. It seems that he had taken over the body of a small human child.

Dr. Fiore: And where's your ship?

Dan: I'm a little kid, no ship, no responsibility. Just a nice summer day. Nothing to do. All day to do it. Just exploring.

Dr. Fiore: Now we see you as this little child. I'm going to ask you to make the connection of how you became this child.

Dan: Two different people. The child has all the memories. It's like retirement. You get a chance to do nothing if you live longer. Be at a nice pretty place.

Dr. Fiore: How did you get to be this child. [sic] . . .

Dan: I joined him on that road. Replaced, really.

Dr. Fiore: Now let's go back to when you joined him, and let's see how you got to be on that road.

Dan: Drunk. Horribly, horribly drunk. Good party. Next morning . . . tour the bridge. Say goodbyes.

Dr. Fiore: Then what happens?

Dan: Just me today. One at a time. Pick your planet. Pick an easy one. Everybody's laughing.

Dr. Fiore: You say you were drunk?

Dan: The night before, terrible hangover.

Dr. Fiore: Where did you get drunk. [sic]

Dan: On the ship, officer's mess. . . . Confusion, drinking.

Dr. Fiore: What kind of ship is this?

Dan: Class M. Large. Battlecruiser; fourteen drop ships; 3500 people. Armed to the teeth.[17]

This questioning validated what the subject was saying and subtly acted to confirm its authenticity. Fiore says later that Dan's recollection gave him an "improvement in his self-confidence and a wonderful inner peace of mind." And she believes that each of the experiences her subjects remembered "actually happened very much as they were remembered."[18] Clearly, this scenario in no way fits the abduction scenario as we know it, although there are a few similarities (adult hybrids sometimes wear quasimilitary uniforms).

Rather than focusing on one incident and gathering data carefully and critically, Fiore skips to nine different "encounters" in her first hypnotic regression with Dan—which, in the hands of an inexperienced abduction hypnotist, can lead to a confused and superficial accounting. Furthermore, Dan knows the answer to virtually every factual question that Fiore asks about life on board the military vessel. This omniscient factual assurance is usually a strong indicator of confabulation.

Dr. Fiore: Is there any homosexuality?

Dan: Some.

Dr. Fiore: And how is that seen?

Dan: Tolerated. Not favorably, but tolerated.

Dr. Fiore: Is there any problem with contraception?

Dan: No.

Dr. Fiore: Why is that?

Dan: Medicines, injections.

Dr. Fiore: How often is it given?

Dan: Every tour.[19]

The chances that this is dissociative fantasy are extremely high. In 1989 when Dr. Fiore investigated the case, she might have been better served by instituting a criteria of belief in which she accepted only material that was confirmed by others unaware of previous testimony. But Fiore and Mack were trained as therapists and not as investigators. Their approach to abduction accounts is very different from that of researchers who are more empirically oriented.

It is important to understand that in spite of their methodological problems, Mack and Fiore, like other hypnotists, uncover much of the standard physical and reproductive procedures that make up the core of the abduction experience. However, because of their training, they are not particularly interested in what has happened to the abductee. For Mack, as for many other therapists, investigation into the actual circumstances of a client's experiences is not a primary concern. Finding out exactly what happened to the abductee is less important than what the client *thinks* has happened to him—the account's accuracy or truthfulness is of little concern. As Mack said, "The question of whether hypnosis (or any other nonordinary modality that can help us access realities outside of or beyond the physical world) discloses accurately what literally or factually 'happened' may be inappropriate. A more useful question would be whether the investigative method can yield information that is *consistent* among experiencers, carries emotional *conviction*, and appears to *enlarge* our knowledge of phenomena that are significant for the lives of the experiencers and the larger culture" [italics his].[20]

Thus, when Mack conducts hypnosis, he first explains to his clients that he is "more interested in their integration of their recalled experiences as we go along than in 'getting the story.' The story . . . will take care of itself in due time."[21] The truth or falsity of a person's experiences—the chronology, the procedural logic, and the accurate perceptions of the events—play a secondary role in Mack's methodology. But he states that his "criterion for including or crediting an observation by an abductee is simply whether what has been reported was felt to be real by the experiencer and was communicated sincerely and authentically to me."[22] Facts have a limited role to play in Mack's confrontation with an abduction event.

Fiore has a similar agenda. She states, "Because my main concern is to help people, it is not important to me if the patients/subjects report correctly the color of the aliens' skin, for example. What is important is that the negative effects of encounters be released through regressions."[23]

Mack's and Fiore's dedication to helping abductees is unquestionably appropriate. They deserve praise for their selfless dedication to helping people come to terms with the abduction phenomenon. Therapy should be the first priority for all researchers. But their (and other hypnotists') reluctance to separate fact from fantasy leads to a naive acceptance of accounts that should be treated suspiciously. This shapes their research techniques and leads to validational questioning and mutual confirmational fantasies.

This mutual fantasy—a subtle form of leading—is a far more significant problem for abduction research than just asking leading questions. For example, psychologist Michael Yapko polled a group of therapists to learn how they think memory works. He found that a large number of clinicians are unaware of the problems of memory and believe that hypnosis always reveals the truth.[24] Many researchers have succumbed to the mutual fantasy trap by taking at face value virtually everything an abductee says. Researchers who have New Age agendas perpetuate the problem by uncritically accepting a wide range of "paranormal" accounts. Past lives, future lives, astral travel, spirit appearances, religious visitations—all assume legitimacy even before the believing hypnotist begins abduction research. When the abductee relates stories with false memories, the believing hypnotist is unable to recognize them and is therefore more than willing to take them seriously.

It is easy for inexperienced and naive hypnotists to "believe" because the majority do not have a fact-based knowledge of the abduction phenomenon. Some hypnotists even pride themselves on their lack of knowledge about abductions. They argue that their ignorance gives them a "clean slate" so that their questioning is not encumbered by what they "bring to the table." However, what they bring is their inability to separate fact from fiction. By uncritically accepting (and not challenging), by naively assuming that what is sincerely told is correct, and by defending this as "reality," inexperienced and naive researchers muddy the waters for competent investigators, allow people to think that events have happened to them that have not, and add to the incredulity of the general public.

Abduction Confabulation

Abduction confabulation is a frequent problem, especially in the first few hypnotic sessions. The initial hypnotic session is always the most difficult because it can be very frightening. Many people erroneously think they will blurt out intimate details of their personal lives, or be at the mercy of the "evil" hypnotist. Once the first few sessions are completed, however, the abductee feels more comfortable with the hypnotist and with hypnosis. As a result, his memories become easier to collect and more accurate as well.

Confabulation typically occurs in three characteristic areas.

1. *Physical Appearance of the Aliens.* The most prevalent area of distortion is the description of the physical appearance of the aliens. Many abductees at first maintain that they can see every part of the aliens' bodies except their faces. Some abductees think that the aliens are purposely distorting or limiting the field of view to help prevent the shock of seeing their faces. The evidence does not support this. Because the abduction phenomenon begins in infancy, most abductees have seen the faces of the aliens many times. Once an abductee becomes accustomed to remembering events and less frightened about what he encounters, he usually sees the aliens' faces clearly.

   Also, at first abductees tend to describe the aliens as much taller than they are, not realizing that they are gazing up at the aliens because they are lying on a table. They also describe the aliens as being different colors and having different features. In fact, the majority of aliens are small, gray, and almost featureless except for their large eyes. During competent hypnotic investigation, the abductees recognize their mistakes and correct themselves without the hypnotist's aid or prompting.

2. *Conversation.* Another prevalent area of confabulation is alien dialogue. Although alien conversation has given us our most important insights into the abduction phenomenon's methods and goals, researchers must be extremely cautious.

Abductees report that all communication with the aliens is telepathic, as is communication among the aliens. When asked what "telepathic" means, the abductees usually say they receive an impression that they automatically translate into words. We know that an abductee can receive an impression from his own thoughts, translate it into his words, and think that the words are coming from aliens. Naive researchers often accept alien dialogue at face value, not realizing that all or portions of it could be generated from the abductee's mind. Abductees sometimes slip into a "channeling" mode—in which the abductee "hears" messages from his own mind and thinks they are coming from outside sources—and the researcher fails to catch it. Some researchers have based much of their knowledge on suspect dialogue. Only experienced researchers can separate characteristic alien conversational patterns from confabulated dialogue.

3. *Alien Intentions.* The third area of confabulation is interpreting alien intentions and goals. For example, when asked about the purpose of a specific mechanical device during an abduction, most abductees answer "I don't know." Some, however, supply an answer because it seems reasonable: "This machine takes pictures of my muscles, sort of like an X-ray machine." Unless the investigator firmly and reliably establishes that the aliens told this to the abductee—and that the abductee did not invent the dialogue—the correct assumption is that the abductee does not know what the machine is for and is simply filling in.

The investigator must also be extremely careful with abductee accounts of what the aliens are doing. The aliens rarely describe the reasons for specific procedures, but some abductees routinely supply the reasons. Again, naive therapists and investigators tend to take these accounts at face value.

Some researchers reinvestigate the same material repeatedly in different hypnotic sessions, not realizing that if the account contains unrecognized confabulation and distortion, it can enter into normal memory as "fact." Repeated hypnosis on an event tends to confirm the "fact," and it often becomes impossible to tell what is real and what is not. On the other hand, the more sessions on different events an abductee has with a competent investigator, the greater the likelihood that confabulation will be uncovered and the accurate account will be told.

Competent Hypnosis

An experienced and competent hypnotist tests the suggestibility of people who recall abduction accounts. By asking purposefully misleading questions, he can easily tell whether the subject can be led. For example, in the first hypnotic session, I often ask if a subject can see the "flat, broad" chins of the aliens. I ask if a subject can see the corners of the ceiling; I ask if the aliens are fat. The answer to these questions should be "no" according to all the evidence we have obtained. If the answer is "yes," I allow for the suggestibility of the subject when I evaluate the truthfulness and accuracy of the account.

Researcher John Carpenter of Springfield, Missouri, has fashioned this line of questioning into something of a science. He has developed a list of misleading questions—some obvious and some subtle—that are calculated to place wrong images into abductees' minds. In the first hypnotic session, he poses these questions to the new subject, who almost never answers "yes"; most abductees refuse to be led and nearly always answer misleading questions negatively, directly contradicting or correcting the hypnotist.

The first abduction incident that received widespread publicity, the Barney and Betty Hill case, published in magazine and book form in 1966, is an excellent example of the lack of suggestibility among abductees. Using hypnosis, psychiatrist Benjamin Simon tried to trap the Hills in contradictions and to suggest to them that

they had invented the account. He could never get the two to agree
with him.

Simon: Was that operating room in the hospital blue?

Barney: No, it was bright lights.

Simon: Did you feel that you were going to be operated on?

Barney: No.

Simon: Did you feel that you were being attacked in any way?

Barney: No.[25]

During another session Simon tried again to trip up Barney.

Simon: Just a minute. Didn't Betty tell this to you while you were
asleep?

Barney: No. Betty never told me this. . . .

Simon: Yes, but didn't she tell you that you were taken inside?

Barney: Yes, she did.

Simon: Then she told you everything that was seen inside and
about being stopped by these men?

Barney: No. She did not tell me about being stopped by the men.
She did not have this in her dreams.[26]

At another point, Simon suggested to Barney that the incident
could have been a hallucination. Barney disagreed.

The accuracy of abduction accounts depends, to a large degree,
upon the skill and competence of the hypnotist. Memory is fallible
and there are many influences that prevent its precision. Hypnosis,

properly conducted and cautiously used, can be a useful and accurate tool for uncovering abduction memories. Competent hypnosis can illuminate the origin of false memories and can untangle the web of confusing memories. What emerges are accurate, consistent, richly detailed, corroborated accounts of abductions that unlock their secrets and add to our knowledge of them.

Are Abductions Believable?

With the problems of memory retrieval and memory interpretation, is it possible that the abduction phenomenon is a psychologically generated fantasy? The answer is *no*, due, in part, to the fact that the evidence for the abduction phenomenon is not based solely on memory and hypnotic recounting. There is also physical evidence. When abducted, people are physically missing from their normal environments—police are called, people search for the abductees, parents are distraught.

An indirect example of being physically missing during an abduction occurred when abductee Janet Morgan's younger sister, Beth, came to babysit for her niece, six-year-old Kim, while Janet went out on a date. Both Janet, a single mother working as a legal secretary, and her daughter had had a lifetime of abduction experiences. Beth, who had also experienced suspicious, but uninvestigated events, had babysat for Kim before and was familiar with her routine.

This night Kim was sitting on the couch in the living room watching television, and Beth decided to take a bath, since the child was occupied. She ran the water, got into the tub with a novel, and began to read. A "mental haze" came over her and she sat in the tub with her eyes trained on the same page in the book for over an hour. Suddenly, she snapped out of it, jumped up, and thought, "Kim!" She threw on her clothes and raced downstairs to see if the little girl was all right.

Kim was not on the couch. Beth went into every room of the row house and called for her. She ran back into the living room, looked behind the couch and in the closet. Then she searched through the rooms a second time. Panicking, she ran outside and looked up and down the street, shouting for Kim. The next-door neighbor was outside and asked what the problem was. Beth told him that Kim was missing. The neighbor ran into the house to search for himself and found Kim sleeping on the couch in plain view. Kim had been abducted, Beth had been "switched off," and when she came to consciousness a little too soon, Kim had not yet been returned from the event. Kim was physically gone from the house, and her absence was conspicuous.

Many abductions occur with more than one person, and as further proof, people who have never heard of the abduction phenomenon have been abducted. A worried Allison Reed called to tell me that her panic-stricken children were remembering abduction events without knowing anything about the subject. She and her husband have a history of unusual personal experiences that suggest abduction activity. At the time of Allison's call in June 1993, her son, Brian, was seven years old and her daughter, Heather, was four. Both had drawn pictures of aliens and described how they floated out of their rooms and through the window into a waiting UFO. The children reported details of incidents that are known only to veteran abduction researchers and that they could not have absorbed through the media. For example, Heather told her mother about a conversation between herself and a female alien: "She tried to make me think that she was my mommy, but I knew she was trying to trick me." Heather said this to reassure her mother that she was on to their tricks and knew who her real mother was.

The fact that two people might be abducted together and can verify each other's presence during the abduction is additional proof of the phenomenon. Janet Morgan and her older sister, Karen, have been abducted together many times along with other members of their families. Each can independently remember the abduction and can describe in detail what happened to the other without having spoken about the event.

In spite of all the difficulties in studying the abduction phenomenon, it is finally yielding its secrets. The procedures that the aliens employ are lending themselves to study and analysis. And the reasons for the procedures are both bizarre and terrifying.

4

What They Do

Virtually everything that aliens do is in service to their abduction program. Every seemingly incomprehensible or absurd alien activity has, upon examination, a logical basis. One by one, these actions have begun to lose their mystery and reveal their true purposes.

When researchers first learned about the abduction phenomenon, they generally assumed that, if it was real, its objective was to investigate humans. That was why aliens abducted humans, examined them, and then released them. Because this scenario occurred repeatedly, researchers concluded that the aliens were conducting a long-term study and benignly collecting data. That belief gave the public a comfortable feeling because it suggested a scientific, and therefore nonhostile, intent.

We now know that the abduction phenomenon as a whole is not for the purpose of research. The evidence suggests that all the alien procedures serve a reproductive agenda. And at the heart of the reproductive agenda is the Breeding Program, in which the aliens collect human sperm and eggs, incubate fetuses in human hosts to produce alien-human hybrids, and cause humans to mentally and physically interact with these hybrids for the purposes of their development.

Extrauterine Gestational Units

A significant component of the Breeding Program is the creation and nurturing of *extrauterine gestational units*. It was only after years of research and hundreds of abduction reports that I understood this procedure and the reasons for it.

For years women have been telling researchers about mysterious gynecological procedures that were performed upon them during their abductions. Some women described "pressure," as if the aliens were filling the area around their reproductive organs with air, and their lower abdomens distended giving them a bloated and uncomfortable feeling. The women often said that their organs were being "moved around" or displaced in some way, and they got a sense that the aliens were "enlarging" or creating more space within the uterine cavity or elsewhere in the pelvic area.

Various abductees have described these gynecological procedures in similar ways. Abductee Barbara Archer, in 1988, reported:

And I started to feel pressure. It was like all this pressure.

Is this a diffuse pressure, or a specific pressure?

Inside.

But not [specifically] on the left side, or right, or middle?

Middle, inside. Just getting blown up or something, I was feeling really big. I felt really big.[1]

This type of procedure occurred many times to Lucy Sanders:

It's on my right [pelvic] side. It's making me burn! It's making my insides burn! They're blowing me up! He's pulling it out now, he's patting my leg and saying it's all right, that I should calm down now. Holy Lord!

What do you think they're doing there, or do they say?

I don't know. It hurt, burned. I feel like I'm blown up.

How do you mean?

Blown up.

Like a balloon?

Mm-hmm. Now the feeling is going away, but I feel puffy. He's pushing on my stomach area, pushing it in and moving his fingers, like this.[2]

Laura Mills described a similar procedure:

What do you think he's doing down there?

I really don't know what the heck he's doing.

Okay. If you had to make a wild guess, what do you think he's up to?

I know it sounds silly, but they're trying to figure out how much space I have inside or something.

So they might be measuring, or whatever?

Inside. Like the uterus or something. I'm not sure.[3]

Belinda Simpson experienced the same procedure even though she had undergone a hysterectomy some years before:

It just feels like somebody's rolling something inside me. . . .

Tell me what you . . . sense that they're doing.

I feel like I'm being blown up. . . . My side's being swollen up. It feels like a balloon. This is weird. I feel like somebody's blowing up my side, this is stupid. . . . It's real warm, and my side's blowing up. . . . Something hurts. I feel like I'm pregnant. Something is real hard in my stomach, on the side.[4]

Some abductees have suggested that the introduction of air into their bodies is similar to a laparoscopy, a technique physicians employ for the treatment of endometriosis and other gynecological problems. I suspected that perhaps the bloating meant the aliens were introducing air as part of the procedure for taking eggs. But I decided to put these puzzling cases on the "back burner" and wait for more information to reveal the purpose of the procedures.

It is noteworthy that hysterectomies are common among abductees. During my ten years of abduction research, I have worked with a number of women abductees who have had hysterectomies or suffered from gynecological problems resulting from their abductions. Several women told me that the surgeons who had performed their hysterectomies have commented on the position of their ovaries, which seemed "pushed" to one side or "pressed" toward their fallopian tubes. Some women reported anomalous ovarian scarring, which is consistent with the theory that the aliens sometimes take eggs directly from the ovaries. Other women have reported vaginal scarring for which neither they nor their gynecologists could account. Others have complained of aching, swelling, and general gynecological pain.

Gynecological pain played an important part in an incident with the first abductee I placed under hypnosis. Melissa Bucknell was twenty-seven years old and intermittently sexually active. In hypnotic regressions she had talked about having "implants" placed in her during her abductions. One morning in March 1987, she awoke with gynecological pain so severe that she was having trouble sitting and she told me that she was now certain the aliens had put an "implant" in her. (My own research had shown that implants were usually placed in the nose or an ear.) I immediately took her to a gynecologist, Dr. Daniel Treller, who graciously agreed to see her on an emergency basis.

Treller's examination confirmed that Melissa's pelvic area was very tender and he ordered an ultrasound. The ultrasound team quickly found an anomaly. At the right side of her right ovary, but not touching it, was a mass of some sort. It was small, but looked "organic," and it was not supposed to be there. The bewildered ultrasound team summoned Treller, who was equally baffled. None of them had ever seen anything quite like this before. Suspecting an unusual ectopic pregnancy, Treller ordered a blood test to determine if Melissa was, in fact, pregnant. It was negative.

Melissa, meanwhile, insisted that this mass was an alien "implant" and she did not want to remove it or disturb it in any way. She was extremely stubborn on this point. She did not want to have it touched and she immediately objected to any suggestions to the contrary. Finally, much to Melissa's relief, Treller suggested that she come back in a week to see if the mass had changed or "grown." When we left the hospital, she said that she never wanted to come back, and she did not want the implant disturbed, despite the pain it was causing.

For the next several weeks I tried to persuade Melissa to return for another ultrasound, but she refused. Finally, a month after the initial visit, I successfully prevailed upon her. She underwent another examination and the ultrasound screen showed the space where the mass had been, but the mass was gone. Dr. Treller was puzzled and noted that the problem appeared to be "resolving itself." Melissa was enormously relieved that she would not have to face having the mass removed. Her case remained a puzzle for years. I would have to analyze several seemingly disparate cases to finally develop a logical theory about what had happened to her.

In March 1992, Lydia Goldman told me about an extraordinary episode. I had conducted seven sessions with this charming and capable sixty-year-old woman since 1989, and she had come to realize that she had been involved with the abduction phenomenon throughout her life.

In early 1992, Lydia awoke one morning with the distinct feeling that she was pregnant. That was impossible, not only because of her age and because she had not engaged in sexual relations, but because she had undergone a total hysterectomy many years before.

Nevertheless, her breasts began to swell, she retained water, and she had something akin to morning sickness. She recognized the symptoms as those she felt when she had been pregnant with her children. After a few weeks, the right side of her lower abdomen became slightly distended. Then, to her horror, she began to feel something moving around inside as if it were a fetus.

Was she going crazy or was something even less acceptable at work? Lydia was reluctant to go to her gynecologist because he might think she was "losing it." But the physical feeling persisted and she made an appointment with him. A few days before her appointment, she woke up and "knew" that everything was all right; her stomach was no longer distended, nothing was moving around in it, and all the symptoms had disappeared. She canceled her appointment.

When Lydia told me about this episode, I was mystified. At the time, abduction researchers knew that aliens take human eggs and human sperm, fertilize them *in vitro,* add alien genetic material, and then replace the altered hybrid embryo *in utero.* Presumably the subject had to have a uterus in which to implant the embryo. But I had regressed many women who were abducted when they were postmenopausal, or had undergone tubal ligations, or had had their uteri and ovaries removed. I had always assumed that the aliens administered different reproductive procedures to them than to women who were still fertile.

Lydia and I decided to do a hypnotic regression on the events that occurred the night before she woke up feeling pregnant. She remembered that she was asleep at her daughter's home in Florida when the abduction took place. After describing the first segment of a typical abduction event, Lydia turned to the internal examination.

What do you think they're doing internally now? Or can you tell that at all?

They're holding something like you would hold a baby, with two hands, but it's not a baby. It's like a, I don't know. . . . I can't even imagine.

[Gently] Does it look like a baby, or not?

It looks like a lobster. I can't imagine. I can't even imagine. My legs are up, and they are in this position in front of me. You know, almost as though they were inserting a sack.

They were inserting something, then?

I don't know. . . . It looks round and light colored, and I would say about the size of a grapefruit.

So it's big.

And they're holding it. . . . I get the impression like you would hold a baby, like something very precious. . . . They're bringing it to me. . . . This is a terribly repulsive idea. I find this to be *extremely* repulsive, dirty, unclean. It's got me very upset.

That they are bringing this to you?

And making it part of my body. . . . I get the sense, and I have a terrible soreness in here—hot and sore. And I find this to be extremely repulsive. This is a solid unit, it is totally contained. There's something in it. I get the sense like it's a sack, and they have inserted that. And my whole feeling about it is that I don't want that in me.

Where do you think they would have inserted this, then?

Vaginally.

But would this have been in the area where the uterus used to be?

Maybe. Maybe. I don't know.

Do you feel that this is sort of the area they're working on, or in?

As a matter of fact, my bladder felt like there was a lot of pressure, as though my bladder was dropping. And for the last six or eight months I felt that way. . . . I thought well, I'm just getting older, and my muscles are not as strong as they used to be. . . . I always felt that if I stood too long I would feel like I had to lie down for a while and let it go back into position. That kind of thing, like something was pressing on it or it was dropping. But I never felt that feeling that I have right now. Right now I feel such a soreness throughout this lower abdominal area—and hot. It feels so hot. My back hurts.

Do they say anything to you? Do they explain what they're doing, or are they just silent about this? . . .

I found it to be extremely repulsive. . . . And I did not want that. And I'm in charge now. This is something I've got to take care of.

That's the impression you get?

It's not that I was saying no. I wouldn't say no. . . . I won't say no to them. I have a feeling that I'm here to serve. . . . I have that feeling though. I have a commitment to serve, but I don't like it. I'm kind of telling them I find this very repulsive. This is not what I want to do. But they didn't ask me if I want to do this. I don't like this at all, and I'm very upset.

I hope that you told that to them. They don't have a right to do this, Lydia, this is something that's not their right. So it's perfectly okay for you to be upset.

[Crying] I think this is about the worst thing that's ever happened to me. . . . You know what this is making me do? I have to change to conform to this. . . . The way my body operates is being disturbed now, and I have to conform to be compatible, to create an atmosphere conducive for this thing. . . . It's throwing my body all off.[5]

As I was listening to Lydia, I remembered a postmenopausal abductee who had told me about feeling pregnant and feeling something "kicking" in her lower abdomen. At the time I did not know how to interpret the report. Now I knew. I realized that it was possible that the aliens are making women carry babies even if the woman does not have a uterus. Instead of implanting the embryo in a uterus, the aliens could be inserting an extrauterine gestational unit—a sac capable of incubating a fetus without having to be attached to the uterine lining. The aliens place the unit in an area near the uterus, or perhaps even in the space that the womb originally occupied, or behind the bladder, or near an ovary.

This led me to reconsider the situation with Melissa. The "implant" that she had worried about was probably not a technological device, as I had assumed, but an extrauterine fetal implantation near the ovary. In this light, Melissa's adamancy about not removing it became understandable—she unconsciously knew that she must not disturb the fetus.

Now, other puzzling cases also began to make sense. The introduction of air, accompanied by a bloating feeling and the sense that organs were being "moved around," was most likely a preparation of the space into which the aliens placed the extrauterine gestational unit; they literally hollowed out an area for its placement.

The implications of these cases were unsettling. Whatever the reproductive stage or abilities of female abductees, they can help produce babies. They can "house" the standard uterine fetal implants as well as extrauterine gestational units. In addition, these gestational units might help to "camouflage" the phenomenon. They do not trigger the human gonadotropin hormone reaction normally registered on a pregnancy test.

The extensive use of women as hosts for hybrid babies brings into sharp relief the importance of the Breeding Program. Its scope is enormous. In theory, the aliens have produced hundreds of thousands, if not millions, of offspring.

Protecting Pregnancies

When an abductee becomes pregnant, what prevents her from aborting the fetus? Or what prevents her from visiting a gynecologist to detect an extrauterine gestational unit and have it removed? It has become clear during the years of my research that the aliens prevent these actions by removing the critical "evidence" before the abductee can act. On many occasions, abductees have reported scheduling an abortion only to find an empty uterus during the actual procedure. By the time the abductee undergoes the procedure, the aliens have already removed the fetus.

Claudia Negrón, a woman who had raised two children before going back to college and earning her bachelor's degree, described the removal process that had occurred during one of her abductions. First she saw a long instrument that the aliens inserted into her.

Strange object. I don't know if it's metal or clear or. . . . They use it for making babies. They put these things together in a laboratory, in a lab. And then they insert them in the womb so that it will grow there and develop into a baby. At a certain age—they monitor it, they know it's progressing—at a certain time they come back, they take you aboard and they remove the fetus, which by that time is not a fully developed fetus but big enough to be recognizable. They remove it, taking them to this place. I've seen it before. Kind of fluid, they keep them in this fluid, a warm fluid. It's like a tank and that has a lot of fluid, has a lot of what is essential, I don't know, something to keep them growing, keep them living.[6]

Logically, the aliens must be monitoring the abductee's thoughts to protect the pregnancy. But do they monitor and record everything a person thinks twenty-four hours a day, or do they monitor selectively? If they monitor continually, then everything an abductee thinks would have to be received, recorded, evaluated, and possibly acted upon. There is evidence to suggest that this level of monitoring does not take place. For example, the aliens are attracted to anything new on an abductee's body: an appendectomy scar, a bruise, a hair color change, a tattoo, and so on. They closely inspect the changed area and ask the person what it signifies and how it happened. If they were continually monitoring, they would probably know the answers.

Therefore, the aliens must monitor selectively. And they probably target thoughts related to specific subjects. If an abductee thinks about pancakes or shopping, it does not trigger a reaction. But if an abductee thinks about abortion, pregnancy, babies, and implants, these thoughts result in action if there is adequate time. When I rushed Melissa to the gynecologist for an ultrasound examination, the aliens did not have enough time to remove the "mass" they had implanted in her body. It all happened within one hour.

How do the aliens monitor thoughts? They most probably do it through implants. Most abductees have alien implants, which they have been describing for years, and which are high up in the nasal passage, possibly as deep as the optic nerve or the pituitary gland, in the ear, or in a sinus cavity. Abductees with implants suffer from lifelong nasal problems, bloody noses, sinus congestion, diminished hearing, tinnitus, and ear bleeding. Physicians have noted anomalous scar tissue and holes in abductees' nasal passages.

Implants have also been placed in abductees' legs, arms, and necks. Some abductees have reported implants inside their brains. Claudia Negrón described receiving this type of implant during an incident in 1983.

He has some kind of instrument in his hand. It looks like, it looks like a needle, a hypodermic needle, but it's not. [It's] long. It has a long tip to it and he puts that in my ear, all the way inside. And it like just goes right through to the brain, it makes my whole brain just go, I don't know, it does something to my whole head. He said it's important. He communicates, he says, "This is important," that he has to do this.

Does he say why it's important, or is he just sort of vague?

He tells me it's important for me, but actually I have a feeling it's more important to him than it is to me. I think they're inserting something inside my head. It's really tiny, very tiny, small, whatever it is. And he said nobody will ever know it's there.

Do you respond to that?

I'm not saying anything. I just feel the pain. It's like I'm immobilized by this pain. He says it's not going to hurt.

But it is hurting.

But it is. He said it's not going to last long. He says I won't feel anything afterwards, I won't even know it's there. I heard something pop in my ear. Oh! Oh! . . . I asked him what this is for, why are they doing this. He says—he does not talk, he just sends his thought. It's like he projects his thoughts to me and he says that they have to know, they have to know how I see the world, how I see things, how I interpret things as they occur and this is their way of monitoring that. This tells them so they know where I am at all times. They know how I react to every situation at every moment. He said that this is important to them. He says it's important for their research. They have to know this . . . because they want to know how the little children will be. They want to know what to expect as they grow older. It's all for the children.[7]

The exact functions of the implants are unclear, but we can make some informed speculations. They are probably complex multifunctional devices, which might monitor or affect hormonal levels for lactation, menstruation, ovulation, or pregnancy. They probably also serve as a means to locate abductees. Implants in the ear, sinus cavity, and nasal passages might all serve a variety of purposes.

What is clear is that the aliens will go to any extreme to protect a pregnancy. If an abductee has any thought of abortion, they intervene. Often the aliens strongly admonish the abductee not to disturb the pregnancy, but this technique has had limited success. Although many abductees say that they do not want to interfere in the pregnancy, most women who are aware of their pregnancies exhibit shock and horror and quickly overcome any qualms they might have about termination.

Kathleen Morrison's case is a good example. Although she was not sexually active and had undergone a hysterectomy some years before, she suspected that she was carrying an extrauterine pregnancy and she made an appointment with Dr. Treller. A few days before the appointment, she was abducted and subjected to a gynecological examination while an alien communicated with her during a concurrent staring (Mindscan) procedure.

What do you think he is doing when he does the staring procedure?

Well, I think that he's taking a reading on my body and he did a quick pass on the mind but—okay he's going deeper. He's going to give me a word and I should respond to it. He gives me the word "Treller," and I respond that I'm going to see the doctor. He asks if I don't feel well, and I said that I was having some problems. And I get the feeling that I—my mind also said something to the effect of—and I want to find out what's going on. They want to know what I mean by that. My response is, "Well, you know. . . ."

When you say, "You know," how does he respond to that?

The word that comes to mind is ICE. The demeanor changes. I get the feeling that prior to this they were . . . a little more gentle, and the face has been lifted. . . . I feel some kind of heat in the vagina area. It's getting weirder when I say that I don't know if it's heat or extreme cold. . . . My question is, "What do you want?" and the thing is, "We need to make sure everything is okay." "But it's not okay, and that's why I'm going to the doctor." "You should have let us know." I get the feeling I should have let them know, but I don't know how to do that. Not that I would.

What do you think they are doing down there?

Harvesting. . . . Eggs.

They are on your right side? . . .

Yeah. There's one over at my right side. He's putting pictures in my head.

What are you seeing?

Nursery full of children. Not ours, here, up there. It's also attempts at family structure as we know it.

How do you mean?

They're not quite right. They'll be two—what seems older beings— with a group of small children.

Two gray beings, or hybrid?

Sometimes a mixture [one gray and one hybrid, Kathleen added later].

Two older beings would be a mixture, or something?

Right. It's like their concept of family life here. I almost want to say it's like a reconstructed scenario of a picnic. . . .

When you see the family unit together, what are they doing?

It's like a reconstruction of a picnic. But they don't have the picnic bench or anything like that. It's like they are in a park type of environment. Groupings, walking, sitting. . . . [They're] talking. They are trying to engage in activities with the younger beings, the little ones, but it's form, no substance. It's form, no substance. It's a park type situation but there aren't any trees or brooks and grass and stuff like that but it gives you the feeling that that is like a simulation type—an acting exercise. . . . Then they ask me a question.

What do they ask you?

"How could you do that to them?" It's relating to the picture.

I don't understand . . . do what to them?

I know what they're talking about. All right, when they were asking before about, you know, why you have to go to the doctor and all that, I said because I didn't feel well. I wanted to know what was going on. And I know that I had a picture in my mind that if something was there, it wouldn't be there any longer, and that's what they're asking. How could I do that, how could I have something taken out that was them.

But you're not having anything taken out.

Well. I'm not, but . . . that was something that I was trying to deal with—a "What if," and they picked up on it. Damn it! Your thoughts aren't even your own.

Right. So you were thinking that if anything was there you would have had it taken out?

That's right. It would have to go.

They're saying how could you have anything taken out that was from them?

How could I do that to these little beings—these little children? How could I do that to them? That I would have something re-moved. That wouldn't be able to get to their like kind—where they are supposed to be. DAMN IT!

So you were seeing a picture of the little children as an example of what is wonderful and good and you're about to mess it all up?

That's right. The guilt trip. . . . I feel like I screwed up—big time.[8]

Sexual Intercourse

For years abductees have reported being forced to engage in sexual intercourse with another abductee on board a UFO. These reports have been especially puzzling. Since aliens take sperm and eggs and then impregnate a woman with an embryo, there seems to be no reason why they should force humans to have intercourse. A popular theory is that the aliens are interested in the emotional aspects of sex. I have found what could be a simpler reason for this practice.

Intercourse usually takes place after an alien performs Mindscan, arousing intense sexual feelings in both the man and the woman. At this point, the aliens put the man and the woman together and the couple engages in intercourse. Then, just before ejaculation, they pull the two apart and the man ejaculates into a receptacle.

During hypnotic regression, abductees have described a variety of emotional states during intercourse. Some are neutral. Some enjoy it, as they are made to envision a loved one with them. Many feel guilt and humiliation. Sometimes the man experiences remorse at having done this to a woman. Lucy Simpson reported a man who communicated "I'm so sorry" as the aliens pulled them apart. But the aliens seem to pay no attention to these emotional reactions. They focus only on eliciting a normal physiological reaction so that the man will ejaculate.

Although the aliens routinely collect sperm by attaching a collection device to the man's penis, apparently this technique is not foolproof. The evidence suggests that there are times when this procedure and even some masturbatory techniques either fail or cannot be performed.

Joel Samuelson, an easygoing forty-year-old man who owns his own business in Pittsburgh, Pennsylvania, related an extremely puzzling event in which the aliens attached a device to his penis for sperm collection. Then, just a few minutes later, they led him into another room, compelled him to have intercourse with a woman, and collected his sperm. As I listened to this account, it occurred to me that although it is possible to ejaculate twice in quick succession, the time between the two ejaculations was so short that the chances are that Joel would not have been able to generate very much more sperm. In addition, he had the impression that the initial mechanical attempt had failed.[9] It seems likely, then, that most sexual intercourse between humans on board a UFO is for the purpose of sperm collection and not necessarily for eliciting sexual expression.

Abductees are often enlisted to obtain sperm when the mechanical means do not work or have failed. Terry Matthews helped to manually masturbate four men in turn as they lay on tables. Each time the aliens collected the sperm. Another example comes from Carla Enders, who had to help the aliens collect sperm from an older man who was "impotent."

They can't get him to respond the way they want. So they ask me if I would help. I'm like, "I don't understand." They're kind of saying, "It's not like you haven't done it before." They're asking me to do something, and I don't really know what they're asking me to do. "You've never asked me these questions before, why are you asking me these questions?" . . . I'm standing in the middle of them, and they're all around me. They've formed a circle around me. I'm feeling like I just want to throw a tantrum and scream and yell. . . . They're telling me it won't be that bad, just do it, and it will be over with. . . .

Do you fully understand what they're asking you?

Not really. Except they want to get some sperm from this man and they can't get it. And they've tried what they normally would do, and it didn't work. And for some reason they have this impression that he would really like that. . . . But I still don't realize until I go in there what they're asking me to do. They're just saying, "It's going to be different, but don't worry about it," or something.

So what happens next, then?

I'm just feeling kind of puzzled as we're walking over there.

You walk back into the hallway, you mean?

Yes, and there's like two in front of me, and two behind me. And we keep going further down the hall, not very far. . . . And I go into this room to the right. There's other ones in there. . . . I'm getting flashes of it being an older man. . . . He's just sitting down on the end of the table, just sitting there. He's not moving. He's older . . . probably at least midfifties. You can tell he's older, he's not fat, but his muscle tone is different. It's not like a young person. . . . It seems like he wants to get up and leave too. Seems like he can't move. . . .

You can tap into his thoughts a little?

Yeah, and then it seems like they start, like they're doing something so he will feel sexually, some kind of sexual desire or something. It seems like he changes. . . . It's like he's not thinking about leaving anymore. He's not realizing that they're all around him anymore. It's like he's fantasizing or something. . . . It seems like they're asking me to touch his genitals. And I'm not cooperating, but they make my hands do it anyway. . . . I'm starting to get images that I somehow really like this person. I don't understand it. That maybe I'm really in love with this person.

Does this guy look familiar at all?

No. I'm thinking, why am I feeling that? Then it just becomes that I don't really notice any other thoughts. I'm not even noticing that they're there anymore. I don't really remember how I started having, doing oral sex, I just remember there was a flash and I was thinking, "I don't want to be doing this," and my head is going up and down and I can't stop it. It felt . . . like their hands were on the side of my head, kind of pushing my head up and down, but not, like, in a way it felt forcibly, but in a way it didn't. In a way it felt like my head was just going up and down anyway. But then I felt like I wanted to stop, and I couldn't stop. . . . It seems like finally I can pull my head away. And I'm just really feeling sick.

What do they do with him when you pull your head away?

It's like I'm thinking they're hoping that he will ejaculate because it seems like that's what they were trying to get him to do. I don't really know. It's like they're all coming around him. . . . It seems like they're getting what they wanted to. It seems like they're satisfied with the results because, it seems like they've got what they wanted.

So the procedure was successful for them.

Yes. It seems like I don't stay in there very long. They're telling me I'll just forget. Because I'm really angry. I'm thinking, "How did that happen?" and we're just walking down the hall.[10]

Sperm collection is so important that the aliens do not adhere to the accepted "rules" about sex between relatives. "Carole" was traveling in Arizona with two friends and a first cousin when they were all abducted. After her physical examination, Carole was sexually aroused and led into another room. The aliens then brought her cousin to her and the two had intercourse—much to Carole's intense shame and guilt. The aliens pulled them apart when her cousin began to ejaculate and collected his sperm. So again, the purpose of forcing sexual intercourse between human seems to be to collect sperm.

An unintended consequence of intercourse for sperm collection might provide a reason for another puzzling aspect of the abduction phenomenon. Women abductees have reported that they became pregnant under impossible conditions; they'd not engaged in sexual intercourse with anyone and yet they were pregnant. They carried the baby to term and they had a normal, healthy child. One woman remembered seeing a bright light while she was driving, then there was a period of missing time. She became pregnant, and after her child's birth, she referred to him as a "star child." Hearing the story of his birth, the now-twelve-year-old son was convinced that he had traveled to his mother's uterus "on a beam of light." At least some of these "immaculate conceptions" are probably a result of bad timing, and because the aliens are living, sentient beings, they make mistakes. If, during an abduction, the male begins to ejaculate a few seconds before the aliens pull him off the woman, she could easily become pregnant.

While sexual intercourse between two humans is primarily for sperm collection, there is another sexual scenario. Abductees have reported establishing close relationships with other humans, which the aliens arrange during their abductions. A male and a female child meet while on board a UFO, continue to see each other during abductions, and establish a friendship. When they become adolescents, they enter into an onboard sexual relationship. Sometimes they know each other's names, and sometimes they make up names for each other. Terry Matthews knew a boy named Ben Anderson, with whom she had a deep relationship as a young girl and teenager during her abductions. On one occasion she expected to meet him again, but the aliens abruptly told her that he was dead and that "we have somebody else for you to meet." When she became upset, they told her that it was not their fault and that he had died in an automobile accident.[11]

Occasionally two abductees will meet in a nonabduction context where they get a strong sense of familiarity and feel a powerful attraction toward each other. For example, Dena and Ray both knew immediately that they belonged together when they met. They had no idea how or why they felt that way, but the feeling was strong enough for them to divorce their spouses and marry. Hypnosis revealed that they have a long-term adolescent sexual relationship that took place exclusively during abductions.

Budd Hopkins, who first identified this phenomenon, has suggested that the mating of two abductees indicates that the aliens are conducting a study of the abductees' relationships, both social and sexual.[12] This may indeed be the case. It is also possible that the two abductees possess certain genetic properties that the aliens want passed on to their children.

Controlling the Human Subjects

A puzzling aspect of the abduction phenomenon has been the use of Mindscan to sexually arouse women. In Mindscan, which usually comes during or immediately after the initial physical examination, a tall alien places his face very close to that of the abductee and stares intensely at her. The alien can elicit a variety of feelings and he can make the abductee envision specific scenarios of his own choosing. One of the most common procedures is when the alien uses Mindscan to elicit sexual feelings that escalate unabated until the female abductee reaches a high sexual plateau or orgasm.

The question is: Why are sexual feelings stimulated during Mindscan? To answer this, one must pay attention to what the tall alien, who usually performs Mindscan, does at the onset of the abductee's orgasm. He immediately breaks off his staring procedure and goes between the abductee's legs to begin the gynecological procedures. The most frequent procedure that abductees report during orgasm is egg harvesting. Inducing orgasm does not appear to be linked to any interest in or testing of sexual response. Instead, the evidence suggests that the aliens need the physiological effects of orgasm—tumescence, expansion, lubrication, and perhaps ovulation—to facilitate the gynecological procedures in which they are engaged. Although the role of orgasm in ovulation is controversial, physician (and abductee) Gloria Kane felt certain that during Mindscan the alien was provoking the release of an egg from her ovary.

When I was . . . sixteen they said that they were altering the way I worked inside, just after I got my period, that they were altering the way that I worked so that I would be like a rabbit. I would be sexually excited and then produce, or release an ovum. . . . They wanted me to get excited enough to ovulate that way.[13]

Ovulation must take place on cue for the Breeding Program. Hybrids have instructed other hybrids in the intricacies of providing for ova release. Christine Kennedy recounted an event in which one hybrid discussed inducing ovulation with three other hybrids.

He's saying something to the other ones.

When he says something, does he face them, or is he facing away from them, or . . . ?

They're facing him. He's pushing around my ovaries.

What's your position on the table? Straight down, legs straight out and together?

No, they have my feet in these things—the stirrup things.

I see. So then am I assuming that your knees are up and legs apart and all that?

Mm-hmm [Yes]. I can't move my feet.

He's pressing on your ovary.

Mm-hmm.

Now, when he says something to these other guys, can you pick up just a little what he said, a thought here, a thought there?

They're going to make me ovulate.

And that's what he says?

Mm-hmm. He says something about an egg, but I don't know if it's, "Take an egg." I don't think so. I can't see my arms . . . moving around.

You arms are moving? How do you mean?

I was able to move my arms around.

Are you flailing away?

I wanted to smack the son of a bitch.

Good. So, you have some movement.

I can't do anything with them. I put them down. He hooks my
right arm down and the other two, they're on the other side of the
table. They followed suit.

So he's no longer pressing down on your ovary when he does
that?

Mm-mm [No]. I feel like I'm being patronized. He's saying something. Something about why do I want to do that, or
something. . . .

Do you tell him off, or do you respond at all?

No, because . . . he's calming me down, he's coming real close to
my face.

How close does he get to you?

Really close. I feel him touching my forehead.

What's happening?

If he makes me reach an orgasm . . . son of a bitch!

When that happens—he's just sort of standing next to you,
touching your forehead?

With his head. He was staring. He's doing the same shit that they
always do.[14]

The aliens' ability to stare into an abductees' eyes and effect a
wide variety of changes in brain function is extraordinary. At first it
seems almost supernatural or mystical, as if Svengali were peering
into Trilby's eyes, mesmerizing her to do anything he wanted. But
the mystical and supernatural are not part of the abduction phenomenon. The aliens use their advanced knowledge of human phys-

iology to control humans and, ultimately, to make sure that humans comply with the Breeding Program and all other parts of the alien agenda.

The aliens' ability to control humans comes through the manipulation of the human brain. For example, when the alien moves close to the abductee's eyes to begin the staring procedure, almost immediately the abductee feels emotional and physical effects. One way to explain this is that the alien uses the optic nerve to gain entrance to the brain's neural pathways. By exciting impulses in the optic nerve, the alien is able to "travel" along the optic neural pathway, through the optic chiasma, into the lateral geniculate body, and then into the primary visual cortex in the back of the brain. From there he can travel into the secondary visual cortex in the occipital lobes and continue into sites in the parietal and temporal lobes and the hypothalamus. Through that route, the alien can stimulate neural pathways, travel to many neural sites, and cause the "firing" of neurons at whatever sites he wants.

Brain stimulation allows the alien to produce a range of effects. If the alien can connect into the neural pathways, he can reconstitute an abductee's memories. He can inject new images directly into the visual cortex, bypassing normal retinal observations, and cause people to "see" things that become part of their abduction "memories." He can activate sites within the limbic system and cause strong emotions, such as fear, anger, and affection. He can create feelings of sexual arousal that build relentlessly to a peak. And he can institute a form of amnesia that helps to preserve secrecy.

By using the optic nerve, the alien can, in effect, travel down the brain stem, into the autonomic nervous system in the spine, and then branch into the parasympathetic nervous system, giving him contact with virtually any organ. Abductees often talk about feeling physical sensations in their genitals, bladder, or other areas when an alien performs Mindscan procedures. The physiological responses necessary for erection and ejaculation in men, and tumescence, expansion, and lubrication in women can be artificially generated in this manner.

How the aliens engage the optic nerve is, of course, unclear, but there are some clues. When Mindscan or any staring procedure begins, the abductee cannot avert or close his eyes; they must remain fixed and open. The abductee is, in effect, forced to peer into the alien's eyes. Most abductees report that his eyes are dark brown or black, and opaque. Others describe what might be liquid inside the alien's eyes. Others frequently see a moving or wiggling structure in the back of the eyes that generates a "light." It is possible that the light-emanating mechanism engages the optic nerve to begin the alien's journey through neural pathways.

Some abductees can feel the engagement when it happens. Allison Reed often sensed the alien's physical attachment to her brain during Mindscan.

What's he doing when he's inside there?

I feel a little tired. There's that thing again. I can't see it but I can feel it, it's . . . and it goes all around. I don't know, it goes all around, it's like a blue light. It's between my skull and my brain, of course I can't see it, I just feel it. I don't feel much of anything right now. I feel good, I feel relaxed. . . .

The blue light, is that from his own eyes, do you guess, or from an instrument?

No, I don't like to call it a light because it's not a light like you see, it's more like an energy. I can't see it, usually in these places you see certain things but you feel more than you see. Your major senses are no longer sight and smell and touch, it's your sixth sense when you're here. It's from him, it's not an instrument, it's an energy. Somehow he can make this energy go in my head.[15]

Similarly, Courtney Walsh, a young woman pursuing a career in the biological sciences, "felt" her neural pathways being stimulated.

No, it feels like, it's hard to describe, like something is worming around in there. You can feel the different nerve pathways. . . . It actually feels nice, though. I can feel actual—it feels like something is—little currents of energy running around in my head.[16]

Jack Thernstrom, a graduate student in the physical sciences, had a similar reaction and sensed that the alien was physically going through his mind:

Now he's looking in my face again, and this time it's that feeling of a knife prying into my mind.

This is a feeling of . . . a physiological situation that's going on there?

It's like pure mental pain.

What do you think he's doing now?

I have this impression of, as if he's probing his way through a lot of—it's almost a physical sensation, as if thin strings or cables are all closely intertwined, almost hairlike, but under tension. It seems I've seen something like this . . . he's kind of groping in there, and finding paths between them to get at a certain point. It's this feeling of a knife probing through, and forcing its way between things. . . . It's somewhere between active and passive . . . it's not like opening it up and looking at it, it's as if one had a mass of wires and one were pulling and separating them to see what's connected to what.[17]

Some abductees visualize random thoughts and images as the alien traverses the neural pathways, as if the "travel" enervates the pathways as a by-product of the procedure. One woman saw a frame house, a mule-drawn carriage, a "Gibson-Girl's" hair, someone washing the hair on a mannequin's head (no body) in a basin, an iceberg in a fjord, the top of an old house in winter, two children, and a nineteenth-century print of two politicians. Another abductee envisioned a comb, teeth, numbers, letters, parts of a face, a man falling out of a building, a bird in flight, knife edges, a leg, a mouse hole, a pocket watch, and potatoes.

Once joined with the abductee's neural pathways, the alien essentially has free rein to do what he wants. The abductee is no longer in control of his own thoughts. The aliens can exercise absolute power over the minds and bodies of the abductees. They can make the abductees think, feel, visualize, or do anything the aliens want.

The aliens' ability to attach to the abductee's neural pathways is not automatic. They turn and twist their heads to get the best vantage point to hook into the optic nerve. They hold the abductee's head so that she will not make any movements that might disrupt engagement. Kathleen Morrison had an unusual Mindscan in which the first alien could not make an adequate attachment. After the first alien tried without success for several minutes, another alien took over and she could quickly feel the effects of the familiar Mindscan procedure.

But another abductee successfully resisted mental engagement. During a recent abduction, Reshma Kamal found that she had more muscle control than usual and she used it to prevent a neural connection. She shifted her eyes back and forth rapidly while reciting an Arabic religious phrase. The first alien tried to lock into her eyes but could not. He diverted her attention by causing a pain in her head, and he threatened not to take her home, but she refused to give in. Another alien took over and increased the threats. Still she refused to stop, although she was getting dizzy moving her eyes back and forth. A third alien tried, and then a fourth. They could not stop her from shifting her eyes. Eventually they gave up and said that they would continue the procedure at the next abduction.[18]

Abductees have said that in some way they know the mental procedures are related to the hybrids. The abductees suggest that aliens record information from them and then transfer it into hybrids' minds so that they can learn how humans live and feel. There are also procedures in which hybrids directly transfer information from human minds into their minds. An alien attached Allison Reed to an adult female hybrid with wires, and as the two sat facing each other, Allison could feel her thoughts and memories flowing out of her and into the hybrid. The hybrid "absorbed" Allison's thoughts and experiences and apparently derived some benefit from this procedure.[19]

The mental procedures must be viewed in relation to the aliens' reproductive agenda. Without the ability to manipulate the human brain, the aliens would be unable to control the abductees physically or mentally and the Breeding Program would not be feasible in its present form. Abductees often feel even more violated by the mental procedures than by the reproductive ones. They know that their private thoughts are not their own and that they can be "tapped into" and manipulated. Although I often try to reassure them that in spite of what happens their thoughts are free, they know that this may not be entirely true.

Who are these powerful beings who can control humans? What kind of society do they live in? How do they live? Through abduction accounts, we have been able to piece together facts that provide some answers to these all-important questions.

5

What They Are

Abductees have painted a clear picture of how the aliens behave. They present themselves to the abductees very professionally—a cooperative society operating like an efficient factory. But the aliens have been very private about their "personal" lives and the society in which they live. Still, over the years they have "leaked" bits and pieces of information, and a picture of their life and society is slowly emerging.

Where Do They Come From?

Do aliens come from outer space, another dimension, or a parallel universe? At first, researchers believed that outer space was the most logical explanation: that the aliens flew here from Mars or Venus or elsewhere in our solar system. But as scientists learned more about our solar system, it seemed certain that Earth was the only planet bearing intelligent life. Therefore, researchers concluded that the aliens would have to come from another solar system. But even the nearest one is light years away, and flying here would be a daunting task, even at the speed of light.

The problem of how UFOs can travel to Earth has been an intellectual "stopper" for many, and scientists have developed various theories over the years to overcome this hurdle. Astronomer and UFO researcher J. Allen Hynek posited that UFOs come from somewhere else via the "astral plane." They in some way "will" themselves here, as if traveling on thought patterns. UFO researcher Jacques Vallee and others have suggested that UFOs come from an alternative reality that mankind somehow calls into consciousness; this alternative reality presumably exists alongside our own. Other researchers have hypothesized that the aliens "pop" out of a parallel universe that might be made of antimatter or some other substance.

This intellectual dilemma—how to reconcile space travel with current scientific knowledge—has been a key issue that has prevented the astronomical community from exploring the UFO phenomenon on any serious level. Yet this intellectual dilemma is a spurious problem. Instead of asking where the aliens are from and how they get here, it is more appropriate to ask: Are people really seeing the anomalous, artificially constructed, and intelligently controlled objects they are reporting? Are people really having the abduction experiences they describe? The question is not how aliens get here but whether they *are* here. The "how" is ultimately a technological detail.

Abductees have, of course, asked the aliens where they come from. And the answers indicate that they are indeed from another planet somewhere in the known universe. Since there are billions of stars and therefore billions of possible planets, this explanation seems reasonable and abductee testimony seems to bear it out.

When abductees have asked the aliens about their "home," they sometimes point to an area of the sky; they do not talk about parallel universes, time travel, dimensions, or other exotic "locations." In one instance, Michelle Peters, a woman with two children living in New Jersey, had a conversation with an adult hybrid:

I asked him where he's from and he said the North. I sat up and looked at him. . . . He pointed up at the stars, and he said, ". . . It's about right there, but you can't see it. You can see stars around it if you had a telescope; three little stars and a planet, then there's a cluster, and then there's that. It's like a helix." First there's a few little stars, then the planet, then the cluster. And then their planet. It's real far away.[1]

Kathleen Morrison found herself with an adult hybrid staring out a window into space. The hybrid explained to her that travel through the stars was accomplished in stages.

He's pointing out constellations and stuff. Not just constellations like we know them but points out farther things. It seems that there's a link between certain of the systems that stretch out into space. I don't know. All I think of it is if you're crossing a river and you have stones and you jump from one stone to the next stone to the next stone, that's the best analogy that I can think of. But he points that kind of stuff out, stepping stones.[2]

Other abductees have described being in space and looking down at Earth. Their UFO did enter another universe.

Many abductees have reported being in desertlike terrain. Although the meaning of these settings is unclear, there are indications that such terrain may be a home environment for the aliens. Susan Steiner remembered an incident when she was in one of these environments walking on sand.

The sky is like reddish. There's like cloud formations that are sort of hanging in the air very low, like very, they're not like cumulus clouds. They're more feathery type clouds. And they're like all different colors. Like multicolored and they're hanging in the air, almost like cotton candy or angel's hair. It looks sort of like angel's hair hanging there in the air. It's just like all over the place. There's like three, looks like there's three suns in the sky. One of them has like little, like smaller things sort of like . . . I don't know what you would call them but like rotating around one of the suns. The other two don't have that, the other two are just plain. We start walking out into this stuff and then. . . .

You were walking on the sand?

Right. But it's like hard sand. It's not like beach sand, it's like harder than that. But it's definitely sand, just not like a beach. And then we're like walking and he's grabbing my hand, he takes my hand and it seems like we're walking up steps but there's no steps. We're just floating and we float up toward this building, these big glass doors.

She floated into the building where two tall robed beings met her. She then underwent the standard alien procedures.[3]

We do not yet know where the aliens come from or how they get here, but a picture is emerging, again from abductees' accounts, of what their lives are like aboard the vehicles that appear to have transported them.

The Organization Chart

The aliens seem to have a recognizable chain of command and clearly defined roles aboard their spacecraft. In my book *Secret Life,* I pointed out that the shorter gray aliens act as assistants to the taller grays. The shorter aliens bring abductees to the UFO, take their clothes off, escort them to the "examination" rooms, and even do some nonspecialized procedures. Shorter aliens rarely engage in extended conversation, and what they do communicate is usually limited to palliatives and reassurances for the frightened abductee.

Researchers now know that the taller alien, whom abductees sometimes call the "doctor" or the "specialist" to differentiate him from the others, often joins the abduction after the shorter aliens have performed an examination of the abductee. The taller being conducts the more complicated procedures. He takes sperm and harvests eggs. He implants embryos into female abductees and a few months later he extracts the fetuses. He conducts staring procedures in which he can extract memories or information from the abductee and in which he can also elicit sexual arousal and orgasm. He engages in visualization procedures, during which he can make the abductee see and even relive life events, or he can create entirely new "events" for the abductee to experience.

The taller aliens appear to have more of a personality than the shorter ones. They will engage in a dialogue with the abductee but remain coy about the objectives of the abduction and about the specific procedures.

There are suggestions of further differentiation of task—according to sex. I have received no reports of female smaller beings; all the females seem to be the taller variety. Female aliens perform the specialized tasks, including gynecological and urological procedures and visualizations; occasionally, they engage in Mindscan and staring procedures. The main distinction is that the female aliens attend to the hybrid offspring. They bring the babies for the important physical interaction that they must have with the abductees. They also watch over and direct the activities of the hybrid toddlers and young children.

This differentiation of task could be an artifact of the abductees' cultural perceptions, but the descriptions of the female alien militate against this. The females have no physical attributes of their sex as we would expect if human cultural perceptions informed these descriptions. They have no breasts or any secondary sexual characteristics that are noticeable to the abductee. Instead, the abductees say that the female aliens seem "kinder," "gentler," or more "graceful" or "feminine" in some ill-defined way. Regardless of the vagaries of their descriptions, the abductees are all absolutely certain that these aliens are female.

In my earlier research, I focused on the gray beings because they are the most predominant life forms that abductees see. But it is now important to note that abductees have also reported other subgroups. Sometimes they report shorter beings with different skin color—tan or white are the most frequent. They also describe varying facial characteristics in both taller and shorter beings. By far, the most prominent differentiation is in overall appearance. There are the standard grays, but there are also "Nordics," "reptilians," "insectoids," and robed, or hooded, tall beings.

Because most aliens are small and gray, for years I thought the Nordics were examples of confabulation and wishful thinking, which transformed the ugly aliens into handsome, blond, blue-eyed humans. After listening to many accounts of these more human-looking aliens, I concluded that the evidence clearly suggests that the Nordics are most probably adult hybrids, the products of human/alien mating. They hybrids are critically important and I will describe their crucial roles later.

The reports of "reptilians" or "insectoids" may simply be a matter of word choice, and some abductees apply these descriptive terms to aliens whom other abductees might describe as "standard" grays. Assuming, however, that reptilian and insectlike beings are actually different types, it is noteworthy that abductees almost always see them with the gray aliens, not alone, and that the tasks they perform are all within the standard alien matrix. They generally perform the taller being's more specialized functions. Abductees often express dislike or fear of these aliens, sometimes characterizing them as "mean" or "evil," although they have no evidence for these assertions.

Although we have not yet delineated the "reptilian" beings' roles, the "insectoid" beings are coming into sharper relief. Abductees have reported an alien who seems to have a higher "rank" and supervisory status than even the taller beings. He is very tall and is usually wearing a cape or long robe with a high collar. He often is described as an insectlike being who looks somewhat like a praying mantis or a giant ant. He examines abductees only infrequently and most often engages in staring procedures. When he communicates telepathically with humans, his talk is often more substantive and he is sometimes more forthcoming in the information he imparts. But generally he stands back, observes the abduction proceedings, and may issue directions to the taller beings.

The existence of task-specific beings suggests a hierarchical "society" and the probability of a "governmental body," with a downward-flowing chain of command from the insectlike beings to the shorter gray aliens. Other aliens appear to act somewhat subservient to the insectlike beings. If this is the case, then we can hypothesize that they might possess the highest authority for the entire Breeding Program, and therefore might be the group that initiated it.

Abductees frequently comment that the aliens display a "hive" mentality. The shorter aliens especially look alike, dress alike, and act alike, and on board the UFO, they do nothing that suggests unique personality traits. All individual activity is directed toward the abduction goal in a clinical and dispassionate way. The taller gray aliens appear to have more individuality and the robed insect-like ones even more.

Although the aliens might have disagreements and annoyances among themselves, they generally present a united and positive front to the abductees. They constantly tell the abductees about how important the program is and how thankful they are for the abductees' "help."

Communications Skills

The aliens communicate telepathically with humans and with each other. When abductees describe the communication process, they say they receive an impression in their minds that they automatically convert into their own words for comprehension. Most of the time abductees seem to understand alien messages extremely well. Yet the subtle and wide range of expression that humans can use—cynicism, irony, sarcasm, drama—seems to be limited for the aliens, and the range of communicative expression that comes from subtle facial movements is almost nonexistent.

Quite often abductees can "tap" into conversations between aliens, which usually relate to the procedures in the abduction. "Hearing" aliens talk among themselves seems to depend on proximity. Abductees report that they do not "hear" a cacophony of sound in the UFO; they only "hear" in the right proximity.

The aliens, however, seem to "hear" and understand both human communication and human thought. Accounts from abductees strongly suggest that the aliens seem to know what abductees are thinking privately. For example, take the situation of a woman abductee who is given a hybrid baby to hold. She resists this order and communicates to the aliens that she will throw it on the floor, but the abductee reports that the aliens "know" she will not do it.

Emotional Demeanor

Most abductees describe the aliens as having a narrow and "controlled" emotional demeanor. They are usually calm and collected. When they do become more emotional, they act satisfied, pleased, and gratified, but not joyous; they act irritated, annoyed, and perturbed, but not angry. Extremes of emotion do not seem to be part of their mental makeup.

Their restricted emotional range may help explain why the aliens force abductees to interact physically with hybrid babies and toddlers. The abductees report that this interaction makes usually passive babies become more active, as if the abductees have in some way "charged" the babies or given them more energy.

It is clear from abduction accounts that the aliens cannot provide what the babies need. They have stated as much themselves. The case of Reshma Kamal is a good example. During an abduction, a female alien asked Reshma to hold a baby, but she resisted and questioned the need for the procedure:

She's going to show me how. She's picking up the baby. She's trying to put it against her, but it's like she doesn't know how. Now she's asking me to do it and I said no. She puts it down again. And I'm asking what do they do with these babies, where do they come from. She's telling me I don't need to worry about that, that the babies need to be held, otherwise they can't grow right. Whatever that means. I'm telling her that she doesn't have to worry about them growing right because they're already not right. She doesn't seem to like the way I feel. . . . She's explaining something to me.

What is she saying?

She thinks if she can make me understand something, I'll behave better. . . . I know she's trying for me to cooperate. I'm thinking the more I bother her, the more she will give me information. Now she's telling me that they need these babies. What we need to

teach them is emotions, feelings, that they cannot do. She's explaining to me that they can feed and clothe the babies, they can
grow physically, but they cannot give these babies emotional development, that they need me to help them to do that. I don't understand that. . . . She's saying there's a very big need for these
babies. She's saying something about these babies are not exactly
like them, or not exactly like us. But they need to have
emotion. . . . She seems a little frustrated with me because I'm not
cooperating. I'm just standing there with my hands folded, and I
tell her I'm not doing anything.

Trying to make Reshma cooperate, the female alien took her to
an incubatorium—a room that contained hundreds of containers of
fetuses.

She's waiting to see my reaction. I'm asking her why are they
doing this, and how do the babies survive like that, and how I
wish that we had something like that so I didn't have to go
through the birth pain. She's saying to me that if we did that,
these babies would have no emotions, just like their babies, and
that's where they need our help. These babies can grow
physically . . . but emotionally they're dead. . . . They need us to do
that—nurture the babies. And I'm asking her why do they have to
do all this.

Good question. What is her answer, then?

She's not saying anything. It's like she can't believe I still want to
know more. . . . She's saying that these babies cannot function exactly like they do in their society, neither can they function if they
were in our society exactly like us. . . . So she's saying that we
have to work together so these babies are not wasted. They cannot
work on the babies alone because the way they function, the baby
cannot function like that. And they cannot let us have them because they're not like us. But they need something from them and
from us. . . . She seems real frustrated with me. She's not saying
anything. She's just saying we need to do that. . . .

She says in time I will know. I'm suspicious of her, so I ask her do you want my kids? And she says not the way I think, to adopt them or something. There's no use for them here. That's all she says. I'm angry, and I'm saying to her that if they keep those babies in the wall like that, of course they're not going to have any emotions. She's saying to me if they kept these babies in our stomachs for nine months, that there would be too much confusion. So it's better to take these babies out when they're very small so we don't know, and they keep bringing us back to help them out. They have to take them out so we don't know what they're doing. I'm looking at all the boxes in the wall. She's asking if I'll help them. I said no.[4]

Eventually, although Reshma did not want to, she relented and held a baby. It is rare that an abductee can resist what is being requested of her.

Basic Alien Biology

All life on Earth requires fuel to exist. Plants obtain fuel from the sun and the soil, animals from plant and animal material. We might assume that aliens would function in a similar way. Abductee reports suggest, however, that they have no mouth, teeth, esophagus, digestive tract, abdomen, or orifices for the elimination of waste products. No abductee has ever reported aliens eating or being in an area that could be reasonably deduced to be a human-style eating room. When the abductee Lynne Miller directly asked the aliens whether they eat, after a pause one answered: "We need no human consumption of the matter that you eat."

Until now, how aliens obtain fuel has been a mystery. My earlier research showed that alien biology was different from human biology, but with no obvious sign of ingesting food, one could easily surmise that these beings were robotlike, stamped out by a die with an internal power source. One of Allison Reed's abduction experiences gave me the key to the puzzle. During a four-and-one-half-day abduction, a hybrid took Allison to rejoin her escort, who had been with her since the beginning of the abduction. The hybrid mistakenly took Allison into a room that apparently was "off limits." It was large, circular, and had a vaulted ceiling. Allison saw approximately forty tanks filled with liquid in a horseshoe arrangement around the circular wall. She heard a humming sound and saw a yellow light streaming to the center of the room from the ceiling.

So, what happens next then? You walk in there. You absorb this scene—

The light in the center, it withdraws. I'm standing there for a while. . . . Eventually, the light in the center it kind of sucks itself up. It goes into the ceiling. . . . Now these things [tanks], they're, like, tilted back just ever so slightly but randomly they'll "sit front" and then the water, I say water, the liquid just goes. It just goes. I don't know where it goes. It just goes. It may be sucked into–I don't know.

Do you hear a gurgling sound or anything?

I hear "wissssshhh." They are sitting back at an angle and every time one is moved ever so much forward, it goes "wisssshhh," like that, then it's forward and the liquid is dissipated. It's gone. I don't see, like, a hose coming out of the top.

Now this happens when the light withdraws?

Right. The light withdraws first, the yellow round thing in the center but then it's, like, intermittently—they don't all sit up together at once and everybody comes piling out—it's more, like, randomly one will pop up here, there, you know, from this side, that side. Some are in longer and some come out. . . .

And what happens then?

Well, some of them they start to come out. They come out.

How do they come out?

They walk right through it.

They walk through it? They don't open the door or anything?

Hm-mm [No].

They walk right through the glass, in other words?

Right. Just like they do at my house.

Are they surprised to see you or do they just go about their business or—? What do they do when they come out?

They just walk past me. They walk past me. And I'm waiting there. Isn't this stupid? I'm waiting there for this gray guy. I'm so stupid! Why do I do that? I'm remembering this and I'd like to beat myself over the head. I'm such a jerk! Any other time I'm bitching that I want to run away from them and here I stand waiting for him!

When Allison's escort walked up to her, he was shocked to see her there. For him, the shock was compounded because she was wearing hybrid clothes. He quickly told Allison that they would have to go back to the shower room and return the clothes.

After I get that understanding that I could have caused problems for myself, I say to him, "What were you doing? What were you doing in there?" I think it, you know. . . . He just puts it off like, "Eating and sleeping," like it's so simple. It sounds too simple to be right but that's what I understand.[5]

If this is true, it suggests that aliens obtain their fuel by absorption through their skin rather than by ingestion. The absorption theory is supported by reports of fetuses floating in tanks in "incubatoriums." Many fetuses do not have umbilical cords, suggesting that they do not receive nourishment from a placenta. An alien told Diane Henderson from southern Illinois that the fetuses were in the liquid for "feeding," and that it was "nutritious."[6] They gave Pam Martin the same explanation. An alien took her into an incubatorium and explained the function of the liquid environment in which the fetuses were floating. He told her that they "get everything" from the liquid.[7]

Susan Steiner went into a nursery where an alien presented her with a baby. First the aliens directed her to have skin-on-skin contact with the baby by rubbing its head and abdomen. Then they wanted her to feed the baby, but she refused. When they could not force her to feed it, they brought out a bowl of brown liquid with a "paintbrush" and told her to paint it on the baby. She asked them what the point of this was. They told her it was for "nourishment."[8]

Thus, whatever the specific and still unknown biological processes, we now know that aliens obtain fuel differently from humans, that their skin has a unique function, and that they convert "food" to energy very differently. But these are mere glimpses into alien life and biology, and the reason we do not know more is that the aliens do not want us to know. They have implemented a policy of secrecy that has effectively prevented us from understanding them or their intentions. Secrecy is the cornerstone upon which the abduction phenomenon rests. The success of the alien agenda depends upon it.

6

Why They
Are Secret

Why don't the UFOs land on the White House lawn? Why don't the alien occupants step out and say "Take me to your leader"? Why don't they make formal contact? These obvious questions, which people have posed for years, deserve thoughtful consideration. Yet the questions themselves are problematic because they are based on the assumption that the aliens want to make themselves known, establish contact with humans, and speak to our leaders. This assumption is incorrect. The evidence surrounding the UFO and abduction phenomenon strongly points, not to revelation, but to concealment as the goal.

Why should the aliens want to keep the UFO and abduction phenomenon a secret? Secrecy benefits the aliens and befuddles the humans. It hides the facts and fuels endless speculations. It is responsible for prolonged and rancorous debate between proponents and debunkers over the phenomenon's legitimacy. Secrecy also has a powerful and negative influence on abductees. It causes them and the public to question their sanity. Without secrecy there would be no UFO and abduction controversy.

Yet millions of people around the world have observed UFOs. Numerous photographs, motion pictures, and videos of UFOs have stood the test of scientific analysis. Radar traces have been part of the hard evidence for many years. How can we reconcile all the overt evidence with a policy of secrecy?

Ultimately, UFO sightings do not compromise secrecy. It is impossible to base an analysis of aliens' motivations and goals on the sightings of UFOs and, occasionally, their occupants. We must conclude, then, that the aliens actively dictate the terms upon which we can study them. They have chosen not to land on the White House lawn. They have chosen not to make overt "contact." In the 1960s, the great French UFO researcher Aime Michel succinctly labeled this "The Problem of Noncontact."

The Early Hypotheses: 1940s to 1960s

A sighting—any sighting—would seem to be inconsistent with a policy of secrecy. If the technologically superior aliens wish to keep their secret, one could argue, they would prevent witnesses from seeing them. But beginning in the late 1940s, researchers struggled with the puzzle of why UFOs did not make formal contact. They offered several hypotheses about noncontact. The first theories focused on human hostility, ethical noninterference, reconnaissance, and various combinations of these three.

The "hostile humans" hypothesis suggested that UFOs were clandestine because they feared human aggression. Instances of jet fighter pilots encountering UFOs in the air and either wanting to fire upon them or actually shooting at them gave credence to the idea that aliens believed we were a hostile species who posed a threat to their spacecraft.

The "hostile humans" hypothesis was particularly in vogue when America was involved with the military mindset of World War II, the Korean conflict, and the Cold War, and was influenced by then-current anthropological ideas that man was an innately aggressive, warlike animal. Humankind's first reaction to extraterrestrial visitation, at least on an institutional level, would be to use military force to control or destroy the UFOs. By maintaining its distance, an advanced, and presumably peaceful, alien species would avoid conflict. As Air Force analyst James Lipp said in 1949: "It is hard to believe that any technologically accomplished race would come here, flaunt its ability in mysterious ways and then simply go away." Lipp suggested that "the lack of purpose apparent in the various episodes is also puzzling. Only one motive can be assigned; that the spacemen are 'feeling out' our defenses without wanting to be belligerent."[1]

This theory first received popular expression in the 1951 motion picture *The Day the Earth Stood Still*, in which a UFO lands near the White House and the U.S. military, armed with guns and tanks, immediately surrounds it. A trigger-happy soldier shoots and wounds an extraterrestrial after he emerges from the flying saucer. When the alien escapes, he completes his mission on Earth only by living incognito with humans. Avoiding overt contact was seen as a preventive reaction to our inherent hostility.

Early researchers also put forward the "reconnaissance" explanation for alien secrecy. Pioneer UFO researcher Donald Keyhoe, in his 1950 *Flying Saucers Are Real*, advanced the idea that "the earth has been under periodic observation from another planet, or other planets for at least two centuries." These inspections are "part of a long-range survey and will continue indefinitely. No immediate attempt to contact the earth seems evident. There may be some unknown block to making contact, but it is more probable that the spacemen's plans are not complete."[2] According to Keyhoe, if we were exploring another planet, we would not make contact until our observations were complete: "If we were to find that the other species was hostile or belligerent, then we would go on to the next planet."[3]

Building upon Keyhoe's theory, Canadian UFO investigator Wilbert Smith speculated in 1953 that when UFO occupants discover that we are a warlike people, they will depart because we are "too primitive by their standards." For Smith and other researchers, UFO occupants were anthropologists practicing a policy of noninterference when they encountered a previously undiscovered tribal society. According to this theory, aliens had a moral responsibility to protect humanity from the problems that interspecies contact could bring. However, Smith suggested to Keyhoe that the aliens would directly intervene if humans became too aggressive:

Suppose, for instance, our pilots discovered a lost civilization down in the Amazon country. We'd investigate from the air to see how advanced they were before risking direct contact. If they were a century or two behind us with sectional wars going on, we'd possibly leave them alone—unless they had something we wanted badly. But they might be only a decade or two behind us. In that event we'd at least keep a close eye on them in the future. . . . But if for any reason they were a danger to the rest of the world, we'd have to bring them under control, by reason—or threat of force.[4]

Aime Michel combined the "hostile humans" and noninterference hypotheses in 1956 when he suggested that UFO occupants did not contact us because it might be physically dangerous for them. Michel said that humans are a violent people and, "considering our bloody past, would they not be justified in thinking that their best protection is an 'iron curtain'?" But, explained Michel, the aliens also had a selfish reason for noncontact: "Contact would be a bad bargain for them. It would teach us far more than it would teach them and in every way reduce their margin of superiority over us. And supposing we found out the secret of their machines? Would we use the knowledge as prudently as they have done?" Still, Michel thought that contact might happen "when contact does more good than harm."[5] He noted with approval that they had "respect for others" because they had "never once attempted to interfere in our affairs."[6]

Aime Michel later suggested that the aliens had deliberately avoided overt contact because of the havoc it would wreak upon human institutions and life—and aliens would supplant us in a Darwinian survival-of-the-fittest model.[7] Contact could, however, take place without our knowledge, said Michel, because the aliens are so superior and clandestine that "we will be as incapable of detecting their activity or of analyzing their motives as a mouse is of reading a book."[8]

In the 1950s, a very divisive element entered the debate over the meaning of noncontact—the infamous contactees. These people claimed that they were having continuing interactions with friendly "Space Brothers." They met with aliens at various places, including restaurants, bus terminals, and isolated areas. This was contact. And although most serious UFO researchers quickly exposed the contactees as frauds, legions of people believed their yarns and concluded that aliens had already made contact and therefore the debate over the secret nature of the UFO phenomenon was moot.[9] The contactees lost their popularity by the 1960s, but ever since, debunkers and skeptics have pointed to them as examples of how UFO proponents can be gullible.

In the 1960s, the "hostile humans" hypothesis declined, but the reconnaissance hypothesis remained strong. Writing in 1962, Coral Lorenzen, codirector of the Aerial Phenomena Research Organization, made the reconnaissance hypothesis part of the satellite program. She said that UFOs were subjecting Earth to "a geographical, ecological, and biological survey accompanied by a military reconnaissance of the whole world's terrestrial defenses." According to Lorenzen this activity had increased since the first Earth-orbiting satellite, *Sputnik*, in 1957, and "succeeding space probes launched by men seem to have generated a closer scrutiny of earth by our 'visitors,' if indeed they are real."[10]

Researchers Richard Hall, Ted Bloecher, and Isabel Davis of the National Investigations Committee on Aerial Phenomena suggested in 1969 that there was no formal contact because the aliens did not understand our civilization. "Even in the simple matter of physical approach to human beings, the behavior of UFOs is above all contradictory; they seem to display a mixture of caution and curiosity." UFOs did not contact humans because "the extraterrestrials . . . may still be as baffled about our behavior and motives as we continue to be about theirs."[11]

However, a real contradiction existed between the hypotheses and the daily events. Thousands of people were sighting UFOs; investigators were collecting thousands of reports of high-level sightings, low-level sightings, and even landed UFOs; and there was an increase in the number of "occupant" reports, in which witnesses said they saw aliens in or near a UFO. The Barney and Betty Hill case, in the early 1960s, also helped bolster the argument that UFOs were making covert contact.

Did this activity mean that UFOs were displaying themselves on purpose? What was the purpose?

The Later Hypotheses: 1970s to 1990s

By the 1970s, some researchers began to theorize that UFOs were revealing themselves slowly so that humans could get accustomed to the idea of alien visitation. Presumably, sudden revelation would be enormously upsetting to all human institutions. Fear, depression, and despair would follow. Suicides would probably rise. Widespread panic, institutional disintegration, governmental crisis, and other forms of catastrophe could follow, leading to societal chaos and anarchy. Gradual revelation would "cushion the blow" of contact and reduce disruption; the aliens did not want to shock humans by showing themselves too abruptly.

Therefore, the aliens allowed humans to sight UFOs as a societal "shock absorber." Researchers hypothesized that sightings allowed us to achieve a higher form of awareness about aliens in a constantly controlled manner, much like a thermostat controlling temperature. Part of the alien design was to allow the idea of UFOs as extraterrestrial objects to creep into popular culture. Thus, researchers theorized, the aliens played us like a fiddle for our own good while they carefully monitored society's knowledge of their presence.

UFO researcher Jacques Vallee expounded a version of this theory in *The Invisible College* (1975). The random appearance and disappearances of single UFOs and waves of sightings held special significance for Vallee. These UFO manifestations were part of a control system designed by the aliens to "stimulate the relationship between man's consciousness needs and the evolving complexities of the world which he must understand." This would lead to what Vallee called "a new cosmic behavior."[12]

For Vallee, the UFO phenomenon resided somewhere between the physical and psychic worlds. It was linked to man's consciousness and was called forth to condition humanity to a shift in world view, presumably about the universe and man's place within it.[13] UFO appearances and disappearances were part of a human conditioning regimen, although Vallee was vague about the purpose of the conditioning.

Similar theories developed. One popular idea among Jungian UFO researchers was that UFOs were manifestations of an alternative reality that existed between the psychic and the objective. Individual people psychically called these forms into being from an "imaginal" realm. While they were here they were "real" and objective, but they vanished into the other realm.[14]

The growing number of "occupant" sightings in the late 1970s and early 1980s added support to the "psychic realm" hypotheses. The occupants seemed to behave in incomprehensible ways. They avoided contact, failed to communicate, seemed to inspect people who stood paralyzed, and then disappeared into their UFOs and flew off. Witnesses reported UFOs swooping down upon their cars and pacing or "chasing" them. Other reports described objects simply materializing in front of witnesses and then disappearing without the observer seeing them fly away.

The celebrated UFO researcher and astronomer J. Allen Hynek wrestled with the problems of noncontact and the seemingly absurd manner in which UFOs behaved. When the UFOs initiated what appeared to be a form of contact—being seen from time to time, buzzing cars and airplanes, scaring people, not giving humans a "gesture of good will"—it made no sense. Why would UFOs and their occupants exhibit such bizarre behavior?

Hynek speculated that UFOs dwelled in a parallel universe or another dimension and "popped" through to Earth. Perhaps they came on the "astral plane" in which they could "will" themselves to be on Earth. Whatever the case, the ease with which they came to Earth suggested that UFOs could do what they wanted without having to make formal contact.[15] Biologist and UFO researcher Frank Salisbury summed up these attitudes in 1974 by saying "The extraterrestrials might simply have their reasons for not wanting to make formal contact, and . . . we, in this stage of our development, simply cannot fathom those reasons."[16]

Although theories have abounded—Earth as a refueling station for UFOS traveling to other places, Earth as a tourist spot for aliens to gaze upon—by the late 1980s most researchers had given up speculating about noncontact. Not enough evidence existed upon which to base a viable hypothesis.

Then in the early 1990s, John Mack revived the debate by postulating that the purpose of noncontact was "to invite, to remind, to permeate our culture from the bottom up as well as the top down, and to open our consciousness in a way that avoids a conclusion that is different from the ways we traditionally require." Humans must look for proof of the existence of aliens in ways other than the purely rational. "It is for us to embrace the reality of the phenomenon and to take a step forward appreciating that we live in a universe different from the one in which we have been taught to believe."[17]

I believe these prior hypotheses to be inadequate to explain the UFO phenomenon. As with most speculation about the phenomenon, researchers have based their hypotheses about noncontact on the most circumstantial evidence. Furthermore, most theories have placed noncontact within a human-centered context: Aliens either fear humans or want to help them. Like Ptolemy, who assumed that Earth was the center of the solar system, most researchers have assumed that aliens have come to Earth because they realize the uniqueness and importance of humans. This is what the Judeo-Christian tradition teaches.[18]

Indeed, most traditional theories of formal contact have been rooted in Judeo-Christian anthropomorphism. These theories have generally assumed that an alien species would have a strong interest in the complex thought processes, civilization, and technology of humans. Aliens would respect us and share their scientific and technological knowledge with us; humans would join with aliens into a community of planets. These assumptions have been based not on evidence but on the ideas and thought processes derived from the society and culture in which its adherents live.

Current Hypotheses and Abductions

The abduction phenomenon has always been more secretive than the UFO-sighting phenomenon. Researchers investigated UFO sightings for fourteen years before they came upon an abduction case. Another twenty-five years elapsed before they understood that abductions were enormously widespread and the central focus of the UFO phenomenon.

When researchers first began to investigate abductions, they assumed that an abduction was a one-time, adult-onset event. Abductions suggested curiosity rather than manipulation on the part of the aliens. As abductees recalled fragments of events, researchers decided that aliens were "studying" or "experimenting" on people. The secretive aliens were finished with their examination of Earth's flora and fauna and had turned their attention to studying humans.

As the number of abduction reports grew, many researchers adopted the ethical noninterference argument and assumed that aliens conducted their study in secret in order not to disrupt the subject's life. Memories of an abduction could be so traumatic that they would negatively interfere with the abductee's psychological well-being. In addition, researchers assumed the aliens gave abductees posthypnotic suggestions not to remember an event so that it would be buried in the subject's unconscious.

Other researchers hypothesized that an abductee would not remember an abduction because the natural defenses of the human brain repressed the traumatic event. The human mind could not cope with the impossibility and terror of an alien abduction; rather than confronting the horrendous events, the mind buried the memories deep within it and only allowed tiny pieces to "bleed" through. Investigators had to use hypnosis to recover these repressed memories.

The argument that aliens operate in secrecy in order not to disrupt abductees' lives might have merit were it not for the fact that the disruption in their lives is enormous even without conscious recollection of their abduction experiences. If the aliens were indeed concerned about not causing personal disruption, they would not abduct people in the first place, or, at the very least, not so often over the course of their lives.

The hypotheses that abductees repress memories to cope with the trauma of an abduction also have evidential problems. The mechanisms of traumatic memory repression are highly debatable, and even if the hypothesis is true, the frequency of abductions militates against repression in every case. There are many abduction events that are not traumatic and they, too, are not remembered. Furthermore, researchers have uncovered no reports of posthypnotic procedures that aliens might use to "bury" the abduction event. If these procedures existed, researchers would be seeing them during every abduction.

Although the exact neurology is not known, it is most likely that the aliens store the abduction events directly in the abductee's long-term memory system, bypassing short-term memory and preventing the triggering mechanism that allows for its reconstitution. Hypnosis restores the trigger that allows the memories to come forth. Reshma Kamal was told that the reason the aliens do not "erase" the memories altogether is that there are aspects of them that must be retained by abductees for future reference. Thus, the memories are intact, but inaccessible through normal recall.[19]

For years, the abduction phenomenon has lain hidden under layers of direct and indirect protection—societal beliefs, scientific hostility, incomplete conscious recall, confabulation in hypnotically recalled testimony, and alien-induced memory manipulation. Unlike sightings of UFOs, there are no radar traces, photographs, films, or videotapes. The evidence is primarily anecdotal, with an occasional artifact. Only one thing is certain: Whatever the reason for it, the alien secrecy strategy has been enormously successful. Most people who have had a lifetime of abduction experiences remain unaware of what has happened to them. They would deny as lunacy any suggestion that they were involved with the abduction phenomenon, even if they had been abducted just hours before.

Methods of Protecting Secrecy

The starting point of secrecy is to prevent the abductee from re-membering what happened, a strategy that is more comprehensive than just inculcating amnesia. First, all those near the abduction event must not be aware of what is happening. Therefore, the aliens routinely immobilize, render unconscious, or perceptually alter po-tential witnesses to the abduction. In effect, they "switch off" prox-imate people so that they cannot interfere in the event. Husbands, wives, friends, and bystanders—all are made unaware of the abduc-tion.

Second, the abductee is separated from a group. For example, if he is at a picnic, he will "take a walk" and not return for an hour and a half; when he returns, he explains vaguely that he "lost track of time," and his friends ignore the incident. Thus, the aliens main-tain secrecy while abducting someone from a large group of people.

Third, to render memory recall more difficult, the aliens cloud what memory the abductee has by injecting confusing and "false" memories into his mind. For example, if the person is abducted from bed, he might remember an unusually vivid and realistic "dream." Other abductions might produce "screen" memories of animals staring at the abductee—owls, deer, monkeys, racoons. An abductee might think he saw an "angel," a "devil," or a deceased relative standing by his bed. Society provides a menu of explanations, and the abductees pick and choose depending on their background and culture.

Secrecy extends to the physical aspect of the abduction, and "cloaking" the removal of an abductee is an integral part of it. When a person is abducted from his normal environment, he re-ports that he floated directly out of a closed window, or through the wall, or through the ceiling and roof and up into a waiting UFO. Yet people on the outside rarely see this because the aliens somehow render themselves, the abductees, and the UFO "unseeable" during this time.

Abductions often take place from automobiles, and the aliens in-stitute secrecy in this situation as well. When a person is driving, the aliens cause the car to stop so that the abductee can walk to a UFO waiting by the side of the road (sometimes the abductee floats directly through the windshield). Typically, the aliens wait until there are no other cars on the road, or they compel the abductee to drive down a deserted road and wait for the abduction. Often, the aliens take the car with the abductee, resolving the problem of having an abandoned vehicle on the side of the road.

Threats to Secrecy

Yet the secrecy policy has not been implemented perfectly. The aliens apparently cannot maintain total secrecy. Witnesses see UFOs. Traces of their existence have been left behind in the form of marks on the ground and physical effects upon the environment. Many abductees have conscious memories of their experiences. Abductees are aware of "missing time." They have unexplainable scars and other physical "clues." In addition to these symptoms of abduction activity, the secrecy policy has many other vulnerabilities.

The first vulnerable point is the mechanical device implanted in many abductees. Walking around with an implant can be risky. The monitoring system that alerts aliens to attempts to remove the implant only works in a nonemergency situation. To my knowledge, on at least twenty occasions abductees who are unaware of their abduction experiences have either sneezed out an implant or discharged it in another way. Potentially, the discharge can compromise secrecy. The aliens have been "lucky" that this has not been the case; the puzzled and unaware abductees have assumed that they accidentally acquired the object ("The wind must have blown it into my nose"). Or an abductee might feel compelled to discard the object. For example, a young woman discharged a two-inch yellow plasticlike object vaginally, which, of course shocked and frightened her. She "knew" that she had to get rid of the object immediately. She flushed it down the toilet, and then she flushed the toilet three more times to make sure that it had disappeared. Then she felt better.

Not being taped on video equipment or photographed is essential to maintain the aliens' secrecy. They are extremely careful to make sure that the abductee turns off photographic detection equipment before an abduction. If necessary, they can cause a power failure in the house or neighborhood to prevent the detection equipment from working. They do not want to be seen.

Protecting the Fetus

The aliens' single most significant area of vulnerability—the one that has, by far, the greatest impact on maintaining secrecy—is the implantation of a gestating fetus. Because producing offspring is a primary goal of abductions, successful fetal implantation and extraction are critical. Virtually all female abductees have had embryos implanted, and after a period of weeks or months the fetus has been removed. Without the fetal implantation-extraction phase of the program, the entire abduction phenomenon would be crippled, if not rendered inoperative. It is absolutely essential that the fetus is protected from abortion during this phase.

Fetal implantation is precisely where security is most likely to be compromised. Once a woman has been impregnated, she continues with her normal life but she is carrying the fetus. Although few female abductees are aware of the fetus, they—and not the aliens—are in control of it and the pregnancy. For the aliens, this crucial shift in control comes at a perilous time. If the woman realizes she is carrying a fetus inserted into her by the aliens, she can elect to terminate the pregnancy. Indeed, many female abductees have sought abortions. Alien monitoring generally reveals a planned abortion so that the fetus can be removed beforehand, but other protective methods must also be implemented.

Deceiving the woman by implanting an extrauterine gestational unit is another way to secure protection for the fetus. The unit does not change the shape, size, or color of the uterus and often does not provoke a characteristic hormonal reaction. Therefore, the abductee has little indication that she is pregnant and takes no action to end the pregnancy.

Another subterfuge is to allow the sexually active woman to think she is pregnant. There is always the real possibility that the pregnancy is a normal outcome of sexual relations even though the couple might have used contraception. If the woman elects to terminate the pregnancy, usually there is enough time between the decision and the necessary testing for the aliens to remove the fetus. In most cases, by the time the woman arrives for the abortion, the fetus is gone. Generally, the physician's diagnosis is pseudocyesis, spontaneous abortion, absorption, or secondary amenorrhea. The woman makes no overt connection between the "disappearance" of the fetus and the abduction phenomenon.

Reasons for Secrecy

The critical question still remains: Why are the aliens so secretive? The answer can be found in the motives and purposes of the Breeding Program. Because the fetus must be protected, the most effective method to prevent the abductee from knowing about the pregnancy is to keep it secret from her. In response to Lucy Sanders's questions one alien was uncharacteristically forthcoming. He told her:

We have our own interest because we are removing your ova and using it for our own genetic purposes. We know this will be very disturbing to the human female because she is a reproductive organ between the two of the species, she is the host for reproduction, and we only remove those that we need.

When Lucy asked him what that meant, he replied:

We sometimes use the female human as a host for genetic reproductive purposes. We feel that if the female of the species knows that her body is being used as a host, she may wish to remove what she feels isn't hers. So we put a very strong blank [block] on her memory process so that she has no idea that the implant has been put there. We will do the same for you when we, as we have in the past, implant you.

We feel that it is better for the female if we do not leave the implant in. We are able to bring the fetus to term using our own females, but the first, within the first trimester it must be removed so that the female human does not realize she is host to an implant.

We find psychologically, within the first trimester, if the female host is unaware of the implant, she goes about her normal routine, and it does not have a debilitating effect on the fetus. Upon removal, we put another blank on the female human host so that in the future we can do this same procedure and she will be accustomed to it.[20]

Beyond protecting the fetus, there are other reasons for secrecy. If abductions are, as all the evidence clearly indicates, an intergenerational phenomenon in which the children of abductees are themselves abductees, then one of the aliens' goals is the generation of more abductees.

Are *all* children of abductees incorporated into the phenomenon? The evidence suggests that the answer is "yes." If an abductee has children with a nonabductee, the chances are that all their descendants will be abductees. This means that through normal population increase, divorce, remarriage, and so on, the abductee population will increase quickly throughout the generations. When those children grow and marry and have children of their own, all of their children, whether they marry an abductee or nonabductee, will be abductees.

To protect the intergenerational nature of the Breeding Program, it must be kept secret from the abductees so they will continue to have children. If the abductees knew that the program was intergenerational, they might elect not to have children. This would bring a critical part of the program to a halt, which the aliens cannot allow.

The final reason for secrecy is to expand the Breeding Program. To integrate laterally in society, the aliens must make sure that abductees mate with nonabductees and produce abductee children. If abductees were aware of the program, they might decide not to have children at all or to mate only with other abductees. Thus, the number of childbearing unions between abductees and nonabductees would decline, endangering the progress of the Breeding Program.

The Breeding Program must be kept secret, not only from women, but also from men and society as a whole. When Claudia Negrón was six years old, a young hybrid girl explained at least part of the program to her.

I ask her why they're doing this. She says it's for the good of everybody and that they have to do this. It's very important and that I'm not the only one. There are many. . . . And one day I will know what it's all about, but not just yet. Because if they tell people what it's all about, then their project is ruined. So they have to keep it a secret for now. I ask her what kind of a project is it. She says to make a better world, to make a better place.[21]

It could be argued that since we have evidence of the Breeding Program, secrecy has effectively been compromised. But this is not the case. The aliens' wall of secrecy will only be penetrated when many people within our society, perhaps the majority, fully realize what has been happening to them and understand the implications for them and their descendants. After fifty years of public awareness of UFO sightings and abductions, the debate continues about whether the phenomenon is "real," and the scientific community refuses to study it.

Thus, at this point in time, the aliens' policy of secrecy has been and continues to be enormously successful, despite the millions of UFO sightings and abduction reports. The vast majority of abductees have the memories of their experiences locked in their minds, entwined within a labyrinth of dreams, confabulation, false memories, and induced images—exactly where the aliens want them to be. And if abductees recover these experiences, they endure societal strictures, ridicule, disbelief, and condescension.

Secrecy is not necessary to protect society from the "shock" of revelation of "contact." Nor is it necessary to protect the individual's life from disruption. Secrecy is necessary to protect the alien Breeding Program. It is a defensive measure, not against the hostility of violent and frightened humans, but against the hostility of a host population who would object to being the victims of a widespread program of physiological exploitation.

Now we can understand why the aliens will not land on the White House lawn. If they were to do so, the reasons they have come to Earth might be discovered, and they might not be able to continue with their Breeding Program. Most of the past secrecy theories have assumed the aliens concealed themselves to hide their existence. It is now clear that the primary reason for secrecy is to keep their *activities* hidden and therefore they must keep their existence a secret.

Because it is covert, the abduction phenomenon that is essential to the Breeding Program has grown to enormous proportions. And both its purpose and its magnitude have profoundly disturbing implications for the future.

7

Infiltration

For many years, UFO researchers thought abductions were rare events that befell unfortunate adults who happened to be in the wrong place at the wrong time. The Barney and Betty Hill case seemed to be a good example of the "There's-One-Get-Him!" theory. In recent years, however, researchers have realized that the abduction phenomenon is lifelong and pervasive.

We now know that abductions begin in infancy. Mothers have described being abducted with their babies. Some abductees have even reported aliens visiting them in their hospital beds shortly before or after giving birth. We also now know that the abduction phenomenon continues into old age. Most important, we now know that abductees experience a lifetime of abductions. Every abductee whom my colleagues and I have investigated has had many abduction events throughout his or her life.

So, how many people have been abducted? This question is virtually impossible to answer, mainly because people do not remember their abductions. But in spite of this difficulty, we know that the abduction phenomenon is enormously widespread. My colleague Budd Hopkins and I have received thousands of letters and phone calls from abductees relating their experiences. Other researchers throughout our society have dealt with or heard from tens of thousands more. Still, the number of people contacting researchers is not an accurate representation of how many people might be abductees because, again, most abductees are unaware of their experiences.

Unaware Abductees

Although unaware abductees are a silent population who confound accurate statistics, they provide an excellent "reality check" for the abduction phenomenon. We can compare reports abductees made before they became aware of their abductions to those they made after hypnosis with a competent therapist. As a group, the unaware abductees consistently report a similar pattern of experiences before becoming aware of abductions.

When unaware, they explain their strange experiences in ways acceptable to society. For example, an unaware abductee will explain his nighttime odd and half-remembered visitations as "guardian angels" calling on him. An unaware abductee might explain a visitation as a deceased relative or friend reassuring him that "Everything is all right." An unaware abductee may think that he has seen "ghosts" and that his house is "haunted." One woman told me she and her family had moved many times to get away from ghosts, but every house she ever lived in was haunted.

Unaware abductees also frequently report seeing religious figures or the Devil. They report having had intense and profound communication with an animal. They describe having unexpected or unwanted "out-of-body experiences" that take place apart from trauma or meditation. They travel on the "astral plane," from which they can look down and see rooftops in their neighborhood.

The case of one graduate student is typical. She told me of seeing ghosts, UFOs, and bizarre occurrences throughout her life. In one spectacular event, when she was a young girl, she looked out of her bedroom window and saw a UFO landing in her backyard. Suddenly her distraught mother came running into her bedroom, yelling that the aliens were going to get them and that they had to hide. The student remembered nothing else in the incident. I asked her what she thought about these unusual events. She answered that her mother had told her this was just part of life, that life has its mysterious side, and that what she experienced was just a part of growing up. She was able to categorize a lifetime of extraordinary events as "normal."

Informal Estimates of Magnitude

Budd Hopkins designed a questionnaire for *OMNI* magazine in 1987 to try to collect incidence data on abductions. Readers of *OMNI* returned over 4,000 questionnaires. Physicist Bruce Maccabee and UFO researchers Don Berliner and Rob Swiatek of the Fund for UFO Research analyzed 450 of them and concluded that about 4 percent of the male respondents and 11 percent of the female respondents might be abductees.[1]

In 1987 I also began to collect incidence data on abductees. I developed a simple survey, based on the *OMNI* questionnaire, for a university student population. Over the years, I refined the survey and continued to give it to students. By 1991 I had collected over twelve hundred responses, mainly from college students aged eighteen to twenty-three. These fell into three categories: possible abductee, questionable, or not an abductee. I based the categories on my knowledge of the unusual experiences that abductees had told me about before they knew they were involved with the phenomenon. The results of my analysis suggested that 5.5 percent of the respondents were "possible" abductees, and that 15.5 percent were "questionable." These numbers were shockingly high.

And there are many other informal estimates. For example, the evidence strongly suggests that the majority, if not all, of "close encounter" UFO sightings are the beginnings or endings of abduction events. Even high-level sightings may be indicative of abductions. Statistics from Gallup Polls on UFO sightings have varied from 9 percent to 14 percent since the 1950s. If a percentage of these sightings mask abductions, then the number of abduction events is high.

The Roper Poll

In 1991, Robert Bigelow, a philanthropist and supporter of UFO research, and another interested researcher proposed to Budd Hopkins and me that we conduct formal survey research to estimate the number of people in America who may be abductees. We agreed.

We knew the challenges. We had to construct the survey so that it would elicit a wide range of information and overcome the problems of lack of conscious memories of abductions. Then we had to find a polling organization that would be willing to take on the task. After interviewing the major polling organizations, we chose the Roper Organization because the people there were enthusiastic about the project. Finally, we had to be very cautious and conservative in analyzing the results.

In the summer of 1991, Roper conducted an omnibus survey of a randomly selected group of adults across the United States. It was an in-home survey, in which an interviewer went to a person's home, asked the questions, and recorded the answers on his questionnaire. The abduction questions were part of other questions about people's personal experiences and politics. There were no questions about product preferences.[2] One question was specifically designed to identify people who felt compelled to answer positively regardless of the facts. Hopkins invented the word "trondant" and we asked if this word had special significance or meaning for the respondent. If a large percentage of people answered the trondant question positively, we would know that the answers to the questionnaire should all be suspect.

Survey research usually covers a population of about sixteen hundred people, which is considered large enough to provide accurate results for most national polls. However, given the controversial nature of abduction research, we wanted to use a much larger population to maximize accuracy. The final number of respondents was 5,947 people, which yielded an error range of a mere 1.4 percent. The Roper Poll thus became the largest and most accurate poll of this type ever taken. It is important to note that it was not an opinion poll, but a poll asking about people's personal experiences, which made it different from nearly all other polls of this nature.

In the initial results, the number of potential abductees was very high—embarrassingly high:

- 18 percent had wakened paralyzed with a strange figure in the room.
- 15 percent had seen a terrifying figure.
- 14 percent had left their body.
- 13 percent had missing time.
- 11 percent had seen a ghost.
- 10 percent had flown through the air.
- 8 percent had seen unusual lights in the room.
- 8 percent had puzzling scars.
- 7 percent had seen a UFO.
- 5 percent had dreams of UFOs.
- 1 percent said the word "trondant" had special significance for them.

The small number of positive responses to the trondant question meant that the poll was not weighted toward those who had the urge to answer positively. The Roper Organization eliminated from the final statistics all questionnaires with a positive answer to the trondant question.

The results of the Roper Poll indicated that millions of Americans might be abductees. Hopkins and I knew that the abduction phenomenon was widespread, but these numbers were breathtaking. For that reason, we took the most conservative approach to the data. We isolated the five questions that had been found in previous research to be reliable indicators of abduction activity. And we included in the final sample only those people who answered at least four of the five questions positively.

The final analysis indicates that 2 percent of the American people—five million Americans—have experienced events consistent with those that abductees experienced before they knew they were abductees. Even if this number is as much as 75 percent higher than actual occurrence, there would still be over one million people who might be abductees. One thing is clear: The Roper Poll confirmed the less formal and anecdotal evidence that there are a tremendous number of people who have had abduction experiences. And we can conclude, therefore, that the abduction phenomenon is widespread and touches almost all groups in society.

In addition to the overall findings, the Roper Poll reported the results by age, sex, race, geography, and social status, and provided data on these subgroups. One important subanalysis focused on age, and a second focused on the group of respondents whom the Roper Organization called *Social/Political Actives*. These people, whatever their political persuasion, are aware of social problems and seek to effect change. For example, they write letters of protest to their local school boards, seek political office, or otherwise have some semblance of social responsibility. They have more education and a greater median income ($38,700 compared to $28,300) than the general population.

The results of the two subanalyses are shown in the following tables. The first summarizes the responses by age group, showing that the eighteen to twenty-nine age group answered more positively to the five abduction indicators than any other age group. This seems to go against logic because older people have had a greater opportunity over their lifetime to have more abduction experiences.

Relationship Between Five Indicator Experiences and Age (Total Sample)

	Overall	AGE 18–29	30–44	45–59	60+
Waking up paralyzed with sense of strange figure	18%	22%	21%	17%	10%
Missing time	13%	14%	13%	13%	10%
Feeling of actually flying	10%	11%	13%	10%	8%
Balls of light in room	8%	11%	9%	7%	5%
Puzzling scars	8%	14%	7%	6%	5%

The second subanalysis concerns the *Social/Political Actives*. This group would not be expected to have experienced bizarre events; they are people who place themselves in the public eye. However, they not only scored higher on all questions, but they scored *significantly* higher.

Relationship Between Five Indicator Experiences and Social Political Activism (Total Sample)

	Overall	Soc./Pol. Actives
Waking up paralyzed with sense of strange figure	18%	28%
Missing time	13%	17%
Feeling of actually flying	10%	18%
Balls of light in room	8%	11%
Puzzling scars	8%	9%

Frequency Estimates

The Roper Poll provides incidence data on the abduction phenomenon, but it does not provide frequency data. We know that abductions occur throughout most of an abductee's life. However, estimating frequency is very difficult. The first and most important problem is that abductees do not remember the vast majority of their abduction events. To collect frequency data, I asked several abductees to chart their abductions. These abductees had a sufficient number of hypnotic sessions with me to be sensitive to the "markers" that strongly indicate abduction activity. Six abductees carefully recorded the events that happened to them. We have confirmed some of these events through hypnotic regression, and we will investigate other events as time goes on.

Frequency of Abductions

Abductee	Period	Events	No. Investigated
Karen Morgan Jan. 25, 1988–Jan. 22, 1989	1 year	9	7
Kathleen Morrison calendar year 1994	1 year	13	7
Christine Kennedy Oct. 1992–Feb. 19, 1993	3½ months	8	5
Allison Reed July 20, 1993–July 22, 1994	1 year	33	14
Gloria Kane July 4, 1988–Feb. 28, 1989	8 months	54	11
Kay Summers Nov. 13, 1993–Dec. 14, 1993	1 month	14	1

The charting effort uncovers some provocative data. Christine Kennedy, for example, correlated her menstrual cycle with her charted abduction events; when there was no abduction event, her period had a twenty-eight-day cycle; but when there was an abduction event, her cycle shortened to as little as twenty-four days. Allison Reed correlated her abduction experiences with her blood sugar level (having diabetes, she took her blood sugar reading every morning); her blood sugar level was often elevated after an abduction, rising to three or four times its normal level. Gloria Kane found that her experience increased in frequency at ovulation and decreased in frequency at menstruation (although ovulation and menstruation were not the sole determinates of her abductions).

The woman who represents the extreme of the abduction phenomenon is Kay Summers, who lives in the Midwest and works in retail sales. Constant telephone contact has allowed me to record the many events that have befallen her. She had as many as 100 abductions during a one-year period, or an average one every three days. The effect on Kay has been devastating and she lives in despair. She receives minimal support from her friends and family, who either refuse to believe her or, if they do believe her, refuse to believe the amazing frequency.

Often tired and depressed because of sleep loss and abduction trauma, Kay has learned to dissociate psychologically from the experience while it is happening, much as a child might during repeated physical or sexual abuse. Still, she is on an emotional roller-coaster. When the abductions ease off, she begins to regain her sunny disposition, but then they begin again and her despondency mounts. As of 1997, her abductions continue. Budd Hopkins and I have investigated many of her experiences, including over fifty of the recent events.

Although the frequency with which Kay is abducted is extreme, it is not as unusual as we originally thought. In the last few years, many abductees have reported dramatic accelerations in the frequency of their abductions. The general trend has been toward a greater number of events for each abductee.

Suppose that these data are wrong—that frequency is much lower. The smallest number of abductions per year reported to me is nine. If the rate is only five per year, and if the phenomenon begins in childhood and continues through old age, the numbers still add up quickly. If the person is forty years old, then he may already have had as many as two hundred abductions, with many more to come. This is borne out by many abductees who have charted their unusual experiences over a period of several years. Charles Petrie, who works as a printer, kept a journal of his experiences over the course of his life and has consciously remembered over two hundred events up to age thirty-eight. His life has been a quest to discover what has been happening to him.

The conclusion from the Roper Poll and from our own research is that, without a doubt, an enormous number of people are experiencing an enormous number of abductions. The aliens have invested and continue to invest a tremendous amount of time and energy in the abduction program. Many people think that abductions are a "study" or "experiment," or that the aliens are "learning" about us. The numbers suggest otherwise. The learning and experimenting, if ever the case, are mainly over. Hence, the evidence clearly indicates that the aliens are conducting a widespread, systematic *program of physiological exploitation* of human beings.

The Hybrid Species– Children

The production of a hybrid species appears to be the means to the aliens' goal. So far, researchers have been unable to uncover any other purpose for the UFO and abduction phenomena, and the Breeding Program. Why are aliens producing hybrids? This has long been one of the fundamental mysteries of UFO and abduction research. Until now, we have had precious little information upon which to formulate a theory. But to answer this question, it is first necessary to understand both the idea of hybridization and the nature of hybrid life.

Producing Hybrids

For years researchers have posited that the aliens are a dying race and must pass on their genes to hybrids to maintain their "life." This theory assumes that the aliens either cannot reproduce or cannot reproduce in enough numbers to sustain their species' viability. Although dismissed as science fiction by many UFO researchers, the evidence suggests that there may be merit to this theory.

The Allison Reed case sheds light on this issue. In her four-and-a-half-day abduction event, an alien escort took her to a "museum" room in which she saw artifacts on shelves along with strange life-sized "holograms" of several beings. Her alien escort explained what these figures represented and why the hybridization was undertaken.

Each of the hologram figures had a "flaw" of some sort. The first had alien features with distinctive black eyes and a thin body; it also had a distended stomach with boil-like protuberances on it. The next hologram looked more human. He had blond hair and human-like eyes, but he had no genitals, and his skin was extremely pale, like that of a "borderline albino." The final hologram was a grouping of smaller beings, about five feet tall. They were very white and Allison received the impression that they were "mentally weak or something."

Allison's escort told her that the most important fact about these beings was that none of them could reproduce. They appeared to have been failures at previous attempts at hybridization. "The human race is not the first that they have found, or that they have attempted to work with," she said. "We are just the ones found to be the most compatible and the ones that it can work with because they can't sustain themselves for an awful lot longer because they [the aliens] are a result of a genetic mix, alteration, manipulation, whatever the word is."

The small one you're looking at can't reproduce?

No. Not any of them. They can't reproduce—any of them. So, besides the parts that were failures, like the white one's mental abilities . . . somehow they just weren't able to get it. But, apart from that, the three that I have told you about, they can't sustain life for themselves. My understanding is that's what's happened to the gray ones. Throughout the creation of the gray ones until through their evolution, we'll say, they've gotten to the point that reproduction of themselves is a problem. Almost like the horse and the donkey syndrome in that you come up with a sexless mule. And that's kind of what went wrong. I don't feel like it happened right away. Somehow they were able to reproduce but, because they are a result of a genetic altering, through the years and through the generations it lessened. I guess it would be almost like if men just became sterile year after year after year until, whatever. . . .

Does he tell you what they were like before genetic alteration?

No. He doesn't specify that. . . . He just claims that he and his gray people are the result of genetic manipulation that some higher species, I guess, played God and mixed and matched and whatever. That's what he tells me. . . . He and his people were created through a genetic alteration through a higher intelligence. . . . I don't know what they were created for. But my understanding is that they were created for a purpose and, through the years, they weren't able to reproduce themselves anymore. From what he told me . . . they didn't start this. They were a result, just like the hybrids are, from something else. From a higher intelligence. That's what I get from him. I guess. That's just what I hear.[1]

This explanation suggests that the aliens had attempted a program of reproduction before they came to Earth, and that they have had periods of trial and error. The idea that the gray beings were themselves products of hybridization experiments was also given credence during one of Reshma Kamal's abductions. The insectlike aliens told her that the gray aliens were products of early attempts at hybridization with humans but the program was flawed and it left the gray aliens without the ability to reproduce. Then the insectlike aliens began a new program of human hybridization with different techniques that has taken more time but has been fruitful.[2] Whatever the case, humans have been successful for them. We can reproduce, and they can reproduce through us.

Creating *Homo Alienus*

In 1992, I began a series of hypnotic regression sessions with a woman who apparently had a sexual relationship with a human-looking hybrid. During one conversation "Emily" and the hybrid had discussed his parents. I asked her if he had discussed the differences between him and us. She told me, "He's a hybrid. His mother was like me, and his father was like him. So he's . . . a degree closer." I was intrigued by what she had said. If true, the implications of her information were extraordinary.

As I thought about Emily's statement, I began to put other information in context. For years abductees have been reporting a variety of hybrid types. Some hybrids look very much like aliens, some look like combinations of human and alien, and some look extremely human. Although the exact hybridization process is not known, a theory can now be put forward that explains the disparate types of hybrids and their activities.

Hybridization appears to progress in stages. It is clear from abduction reports that it starts in vitro with the joining of human sperm, eggs, and alien genetic material. The result of this union, which is "grown" partially in a human female host and partially in a gestation device, is a hybrid being who is a cross between alien and human (hybrid.1). Many of these hybrids look almost alien. They have large black eyes with no whites; small, thin bodies; thin arms; thin legs; thin, nonexistent, or sparse hair; a tiny mouth; nonexistent or tiny ears; and pointed chins. They have no genitals. Some look so much like aliens that abductees often mistake them for "pure" aliens.

The next (perhaps second) stage in the hybridization process occurs when the aliens join a human egg and sperm and assimilate genetic material from the first-stage hybrid (hybrid.1) into the zygote. This too begins as an in vitro procedure and then requires both a human female host and a gestation device to mature the fetus to "birth." The resulting offspring is a cross between hybrid.1 and human. These beings (hybrid.2) still look quite alien. They have an oddly shaped head with a pointed chin, high cheekbones, and only a small amount of white in their eyes; their hair is still quite sparse but there is more of it; their bodies are thin but larger. There is no evidence that hybrids.2 can reproduce. When mature, these early-stage hybrids often help aliens with the abduction procedures and are an integral part of the alien workforce. Abductees see them taking care of hybrid babies and toddlers and executing other important tasks.

The next (perhaps third) stage of hybridization involves taking a human egg and sperm and adding genetic material from hybrid.2. Like the previous stages, the middle-stage hybridization process begins in vitro, progresses to in utero and then to a gestation device. The resulting hybrids (hybrid.3) look very human. If properly attired and wearing dark glasses, they could "pass," although they might be "off" in their appearance. Abductees say that hybrids.3 can have too much black in their pupils or lack eyebrows or eyelashes. Like the previous-stage hybrids, these middle-stage hybrids help the aliens, and some are responsible for more complex jobs— even performing complete abductions without alien supervision.

Hybridization reaches a critical point in a later-stage generation— possibly the fourth or fifth. Once again, the aliens use the standard hybridization process, splicing a human egg and sperm with genetic material from a hybrid.3. The resulting late-stage hybrids are so close to human that they could easily "pass" without notice.

Most of the late-stage hybrids have normal-looking eyes (perhaps only a slightly enlarged pupil). Their skin color is humanlike but sometimes a bit too even. They often have short-cropped hair, but some have curly or long hair. Some do not have eyebrows or eyelashes, and most do not have body hair or pubic hair. Their frames are sometimes thin, sometimes muscular, but never overweight. They are often blond and have blue eyes, although abductees have noted a range of hair and eye coloration. The females have human secondary sexual characteristics and have longer hair than the men. Most males have normal genitals but some penises might be too narrow. The males are not circumcised. It is these late-stage hybrids whom abductees often call the "Nordics."

Late-stage hybrids possess the aliens' extraordinary mental abilities. They can engage in staring procedures, Mindscan, visualizations, envisioning, and so on. They have *nearly* complete command over the abductees, who report having a little more physical and mental control during hybrid abduction activity—not enough, however, to effectively resist abductions.

Late-stage hybrids have a singularly important attribute: They can reproduce with humans. They have intercourse with humans in the "normal" manner, bypassing the standard egg and sperm harvesting phase of abductions. These resulting hybrids are barely distinguishable from "normal" human beings.

Although it is unknown precisely how many stages of hybrid development exist, the evidence points inexorably to the development of an increasingly human-looking and human-behaving hybrid armed with the aliens' ability to manipulate humans. Whether male late-stage hybrids can reproduce with female late-stage hybrids is unknown. Abductees have reported that female late-stage hybrids have had difficulty bringing babies to term.

Once the hybrids are born, the aliens funnel them into specific types of service. For example, Kathleen Morrison was told that some hybrids are for acquiring knowledge, some are for "assisting," and some are for both. She also understood that the later hybrid "models" have greater "power" than the earlier ones.[3] Clearly, hybrids are not all alike in ability and behavior.

Researchers know little about the hybrids' daily lives. Nevertheless, abduction accounts have provided enough information to at least outline many hybrid activities from fetus to adult.

Fetuses

When fetuses are removed from the abductees, they are kept in tanks filled with liquid nutrients. Abductees have reported rooms, some small and some almost cavernous, containing hundreds, and even thousands, of tanks with gestating fetuses—their large, open black eyes dominating their tiny bodies. The tanks are often arrayed in gestational stages of development, from youngest to oldest. A gray alien told Allison that late-stage fetuses are kept longer in utero because they cannot be sustained in incubators for a long time. Early-stage hybrids, he said, can be kept in the incubators for more sustained periods.[4]

Babies

When the "newborns" are removed from the tanks, they are usually phlegmatic, especially the early-stage hybrids. They seem, by human standards, passive and even "sickly." They do not cry, they do not grasp with their hands, and their bodies do not have the same muscular tension as human babies. Abductees often remark that these babies seem "wise" or "mature" for their age; some abductees have said that the babies communicate with the abductee through their eyes, as if they were absorbing information from the abductee through neural coupling. Whether this is true is uncertain, but many abductees have said that the babies, even at an age of less than two, have unusual mental capacities. Susan Steiner once held a baby that impressed her as having capabilities beyond his age:

It seems like maybe it's about three or four months old but it seems more alert than a three- or four-month-old baby. . . . It's not like really physical, but I could see it like looking around. It has almost a curious look in its face instead of the typical blank expression that most three- or four-month-olds have. I get the feeling that this baby's like older than three or four months. It seems older somehow and it seems knowledgeable. When I look at its eyes, I get almost the same feeling that I get from that tall being like when I'm on the operating table. And so I try to avoid looking at its eyes because that makes me a little uncomfortable. It's almost like the eyes can control you so I don't want to look at its eyes too much.[5]

Abductees have fed babies by breast and with bottles and have painted nutrients onto their skin. The early-stage hybrid infants seem to eat by absorbing liquid, the middle-stage hybrids eat by a combination of absorption and ingestion, and the late-stage hybrids ingest through their mouths.

Toddlers and Young Children

Abductees often report having contact with hybrid toddlers (two to six years old) in group situations. The toddler group usually consists of mixed-stage hybrids, and the aliens bring the abductee to the toddlers to have physical contact, play with them, or teach them. If abductee children are present, they are required to take the lead in play activity, directing the hybrids in how to perform. For example, the human child might suggest that they play ring-around-the-rosy, and then she will show the hybrids how to hold hands and go around in a circle.

Hybrid toddlers sometimes play with human toys (trucks, teddy bears, dolls, airplanes, and balls) and sometimes with alien toys (a ball that has swirling colors in it and dances about in midair by itself, or other high-technology playthings). Hybrid toddlers have alien abilities and can execute Mindscan and other optic nerve engagement procedures. Abductees report that the toddlers use staring procedures to gather information from humans.

Unlike the aliens, the hybrid children display definite personality differences. For example, Diane Henderson went into a room containing six or seven toddlers. They all had blue eyes with no whites, fuzzy hair, and small noses and wore white garments. She kneeled and hugged each one. The room had some blocks built into the floor but there was nothing for the children to play with.

They just look at me. Like look into my eyes. . . . They all seem to like me for some reason. . . . There's one little girl that's more shy than the other ones. Some of them seem to be kind of hearty in a way. They're not as slow. They're a little quicker. Not a lot. They just seem to be very peaceful, but I don't think I see any whites of eyes.[6]

Very often the aliens seem concerned about giving the toddlers some sensory stimulation. They sometimes build a nature "setting" in which the hybrid children can play. Sarah Stevenson, a real estate agent from Delaware, entered a "glass-bubble" room where she saw

Cindy, an abductee friend of hers, playing with a group of about fifteen three- and four-year-olds in a barren, outside setting. They were all kneeling on the ground with a few adults around them.

Yeah, it feels like if you were at the zoo, and you were looking at a habitat. It's very brown, like sandy, light, you know, a lot of light. There's not a lot of grass or—more like rock and sand, a lot of brown. The kids are sitting on the ground on their knees. It looks like they're all wearing the same thing . . . a little tunic or something. You don't see any shoes or anything. That's all they have on.

Do they have any toys?

Mm-hmm. It looks like nothing complicated. It looks like some kind of blocks. It seems like maybe there's some adults there too, more human looking. They're kind of playing with them.

Regular humans or kind of humanlike?

They look like regular humans. It's hard for me to see. I think that Cindy is there.

Okay, how is she doing?

. . . She's sitting on the ground with them. She seems to be showing them how to build things with the blocks. I don't know why it seems like there's caves there or something. I don't know why. Like they're playing on the ground, and behind them is . . . something rocky. It feels like the zoo.[7]

The aliens seem aware of the varying needs of the hybrid children depending on their stage of hybridization. An alien took Roxanne Zeigler, a nurse living in New York State, to see a group of toddlers who were playing together. Then an adult hybrid took Roxanne to visit a late-stage toddler who was in a different playroom with climbing equipment; this toddler was dressed in human clothes. The escort said that the child was born in 1990 and it was Roxanne's.

Well, right now he's taking me to this other room that is, there's like another doorway that goes to this other room, and there's a jungle gym type of thing in there. And it's a colorful one, I mean it looks like it's made out of metal. And there's like a ladder and there's all these rods going and connecting like making open boxes that are kind of scrambled in this thing, but they're the rods. One section is painted. It has one color and these are more brightly colored. One step is red, and one bar is red, and the next bar is yellow, and the next bar is like blue, and the next bar green—that type of thing. Okay. And . . . there's a little boy who's climbing around on this.

Is he the same age as the others, or a little bit younger, or—?

I think he's a little older. And, he's, he's a little darker, and his hair is darker. I mean he, just like, like the difference between . . . a Scandinavian-looking, with the blond and light-skinned, to a more of a umm . . . I don't know, Mediterranean, maybe. You know, more bronzy, like, tanner. . . . They're asking him to come, they're asking him to come to me, and he's coming. They had this little boy dressed differently from the other children that were playing in that other room.

He's not wearing that white smock?

No. He's got on a, a multistriped t-shirt. This is, you know, the stripes going around him. And some, like little blue shorts.

Okay. Did he have shoes on at all or . . . ?

Yeah. He had like little brown shoes on. And, yeah he's coming to me. And he's just standing there, and he's looking at the being and he's looking at me. I kneel down and I hold on to him, and you know, I tell him I want to give him a hug, and I put my arms around him . . . [he] put his arms around me too. And, then I pick him up and stand up with him, and the being seems to be very pleased. This being said that I held him when he was a baby. But I can't take him home with me. He has to stay there because they said he won't survive outside the environment they've provided for him. But they made arrangements for us to be together that day. It seems like what they're trying to do is they're trying to get him accustomed to our race, somewhat, because at some point, they want to try to wean him so that he can survive in this society, somehow. But he's different, you know, he'd still be linked with them. He can, this little boy, he can kind of will something to come to him. There was something up on a shelf, and he couldn't reach it, and he wanted to give it to me, and to show me this.

How far away was the shelf?

Well . . . the shelf is across the room, and I probably could reach it, but he wanted to bring this to me. And . . . it's a rocket ship, it's not a spaceship, it's a rocket ship, a little silver one. And the way he's getting it, he's just willing it to him, and it floats to him. And he can hand it to me. And it's a little silver rocket ship. And it's one of those, like pencil-type things, you know, that kind of a shape and silver with the wings pointed back that are close to the body of it.

Yeah, like an old-fashioned rocket ship.

Yeah.

Does this look like an, an American style toy, or is it a little different, or—?

Well, it's metal.

Does it have marks on it, like you know, a toy will have an American flag on it and things like that? You know, stickers you put on it.

There's, there's like a white . . . triangle, you know, that has a short base and a long straight side . . . and inverted on the other side of that is a blue, blue equivalent, on top of the wing.

Okay. So this thing floats over toward you?

Yeah, it floated right to his hand, and he shows it to me, and he's kind of excited about that.

Does he communicate with you or . . . just show it to you?

Yeah. His eyes kind of shine, and he's smiling, and he's pointing to this thing. He's cute. . . .

So you're holding him this whole time then?

Yeah, I'm just standing with him, and I'm holding him in my arms, and he's showing me this thing and. . . . He wants to get down, but apparently he's not telling me he wants to get down. He just kind of floated out of my arms to the floor and let himself down.[8]

Later the little boy showed Roxanne a special room he lived in, with a human-style bed that came out of the wall. He seemed proud of his possessions.

Hybrid children sometimes want to play with human-style toys, but often they do not know how and need instruction. Aliens bring human children on board to teach the hybrid children how to play. When Claudia Negrón was five years old, a female alien took her into a room with five or six hybrids her age. They played together and she taught them how to use a yo-yo.

They want to show me something. They want me to teach them my games. . . . That's funny. They have a yo-yo. It's weird.

A regular kind of yo-yo?

Something like it.

Is it colored?

No. It's like white.

You know, most yo-yos have the company name on the side, Duncan, or whatever. . . .

No, this doesn't have anything. I can tell it's a yo-yo—I knew what they look like, but it doesn't have any markings on it. . . . They want me to show them how to use it. . . . They have these little round balls that look like marbles.

Uh-huh. Where do you see these balls? Do they have them just on the floor you mean, or just in their hands, or in a container of some sort?

One of the children had it and showed it to me.

Do they say anything when they showed it to you? Do they say look at this, or what do you think of this, or something like that?

Nobody's talking. They just show it [the yo-yo] to me and I get the impression that they want me to use it because I know how to use it.

Did they seem pleased or happy?

Oh, yeah. They got happy when I showed them.

Did you show them how to use the yo-yo first, or—?

I showed them. I took it in my hand and I showed them how to play with it. And that sort of broke the ice.

I see. Well, playing with a yo-yo for a five-year-old, that's kind of hard to do.

I had played with it before. . . .

So they had these marblelike balls, how did you play with those?

They're little—they're strange balls . . . they spin.

You mean by themselves?

By themselves. There's something inside them that makes them do that.

Well, do you kind of play with them, or do you show them what you're doing, or what kind of interaction do you have with them?

They show me. . . . It's like they spin around and they levitate and keep spinning.

You mean they're up in the air a little bit?

Yeah, they keep spinning. And they go down. I'm tired of this game, I want to go home.[9]

The hybrid adults who attend to the children are usually not forthcoming about the children's origin or family life. Susan Steiner had a short exchange about this with an adult hybrid when she was taken into a room filled with apparently same-stage hybrid toddlers. The children were playing with a combination of small toys and playroom equipment.

They had sophisticated-looking toys, like maybe they got them out of Edmund's Scientific or something. They didn't look like the typical—except for maybe a ball or something like that. Most of the toys looked more complicated than regular toys.

See any of them working the toys?

Yeah, they were playing with them. Sort of like one kid was playing with what looked like a puzzle toy. And some of the kids were playing with the ball. And some of the kids were playing with this stuff that looked sort of like wet silver sand or something. . . . They were sort of molding it with their hands and stuff, just playing with it. There was no television in there or anything. . . . There was something that looked sort of like a gym that you could play on. Things that they could crawl through and crawl on—you know, like a play gym. So I asked him, "Well, who do these kids belong to?" And he didn't give me an answer, he didn't say anything. Like I said, "Where are their parents?" because they looked like humans. Then I asked him if he was one of the parents and he just sort of looked at me like, you know, "I'd like to give you the information, but I can't."

I see. So he also is not being forthcoming about what this is all about here. What are these kids wearing?

Well, they're wearing little miniature outfits, sort of what he has on. But they're not all black, some of them have a white-beige one, a silvery-colored one, and some of them have black. Like a miniature version of what he's wearing. But they don't all look like him, they're not all blond and blue-eyed like he is.

So they're all sort of wearing these one-piece tight outfits.

Right. But they have different colors of hair and stuff. Some have brown eyes, some have blue eyes, some have hazel eyes. . . . They all seem to move in unison. I don't know if necessarily they move in unison, but they all seem to know when the other's going to move. Then they all sort of looked like they were cloned or something, at least the blond ones.[10]

Youth

As with the toddlers, abductee adults and children are required to play with and at times instruct the six- to twelve-year-old mixed-stage (from early to late) hybrids. Abductees have taught hybrid youths a variety of games, including kickball, hand-clapping games, and other play activities. The hybrid youths' toys are very technologically sophisticated. The youths also apparently have more learning sessions conducted by abductees. When they interact with abductees, they appear to be more curious about humans in general, and about the emotional differences between the two species.

Kathleen Morrison was seven years old when she was abducted with her friends Heidi and Barbara. She played with hybrid toys and engaged in a discussion about emotions with her hybrid friend. Kathleen recalled this event from a child's perspective:

Their toys are different than our toys.

How so?

Their toys *feel*. When you play with them, you feel things. Our toys don't do that.

You mean, they feel rough, or—?

No, they make *you* feel.

What kind of toys were there, then?

They're different colors and they're shapes, mostly. And you get to hold them.

Is there like a ball or block or something?

No, it's more like, it's more like blue glass. But they don't like it when you throw them.

Do they want you to touch one?

Yeah.

How many toys are there?

Maybe three or four. But Barbara's there [her friend who, along with Heidi, was abducted with her], and there's whole bunches of other kids. There's a bunch of us [human children]. . . .

So when you come into the room, what's everybody doing?

My kids are giggling and having a good time. And there are two girls on the side and they're sitting near each other and one girl's talking to the other one.

These are normal kids?

The one is and the other one's not all that . . . no. One of them's like *them.* And this other girl's sitting there talking to her.

Can you see what they're talking about?

Well, the girl who's talking is braiding her hair, her own hair? And it's something about her hair.

So what do you do then?

I walked in and I got near Heidi and Barbara. I needed to be near them. But they don't like us to stick all with our own kind. But we all have to play together. I really do like their toys though, because they make you feel.

Well, do you get to pick up a toy?

Yeah. . . . I pick up the blue glass one.

What kind of shape is it?

Mmm . . . triangle? But it's like it melted? And it's a triangle that melted. You know wax lips? And you put it down on a radiator and it melts all over it? Well, this toy was wax, it kind of melted over something that was round. And it's like shiny from the inside.

How does it make you feel when you pick it up?

Very happy. Makes me feel very happy.

Do you have to do anything to it or do you just hold it?

You just hold it in your hands. And I took it to Barbara and I had her hold it.

Did she like it?

Yes, she did. She thought it was fun. She said she ought to give it to her parents sometimes. We tried something different, because most of them were just being held by one person and we wanted to see what it would be like for two people to hold on to one. So we did and I think I felt happier than she did. I don't know. She didn't smile. Made me feel real good. . . .

Before that, did you get to talk with any of the other different kids, or not?

After I put down the blue glass thing? I didn't go over to her but I still talked to her. We didn't talk through our mouths though. [She] wanted to know why I was laughing. "Because I felt good." Did I always laugh like that when I felt good? "No. Sometimes I just feel good." I don't know, they don't look like they have a very happy house.

Did she say anything else to you?

"Is happy good?" I think I said, "Yes." That's a silly question though, really—"Is happy good?" So I don't think they have a real happy house. You know, nobody laughs up there. I think I want to go home. I want to go home now. I want to go home. She doesn't understand why I'm getting so upset. I want to go home. I want to be with my family. I want to go home.[11]

Not only do abductees teach the children how to play with human toys and learn human games, they also begin to teach about Earth and human society. Doris Reilly, a small-business owner from Harrisburg, Pennsylvania, was ten years old when she taught a group of hybrid youths about the circus. Talking from an uncooperative ten-year-old's perspective, she recalled how adult hybrids observed the proceedings as she interacted with a large group of hybrid children.

The children were so happy to have me there, they were so excited. . . . There's something wrong with these kids. Are they retarded?

How can you tell?

I must be smarter than them because I sure look a lot better. But they're all talking to me as fast as I can talk, and they're talking to me in my language. Their bodies are weaker than I am. They're slower than I am. I would be the ringleader if I stayed. They are so happy to have me there. I seem so wonderful to them. . . .

Are there a lot of kids in there?

I'm going to play with them. I'm enjoying it because they're going to let me be the showoff. There's at least five or more that are really paying attention to me. There's other activities going on way back in other parts of this big giant room. Those kids are busy doing other things. It's not real noisy. They're asking me about the circus. She's telling them what to ask me about.

Which one is this?

It's a female, bigger one, older. She's the one that's supervising their activities. She's telling them what to ask me. The one little boy asks me about the circus, what it's like. They want to talk about the animals, and I want to tell them about the clowns. I keep telling them, "You have to know about the clowns. They're so funny." They don't know what funny is, so I'm trying to show them. I'm trying to explain a playground and what it's like. They don't know what swings are. I feel so sad for them. I want to cry for them. They don't know what it's like to play like I can play. I really don't care about the boys, I feel sad for the girls. I tell them that I'd build them a swing set for them if they'd give me some logs and hammers, but the lady is telling them it's impossible and to stop talking about it.

She's telling you, or—?

She's telling them what to talk about, and she's discouraging them from the playground. I don't pay attention to her because she's talking to them. I tell them what it's like to be in a sandbox.

What are their ages?

They're the same age as me. She's saying to stop talking about the swing set. I hear her telling them that, they wanted to keep talking to me about it, though. So I don't have to listen to her, I don't have to obey her. I'm going to tell you all about big sandboxes. We all sit Indian-style . . . and I explain what a tin bucket and shovel is like. I'm showing them what it's like to shovel out the sand. They're imitating me, they look so stupid, they don't know what it is. She doesn't like that I think they look stupid trying it.

She doesn't like your feelings?

She doesn't like me feeling superior because I know this stuff. . . . I'm telling them stuff they don't know about. They want to go where I am. A couple of them want to see what that's like to play with the other children. She's discouraging them, telling them their life is happier where they are. If they can't come with me, I'll just stay with them. Maybe they'll let me build swing sets, and maybe they'll let me build a sandbox for them. Maybe they can give me metal and I can teach them how to make a big giant sliding board. . . . She's going, "Our children don't do that." But they want to. They want me to stay. She doesn't want me to stay. . . . They're having so much fun with me. They really like me; I'm so different and so strong, and I know so much about having fun, and they don't know anything about that. They want to know more about it, and that's why they like me. I'm telling them, if they can come back with me they can probably look like I do. "Come back into my bedroom, I'm sure God will make you look like me so you can stay and play with me." She's telling them to stop talking like that, to stop it. . . . I feel like she has some compassion for them, but she has to stick by her rules. She's making sure that there's peace and order kept among all of us. There's one little girl I really like, and I'm naming her Maria. She's smaller than I am.

Does she have a name of her own?

I don't care. I'm telling her I'm naming her Maria, and I want her to be my friend.

How does she respond?

She says she'd like that too. She knows my name is Doris. She will have me back to play with her again. They don't want me to leave, I don't want to leave.

Are you still sitting there?

No, the lady is making me go. I don't want to go. There's so much more we can play . . . she's telling me we have to go now. The children seem so happy that I was there, but I'm leaving. There were adult ones observing all this from somewhere. . . . They were in windows along the sides of us, particularly to the right. They were observing us like we were lab rats. I look over and they're in there, observing us. . . . She's going to take me out of the room. My heart is beating very fast all of a sudden. . . . I don't want to go. I promised the children I'd be back, and they tell me to try my hardest to come back. Maria looks so sad. I'm telling Maria that I will be back to play with her, I promise.[12]

At times, abductees see large groups of hybrid children in special playrooms. Interaction between the humans and the hybrids is controlled so that the hybrids get the maximum amount of play enjoyment. Unlike human children, the hybrids appear to have no disputes or disagreements. In 1965, ten-year-old Carla Enders was at a girls' camp in Texas. In the middle of the night, she and approximately twenty-five other young campers were abducted. They were brought into a large room filled with mixed-stage hybrid children and highly sophisticated play equipment. The children immediately began "laughing and running around" in a state of artificially induced hilarity.

It just seems like there's a bunch of things in there for kids to play with.

Is this a large room, or a small room, or . . . can you get a sense of that?

It's really pretty big. It's really big. I can't tell what everybody's doing, but it seems like they're all laughing and running around. It seems like there's girls and boys . . . running around like they're playing on these swings and jungle gyms and stuff like that, but different.

How do you mean?

. . . Like there was just, like a big amusement park where all these different things are there. Like a Disneyland, all compact. I don't know how to explain it. But it seemed fun.

You're talking basically about heavy equipment, things to climb on and all?

It seems like they were just suspended, there was nothing it had to be attached to or anything. Just things, you wondered how they were there, how they were working. I just felt like really amazed. Then I didn't think about a whole lot, I was just running around with the other kids.

Do they tell you anything, or do you just go off by yourself, or . . . ?

They just say, "This is what we wanted to show you." They let go, and I go check it out. I can just remember it seemed like a lot of fun. Like really just different than I've ever seen.

Do you hear any sounds? Are the kids yelling and screaming and laughing, that sort of stuff?

Yes. They're having the greatest time I ever had before.

You can hear them through your ears?

Yeah, they're all laughing and screaming and running around. And they're all getting along. Nobody's pushing or shoving or hitting or wanting to be first. Everybody's pretty much getting to do what they want.

Do you see the girls from camp there?

Yes. I don't remember what they look like. But there's girls there about my age and a little younger and maybe a few years older.

Are they all wearing their nightgowns and pajamas?

They seem like they all kind of have on the same thing. Just like really plain, just something, even the boys. Nobody was really concerned about what they were wearing. They didn't care. They weren't even aware of it. . . . But they're funny, when I think of it now, they're wearing these gowns or something. Like a hospital

gown with sleeves, almost like a dress. We didn't really think anything of it.

When you say "We," do you mean the girls from camp?

All of us, the girls and the boys. . . . It seems like they're just
laughing. I don't know why they just keep laughing. I keep
laughing too, but we don't really ever talk to each other, we're just
laughing. It's almost like they gave us some kind of drug that
makes us laugh. . . .

So now when you're laughing, are you just standing there?

We're all just running around. Then we stop and then we're
standing there all just laughing. We're just having so much fun we
can't quit laughing. I think they're thinking that this is all just too
much fun so we can't quit laughing. We're kind of laughing at each
other too, in a way. It's almost like we don't ever want to leave
there. So we're just running around on these things, hanging from
the . . . they seem like they're hanging in midair. And then there's
things that you can get on and they zip you around. Like a roller-
coaster or something but they don't have any track.

What are they on?

I don't know, they're just zipping around through the air, up and
down and all around, really fast.

Do you get on one of these, or do you just sort of observe it?

Yeah, I ride them too.

This is up above things?

Yeah, you can't see the ceiling. It's like just this big space and you
can't see the ceiling.

When you're up in this ride, do you kind of look down and survey this situation?

It just seems like a big amusement park and there's kids running all over and on these rides. You can't really tell where it begins and where it ends except when you go in that door where you come in. That's all I can see. It doesn't seem like the rides are really high up, but high enough, people are running around underneath and nobody gets hurt. It seems like we were there for a little while and then it was time to go.[13]

When the children are older, the abductees sometimes are required to teach them about life on Earth. In a classroomlike setting, the youths ask questions about a preselected subject. An alien took Susan Steiner to a room with twenty youths who were apparently waiting for her arrival. They were sitting on molded benches. The alien told Susan that she was to teach a class and indicated to her that she should use the screenlike chart on the wall for her teaching. The lesson consisted of Susan answering questions from the curious hybrid children as barnyard and domestic animals appeared on the screen.

There's a regular school-type chart?

Well, it looks like a blackboard but it's not. It looks like some sort of screen. It looks like an Etch-a-Sketch screen, except it's filled with all sorts of stuff. It's sort of silvery and like a dog is on the screen and she tells me that I'm supposed to explain the dog to them, what the dog is.

Was this a picture of a dog?

It's like a picture of a dog appears on the screen, like a real dog.

Color? Black and white?

Color.

What kind of dog is it?

It's like a chow. A big, furry chow chow, the ones with the purple
tongue. And she tells me I'm supposed to explain to them what the
dog is. So I tell them what a dog is, you know, that humans like
them and they keep them as pets. That they used to live in the
wild and humans domesticated them and they became very
friendly and loyal. So, then I asked them if they have any questions after I explain what the dog is and the kids ask me, "Why is
the dog loyal?" And I tell them I don't know, they'd have to ask
the dog. I don't know why a dog's loyal. And they said, "Why does
it like humans?" and I tell them I don't know. And they ask me
questions like, "What does it eat?" and I tell them what they eat.

Well, are they raising their hands or are they just . . . ?

They're just sort of speaking in turn, one will speak up and when
he finishes up, someone else will ask a question and when she finishes. . . .

So they say, "What does a dog eat?"

And I say that a dog should eat meat. And they ask me why the
dog should eat meat and I said because its intestine is shorter than
mine. So they ask me if I eat meat, and they ask me if I have
a dog.

Do you tell them that you do or do not eat meat?

Yeah, I tell them that I don't. . . . And they ask me if I have a dog,
and I said, "I do. I have a dog." And they ask me what I use him
for and I tell them that I use him for companionship. And they
seem satisfied with that, like they're finished with the dog and
then a goat goes on the screen and they ask me about the goat. I
tell them that I really don't know that much about goats, but that
some people use them to get milk from and I told them where I
come from they don't eat goats but in some countries, they do.

They eat goats. They ask me why some people eat the goats. And I said because they don't know any better. They ask me what else you could use a goat for. And I said some people use them to work, like pull carts and stuff and sometimes you can get wool from certain goats and some people use them to make cheese from their milk. They get milk and they make goat cheese and stuff and people eat the cheese. Then a chicken goes on the screen and they ask me what a chicken is and I explain the chicken. And other animals go on the screen and we go through a similar process—I tell them what it is, like it's a cow and a horse goes on the screen. They seem to be interested in the horse and they ask me what we use the horse for. And I say, well, we use it mostly for work, like it does things, like it pulls things and maybe we ride it to take us from place to place—not so much anymore, I tell them, because we have cars now but we used to ride horses. And they ask me if we eat horses and I tell them that we don't, not where I come from, but some countries eat them. And they ask me why. And I tell them I don't know. Then it seems like the screen just shuts off and the kids come up to me and they sort of like touch me, everybody touching me, like curious.

You mean they're touching you?

Like my arms and my hands and stuff. They even pick up my hands and they're looking at my hands and, for some reason, even though I don't have my clothes on, I'm not embarrassed. It's like weird, I think that normally I would be. They don't seem to notice that.

Are they wearing anything?

Yeah, they have like little skin-tight outfits on, similar to the one that the teenager was wearing. Some of the girls have little flimsy little dresses on, looks like a nightgown almost, but some of the girls have the skin-tight outfit on too.

But they're girls?

Yeah, there's girls and boys.

How can you tell?

Because they look like normal people. They look like you or me.

When they speak to you, when you were hearing the questions, were they speaking through their mouths?

No.

They have normal noses and normal lips and all that?

Well, their eyes are like very, very pretty eyes. Their eyes are very big and slightly almond-shaped, not Oriental, but they seem to have big irises but there is white in their eyes, though. And they have cute little noses and their mouths look normal. They look maybe thinner than normal, but they still look normal and their skin is, well some of them have light skin and some of them have skin that looks very normal. . . .

When they come up and touch you, do you touch them?

Yeah. I pat them on the head and I like rub their back and I put my arms around one of the kid's shoulders. They seem to like that. After a little bit of that, the woman tells me that we have to leave. And we go out of the room.[14]

Late-stage hybrid youths sometimes display an awareness of their genetic situation. Some abductees have related conversations that suggest these hybrids are emotionally caught between two worlds. When Carla Enders was eleven years old, she came across a particularly sad situation with a girl whom she had met during previous abductions. The girl was intensely curious about human family life and sensed that she had missed something by growing up where she did. The meeting took place in a large room with a group of adult hybrids observing.

Then we stop in this room. . . . And she's walking toward me, and she looks older now. And I'm really glad to see her.

How old does she look? Can you make a guess?

She's kind of my age.

Eleven or so?

Yeah. It was a year either way, she was my age. We're about the same height. Her head's bigger than mine. But she seems really happy to see me. She can't really smile, but it just feels like she's smiling. I really like her. I guess I kind of love her too. Like she's my sister. Like a sister. Like you would love a sister. . . . Seems like I give her a hug, and she kind of doesn't know how to respond, but almost like she lifts her arms a little bit, and puts her arms around me a little bit, but not like I do around her. She doesn't get hugs very often. She doesn't know, really, what to think of it. But she knows that it means love. It's just kind of sad. I'm sort of sad for her. She wants to be normal like us. She wants to be, it's like she can't get free, like she's trapped or something. She can't have the same experiences. It's sad. . . .

You said you're standing there looking at her.

She's like, she can become part of me or something.

Here comes these odd questions, Carla. Where is she looking?

She's just staring at my eyes.

And where are you looking?

I'm just looking at her eyes.

How close does she get to you?

Half of an arm's length. . . .

Is she touching you?

No. It's like we're trading thoughts. Like she can experience things through me. It's just like she wants to know everything about me—what I've been doing, and what's happened since she last saw me, and how I've changed, and what I'm like now. She seems like she doesn't really have anything to do. She gets to see people now and then. That's the most exciting thing that she has to do. And be with other kids, and when she had fun with us, that was every-thing to her. Like she gets lonely, but not as bad as when she was younger. She's not usually very happy. She doesn't think that she'll ever be happy. . . .

Does she specifically communicate with you?

Yes, she says "Hi" to me, and it seems like she says my name, and how happy she is that we are together again, and she really wishes that we could be together more. She doesn't have much of a life. It's like she tells me there's nothing to do. She doesn't have any-thing to do except what they do around there, and it's really boring. And she would like to be able to do things like we do, just to be like a kid. She doesn't really get to be like a kid unless she's with us. Nobody around there is like us.

So I get the sense that she really wants your company.

Yes. And then I hold her hand. And I don't know what we do. It seems like we just walked over somewhere and we were sitting down and we started looking at some things together, like books or something. I don't know where they got these books.

Regular books, with pages?

They seem like books. And she's saying, "I've got these things to remind me of you and the other kids. They remind me of you when you're not here with me. They have pictures of people in them."

There's English writing in them?

They're like, it seems like they're kids' books.

But it's recognizable letters and all that?

I don't know if she reads them. I think she just looks at those pictures. They got them from us somehow.

The pictures are normal pictures?

Of kids, and older people, and animals, and just, they're probably geared for kids our age, like maybe eight- to twelve-year-olds or something. They have pretty big writing, and there's half the page, some would be writing, and pictures. And she really likes to just look at the pictures. She wants to be in the picture. She just wishes she could be in the picture. I told her it's really not that great in the picture. I don't know why I tell her that. I say it's better probably than what you have, but sometimes it's really not that great in the picture. . . . There are a lot of things that go on that are not very pleasant. In a lot of ways I know she has it much worse, but then in some ways I think she has it better because she doesn't have to experience a lot of the negative things about the way we live. But she still thinks she wants to experience it. She thinks it would be better than what she experienced.

Did she say what she's experienced, or is she just talking in general?

. . . She feels like she's capable of feeling things more than the others are. They can't understand her. She feels like we can understand her. And it's really lonely for her that way because she just wants to feel what it's like to really feel loved and she doesn't feel that she can really know what it's like to feel loved. We're the only ones that can give her that.

I see. Is she leafing through the pages in the book?

She just turns the pages really slow, and she's showing me the pictures that she likes the most, which seem to be the ones with kids and parents in the park or something, and there's a dog running around. And she's amazed, like, "What is that really like to do that?" And I'm thinking, "Well, I guess that is pretty neat, if you don't get to ever do it." She doesn't think she'll ever get to do it, so she's really, she gets excited about looking at the pictures, but at the same time it makes her sad. I don't know how to make it better for her except to tell her they're just pictures and it's not always like that. Animals are fun, and it's nice to have trees around, and there's a lot of nice things about nature but there's a lot of scary things that happen. And people aren't always that nice to each other, and there's a lot of things that happen. People starve, and people are killed, and I just tell her there's bad things too.

So you're trying to make her feel better by having her appreciate her own situation a little more.

I guess it's like she doesn't understand what it's really like, and I just want to explain to her that it's really not all good. There's a lot of good things that I wish she could see. But I'd like her to know that. . . . I think there are some good things from her. . . .

How many books does she have there?

There's lots of books, all different books for different kids, different ages. . . . Stacked in piles. . . . It seemed like she would just like to go with me for a while. I'm wondering if she goes with me sometimes. Maybe she can read my mind so much that she can, she doesn't have to go there, she can see it in my mind, and she's there, kind of. And it doesn't seem like quite enough. She would still like to be able to go with me, not having to be in my thoughts.

Right. What happens next, then?

It seemed like we just were standing up, and I was holding her hand, and we just walked around the room a little bit together. And just so we could be together a little longer. We just walked around the room. And I told her that she was a very good friend, I really liked her as a friend, and I would always be her friend. And then it just seemed really sad because we had to say goodbye.

How do you know?

She just stands there, looks at me really sad. Like when she first saw me she was so happy and now she's standing there looking like she doesn't have anything to be happy about. Then I say well, I'll see her again. I'll probably get to see her again, but I don't know for sure. It seems like I tell her that I'll try to send her thoughts. . . . I don't know. It just makes me really sad.

So you say goodbye?

Yeah. She has to go, so she turns and walks, one of them walks off with her, out the other side of the room from where I came in. And then somebody walks with me out the other way.[15]

The evidence suggests that the toddlers and youths are involved with a dual instruction process: gaining knowledge about their own lives and duties, and learning about Earth and life on it. But rather than dealing with Earth's political, economic, and social institutions, their lessons appear to focus on the ordinary events in the day-to-day lives of humans. Much of what is taught involves getting along with humans and acting human—evidently in preparation for the time when the hybrids will be able to live among us.

The Hybrid Species—
Adolescents and Adults

By the time young hybrids have reached adolescence, the aliens have given them new tasks and responsibilities within the abduction program. Although they still learn from the humans, they now begin to interact with abductees more on a sexual and social level. The aliens' use of the adult hybrids demonstrates the scope of their Breeding Program. Adult hybrids assume complex duties within the abduction program which, like those of the adolescents, sometimes involve sexual relationships with abductees. But the adults have interactions with humans that go far beyond that.

Adolescents

When hybrids reach adolescence, the aliens begin to give them tasks to perform. They sometimes help retrieve the abductee from his normal environment, they help with some procedures, they escort the abductee from room to room. Their work ranges from menial jobs to helping the grays with specialized duties. In effect, they become "apprentices" to the smaller gray aliens.

Although the adolescents "work," they are young and, unlike the aliens, amuse themselves. Susan Steiner recounted her experiences with an adolescent hybrid who had some sort of "game." The fif-teen-year-old boy escorted her to different rooms, but at one point sat down with her to play with a machine.

He just smiles at me and he runs his hand down my arm and takes my wrist. And I kind of like him because I'm kind of happy to see him. . . . And he has this thing sort of tucked under his arm, the little machine, and he gives it to me. . . . It's like some kind of wonderful thing and I should be glad that he gave me this thing. . . . And then I kind of like take the thing and I sink down on the floor, you know. I'm sort of like playing with it, because I can tell he wants me to play with it. And I'm thinking, "Oh, well. I'll play with it even though I don't know what it is, and I don't understand what I'm doing." I just sort of start pressing buttons on it . . . I get the feeling from him that I'm supposed to know what it is, that I might have seen it before.

You said that there was some sort of a green kind of glow coming from part of it?

Light-emitting diode kind of thing. LED? It was like maybe pencil-thin and it was in the center of the metal piece. . . . He gives it to me and I, well, first I sort of turn it over and look at it. I'm looking at it and I'm trying to think, "What is this? Is this the stereo? Did he take the stereo?" Then I realize that it's not the stereo. Then I start hitting all the different buttons. I'm sitting cross-legged—and I put it down on my knees and start hitting all the buttons, trying to get something different to happen other than just the lines moving in the LED display.

. . . Can you get something different to happen?

No, nothing's happening. Then he takes it from me and he presses a button, gives it back to me and I'm supposed to press the same button. I press the button and he takes it back. Then he presses a button and I'm supposed to press the button. This goes on for a while and then he gives it to me and I press a button and there's this flash.

You mean the flash comes from the box itself?

Yeah. . . . It seems the whole box just flashes . . . and I drop it because I'm afraid of it. I think it's electrical.

You mean, you dropped it on the floor?

Yeah. . . . He seems amused . . . that I dropped it because I was afraid. He thinks it's very humorous. . . . He thinks it's funny— almost like he thinks it's funny.

Does he smile? Or do you just get a sense that he thinks it's funny?

I do see a smile and I get a sense, but he doesn't laugh like we do. I get the feeling that he's like laughing, but he doesn't laugh like a regular child would laugh. His mouth does curve into a smile. Then I think those three other beings come into the room. And they look more serious than the others, like I'm a little afraid of them. They look very stern and they look different than the ones in the operating room. . . . And they're watching us interact. . . . And they look at me like really stern, really stare at me. And I'm a little afraid but then the little boy touches my shoulder and I'm not afraid any more. . . . He tries to bring my attention back to the toy, that thing, whatever it is. And then I'm sort of not paying attention to them anymore, I'm playing with that metal box again.

You mean you were starting to push the buttons again?

Um-hum.

Did you push them in a sequence with him? You push, he pushes, you push, he pushes, or are you doing it by yourself?

Yeah, we're doing that. He's pushing a button and giving it back to me. I'm pushing a button and he's pushing a button, I'm pushing a button, he's watching. But nothing else happens. No flash like that.

It doesn't lead to another flash?

No. I'm getting kind of frustrated. The little kid just thinks it's funny, that I'm frustrated.

So he thinks that's amusing too?

. . . Yeah, he just seems amused that I can't figure out what it is. And I get this, like, I don't know, some kind of feeling from this kid, but I can't figure out what it is though—almost like he can understand why I can't figure it out, like he knows why I can't figure it out or something. I don't know.

You get a sense that he knows why you're confused?

Um-hum. Like it's not a feeling of superiority, but it's a feeling of like, "Well, I wouldn't expect you to understand." That type of thing.[1]

The late-stage hybrids who display a strong sexual drive often begin their sexual activity in adolescence. When Kathleen Morrison was eight years old, a sixteen-year-old hybrid, whom she would know through out her life, engaged in what was clearly masturbatory activity with her. First he put her on his lap and began rubbing his body on hers while he generated sexual feelings in her through a staring procedure. Kathleen recalled the episode from an eight-year-old's point of view.

He's done this before?

. . . It's when we've been quiet together. It's usually when I'm sitting on his lap. I'm sitting on his lap, and I straddle his body, and I face him. He gives me wonderful big hugs. And then sometimes he looks at me and makes me feel different. . . . He says he likes me to sit on his lap and be very close to him.

. . . How old are you . . . ?

Maybe eight or nine. We don't do this all the time though. Just sometimes. When we're quiet and alone. He does like to rub on my body though.

Does he usually wear some kind of outfit when you see him?

Not always. Sometimes he doesn't have a lot on.

When he doesn't have a lot on, you mean he's sort of naked and all that?

Sometimes.

When you sit on his lap, what does he do then when he's not wearing clothes?

He just bends his knees up and I just sit on his lap and sit back up against his legs. And his legs are like this and I sit right here but I can lean on his legs and he holds me, and he breathes pretty heavy sometimes. But he always makes me leave.

He makes you leave?

I always have to get off his lap. . . . I just kind of sit off on the side, and kind of go into a "comatose" thing. When he's breathing kind of heavily he tells me to get off his lap.[2]

Hybrid adolescents are encouraged to have sexual relations with abductees. Christine Kennedy recounted an incident when, after Mindscan, she had to get on top of an adolescent hybrid who was reclining on a pad on the floor. The young hybrid, who appeared to be fifteen years old, engaged in intercourse with her. She was extremely angry and thought that she was being used simply to satisfy his needs.

I feel like I was a "treat" that was tossed to this little fucker. . . .

What are his reactions like? I mean, what does he do with his arms? Are they just laying at his side, or does he—?

No. They're wrapped tight around me. I can't . . . move. My head is laying like over at his shoulder. I'm looking away, and it's just . . . I'm totally gone. I'm not even a part of my body.

. . . Do you think they're doing this for reproductive purposes or for other purposes? What's your best guess on that?

I wouldn't say for reproductive—not when it comes to me, because I have my tubes tied.[3]

Some abductees feel that intercourse with an adolescent is almost like a hybrid "training" session for the future. On some occasions, an adult hybrid actively directs the adolescent on how to have intercourse with an abductee. The adolescent hybrid learns from these experiences and then engages in more active sexual behavior as an adult.

Adult Hybrid Life

Once the hybrids become adults, their responsibilities increase and, according to abductee reports, they are more involved in the abduction routine. Although still in an "assistant" or subordinate capacity, some adult hybrids conduct the full range of physical, mental, and reproductive procedures. They work alongside the gray aliens—and become partners working toward a common goal. In recent years, abductees have reported events in which hybrids perform complete abductions without any grays in evidence.

Some abductees prefer being with the hybrids rather than with the grays. For them, hybrids offer the comfort of human familiarity. Other abductees find the late-stage hybrids frightening and prefer the more predictable gray aliens. The grays act according to a well-defined system, and over time many abductees have grown comfortable with them. For the most part, the hybrids act like the grays: task-oriented, efficient, and clinical. But their presence injects a note of emotionality and unpredictability. Their very humanness almost makes them party to a crime involving the kidnaping of men and women. Many women feel more emotionally vulnerable around late-stage hybrids. Allison Reed put it best when she said:

It sounds crazy but I feel more comfortable with the little gray guys than being left alone with these people-looking [hybrids]. . . . They don't have that compassion, I don't feel it. I don't know if they're anything like human beings. Maybe that's why I'm scared, because human beings can be so cruel. Whereas the gray guys, they do their job and they don't want to hurt you but they don't want to, you know, give you kisses and love you either. They're just kind of neutral in a way. But human beings can be so cruel.[4]

Little is known of the private life of hybrids, but some of the most suggestive testimony comes from Allison's four-and-a-half-day abduction, which provided a rare opportunity to glimpse aspects of daily hybrid life. Her experiences reveal that the hybrids have a cleaning routine; they communally groom themselves and check one another for health problems. At one point, an alien escort took Allison to a cleaning and grooming room. Many naked male and female hybrids between the ages of eighteen and thirty were in the room. Allison, accompanied by an eighteen-year-old female hybrid, and the other hybrids walked in a line to a "shower" area. They stood in front of jets in the wall that sprayed a fine mist that dried on contact. The jets were about chest high. Allison turned around slowly so that the spray would spread evenly around her body. She thought that the mist not only cleaned but protected the skin in some way.

After the shower, she and the others went to a central area in the middle of the room. The hybrids paired off and began to groom and inspect each other. The adolescent hybrid inspected her and then showed Allison how to check her—Allison had to look at the hybrid's hair, the back of her neck, and her eyes; she was required to pull the adolescent's lower eyelids down and look for spots of red in the bottom of each eye. The adolescent told her that the hybrids are prone to rashes under the armpits and Allison had to check her there, too. The adolescent hybrid had "soft" hair, pinkish color in her eyelids (with no red spots), no eyelashes, and taut skin. Her body was long and thin with no hips. It reminded Allison of the animated character Gumby. After the inspection, the other hybrids cut each other's toenails. Allison did not have to perform this task because her adolescent had no fingernails or toenails. Finally, she and the hybrid brushed each other's hair with a tool resembling a normal hairbrush.

The hybrid went to another area to get her clothes—a white shift. She got it from a slot in the bottom of a floor-to-ceiling cylindrical dispenser, and Allison helped her put it on. A short time later Allison's alien escort took her to a huge sleep room. The hybrids were sleeping in tiers, suspended in the air, hooked up to cables attached to the ceiling. The scene was reminiscent of the motion picture *Coma*.[5]

Susan Steiner also saw a hybrid sleep room. It had bunk beds arranged in tiers of three.

It could be just as large [as an airplane hangar]. I can't see the whole thing because it's divided. There's areas that are divided and there's like bunk beds all over the place and there's people on the bunk beds. . . . They're sort of like molded into the wall, and it looks like they're three on top of each other. And the room is sort of like divided so I can see, like areas. And on each side of the wall there's bunk beds. So there's a lot of them.

They're in tiers of three, you mean?

Right, in tiers of three. And maybe . . . they're partitioned off and there are some on the opposite sides of the wall and there must be others. I can't see what's on the other side of the partitions but I have the feeling that there are others. Because it all looks the same, it's a very homogeneous environment.[6]

The adult hybrids appear to have a life that resembles the life humans lead, although the indications are that they lead that life more communally, and less privately, than humans do in modern industrialized society. They bathe, sleep, dress, and work together. Like humans, they have health problems. On an emotional level, however, their lives bridge the area between human and alien.

According to abductee reports, the hybrids have no memories of parents, siblings, family life, nurturing, or other emotionally important events that bond humans to each other. In a long conversation, one late-stage hybrid told Reshma Kamal that his memories were quite different from hers.

And then I'm asking him does he have parents like I do or kids and things like that. He kind of looks sad. I don't know, he looks down and then he looks at me and he's saying no. He says, "We just belong here." . . . I almost feel sorry for him. And I'm asking him like I have a mom and dad, does he have it?
He looks down again, then he looks up at me and he goes, "I know where I'm from but I don't have bonding like you do." I said, "What do you mean, bonding?" And he's saying, "files." . . . I ask him again "What do you mean by files?" . . . And he's saying like, he's kind of explaining to me like when we look at our ancestors, we have memories and histories. He's saying when he looks at *his* background, he only has to look at files. There's no bonding and no memories. . . .
He says, "When you remember your mother or your sister, you're remembering memories of being there, of seeing them." He's saying, "When I want to do those things, I have to see files. I don't have that bonding or memories." So I'm saying, "Haven't you seen your parents?" He said, "I have seen them but I don't have the same bonding." He said, "We are just told who they were or what and they're on files." I don't know what he means by that.
He's saying to me something like, I don't know, he's explaining to me like when he was a little boy or something. It's like he's really,

really, really sad and he's saying that when he was a little boy and
when he questioned them [because he looked different than
them]—I think he means "them" by aliens because he looks up
there [to aliens in the room] . . . he was always shown a file. . . .
And I said, "A file? You mean like pictures and things of your be-
longings?" He's saying, "More in a medical way." . . . He's going
into like medical stuff, the genealogy of the medical stuff of his
parents and things but not in photographs or. . . . He says, "Not like
picnics you might have or parties but in a medical way. Do you understand?" I just kind of shrug my shoulders like I do, but I don't.
. . . I'm saying to him that can't he come, you know? And he goes,
he's asking me, "Come where? You mean to your home?" And I
said, "But that's *your* home, isn't it?" He's saying, "I have no
home. Not in the same sense you do." He's saying, "I don't belong
anywhere." I'm asking him like where does he live and he looks at
the aliens and he's saying like them. And I said, "What do you
mean you live with them? Don't you have a home like I do?" He
seems to be saying that he has a home but not the same meaning
that I have attached with a home.

He's asking me a question, "Do you know what a robot means?" I
said yeah. He's asking me like what. And I'm saying, "Well, a robot
is something that you create and it does what you want it to do
and nothing else." When I give him that answer, he goes, "Now
you know how I feel." And I'm saying, "You're a robot?" He seems
a little annoyed with me. He says no, but the meaning is the same.
That that robot has no bonding. It just does what it's programmed
to do. And he said, "Do you see that I'm doing the same thing?"
And I said . . . "I understand that, but don't you have emotions of
your own?" And he's saying to me, "Even if I had those emotions,
what good are they because nothing will happen?" And I'm asking
him, "What do you mean by that?" He doesn't answer me but he
looks really sad. And I'm asking him like is he happy? He's asking
me like what do I think or what do I perceive looking at him. Like
I don't answer him because I don't want to hurt him, but he looks
like he has really practically no life. He's just alive and breathing.
He said, "We're just here to do work."

And then he looks at them, the aliens again. He's saying, "We have to do everything they say." I said, "Do you have a bond with them like I do with my family?" And he's saying, "Not the same bond that you have." Like we have relationships and we feel love, hate, sorrow, and all that. He said not in that manner, he doesn't have a relationship with them. It's just like they're in total control of everything. That he's just their creation, whatever they did, and he's to do whatever they say. Then he looks at me and he said . . . "If you want to understand me, just think like robots. That's all there is," he says.[7]

We do not know the effects of the lack of familial ties or memories. Whatever the consequences are, the hybrids' emotional development in that regard would be devoid of a commonality that most humans share and their emotional lives would have to be very different from ours.

Hybrid-Human Information Transference

As they do for the younger hybrids, the abductees are often required to instruct the adult hybrids. Instruction takes two forms: directed, and involuntary thought transference. Allison Reed's case provides a good example. She was directed to instruct four female adult hybrids on how to bond with a child; the hybrids told her that they wanted to raise the children in a nonsterile environment more like "normal" humans and less like their own childhood experience with the gray aliens.[8]

Like the older children, the adult hybrids show interest in earthly activities. For example, Claudia Negrón awoke one evening to see two hybrids in her room—a male and female in their early twenties. They wanted to know why she was hanging her clothes around the room instead of in her closet; she explained that she was remodeling the closet. They asked her other questions about her room and then left.

Sometimes an abductee is required to transfer his memories to a hybrid, almost as if the transfer were a "data dump." Kathleen Morrison cupped her hands around a multifaceted orb that glowed red while a hybrid gazed at her and cupped his hands around hers. He "downloaded" information from her brain—what school papers she had been writing and how she went about doing it. He also mentally examined an argument that she had with her sister.[9]

Data transference to hybrids also includes emotional responses. Allison found herself "wired" to a female hybrid who sat opposite her and performed Mindscan upon her. Allison saw sad and painful things in her life, such as her grandfather dying, and she also saw things that had made her angry. After the procedure was completed, the hybrid said she felt fortunate because Allison had such a wide range of emotions.[10]

Hybrid-Human Reproduction

The most problematic aspect of abductee interaction with late-stage hybrids is the frequency of sexual activity. The hybrids want sex, not only because it is critical for the Breeding Program, but also apparently because it satisfies them. Hybrids have total control over the sexual encounter, and the male hybrids require female abductees to have a full range of sexual response. To ensure this response, the hybrids perform a separate procedure in which they physically stimulate a woman almost to orgasm, while an alien stares into her eyes in what amounts to "fine tuning" the precise neural response in the brain. "Beverly"[11] had this experience while she was lying on a table, hooked up to a headgear device:

There's a monitoring type procedure done. There's . . . like something put on my head that I feel . . . monitors brain activity, brain waves . . . something to do with brain. It's something to do with brain and monitoring brain waves, brain action, whatever it does. This gray one, he's here on my left.

Is this the escort, you mean?

Yeah, same guy. . . . There's a hybrid man on my right, I'm a lot
more nervous than before and . . .

The anxiety has gone up?

A lot. A lot. Especially because of this . . . I want to say "man" but
I don't want to humanize it. The gray guy . . . he doesn't come
really close to my face but he, using telepathy, he can pass on to
me calming energies but they don't want me zonked out because
then my brain responses won't be legitimate. If they mess with my
brain and probe in there or whatever and do something to make
me calm down and be vegetablelike, then it will mess up their . . .

So, they're allowing you to be nervous?

Yeah. . . . The hybrid is talking about being calm and stuff but I
don't trust him. He's being nice but I don't like being in these situations. I just do not like this at all. And, again, I don't think either
one of these guys means any harm and I don't think any harm is
going to come to me but . . . they're doing their job, whatever that
is, and I just don't like the things that they do. This guy here's not
being mean, like, some can be mean. He's not being mean. He's
just being there and what happens is, he touches me everywhere.
Touches me everywhere and in different ways. He just touches me
and my feeling is that my responses are being monitored to different touches in different places. . . . It's just, you know, monitoring . . . for sexual zones, sexual stimuli. You know, some people
are sexually stimulated when touched here, some sexually stimulated when touched . . . of course, there's the obvious, you know,
that we all have in common. But other people have different areas
that raise more of an excitement than, maybe, someone else. . . .

Well, how do you know he's doing that?

. . . There's no dialogue. This is a just "knowing" one—one of
those things I'm sorry I can't tell you how I know. I just know.

Are you reacting when he's doing this? Are you saying to yourself, "Yes, this is nice," or, "No, that's not," or whatever?

I'm . . . in a layer of denial. That nothing you do is going to be pleasurable to me. And that's where I am, but the other layer is registering, regardless, on whatever mechanism they're using to register it. . . . It's a violation. I don't like it.[12]

Similarly, "Paula" was visited by hybrids in her bedroom. They hooked up an "electrical" device to her genitals and she had intercourse with a hybrid. At the climactic moment, the hybrid abruptly removed himself. Her orgasm was so unnaturally intense, it was almost painful. While this was happening, one of the hybrids stared at what appeared to be a "readout" on the machine and told her that it measured "electrical impulses." The device was removed and Paula felt excruciating physical pain followed by nausea. It created a lesion on her clitoris that caused her to seek the help of a gynecologist, who was mystified about how she had received such a wound.[13]

During intercourse with abductees, some late-stage hybrid males have "normal" sexual response and physical movement. Others, however, do not engage in the normal thrusting movements. Abductees describe more of a "pulse" or a quick penetration and ejaculation. The hybrids also routinely generate orgasm in women with the help of Mindscan. Thus, it is possible that female orgasm during hybrid intercourse produces ovulation or the facilitation of conception.

The hybrids often note the pregnancy to the abductees. For Stan Garcia, a rehabilitation counselor, this was a fact he wished he had not heard.

She's right directly in front of me, standing and looking at me. . . . I felt disgusted.

Because she was a female, or because of what she was doing?

What she was doing.

What is she doing?

When I say what she was doing, it's like she was chosen, or she was the one for me. And I felt disgusted, because I didn't have a say. I'm just disgusted by the whole thing—that I had no say about it.

When you say she was the one for you, how do you mean that?

She's going to have my kids. . . . I'm not thrilled at all.[14]

Physical Problems

Some hybrids are born disfigured or with other abnormal characteristics. For example, the aliens showed Kathleen Morrison five malformed hybrid babies. Their legs and arms had either improperly developed or not developed at all. Terry Matthews saw an older hybrid with a distorted chin, giving him a vaguely "Popeye" appearance. At another time, Terry saw an adolescent hybrid whose deformed head was too wide and had "bumps" on it.[15]

The hybrids have other physical problems. Allison Reed observed young hybrids with red blotchy marks on their skin. During a 1994 abduction she was told that her "sister" was "sick" and needed her help; the aliens inserted a needle into Allison's neck and drew blood from her jugular vein. In a similar scenario, hybrids brought Susan Steiner to a sick adolescent hybrid boy. They drew blood from her (they said they wanted "hemoglobin") and extracted a small section of her liver. The aliens explained that they needed these things if the boy was to survive.[16]

Female hybrids have reproductive problems. Abductees have reported that the females seem to have difficulties with stillbirths. There is also an indication that female hybrids have more problems reproducing with human males than male hybrids have reproducing with human females.[17] Reshma Kamal once asked an adult hybrid why there were no females around.

I'm asking him how come I didn't see any females. And he looks up at me and I'm saying like, "Females, like I am. I'm a female, you're a male. Like in your group or race"—I don't know what he is—"aren't there any females?" He goes, he's asking me if I mean him or the aliens and I'm saying him. Where are the females? And he seems to be telling me that they're used for some other task. I'm asking him what task and I'm asking him are they the same as me. He said, "Not all of them are like you." He's pointing toward his stomach and he's going like this with it. He goes, "They can't."

He's making a rounded gesture with his stomach as if they were pregnant or something?

Exactly. He said, "They can't." And I'm saying to him, "What do you mean, they can't?" He goes, "Like the parts that you have, theirs doesn't function like that." And I'm saying, "How come? Aren't they humans?" And he's saying, "Not like you. They don't have the same functions. They cannot be used for that." He says some of them can but not quite. It's not the same. So I'm asking him what does he mean by that and he's saying to me that of course they have tried to impregnate them and all that, and he said that it didn't work. The fetus or whatever—the baby didn't develop all the way for a normal survival.[18]

Allison Reed saw a hybrid female giving birth to a stillborn fetus. The aliens led Allison to conclude that "the fetus was able to sustain its life in [the hybrid female] for some time and that in itself is quite a step."[19]

Emotional Reactions

Most hybrids who assist the aliens on board a UFO go about their duties dispassionately. At times, however, abductees can elicit emotions from the hybrids. Take the report of abductee Doris Reilly. When she was five years old, two adolescent female hybrids escorted her to a procedural room, where they placed her on a table.

She kicked her feet and flailed her arms, and they had to hold her down to subdue her. She reached up and grabbed a hybrid's hair, giving it a strong yank. The hybrid uttered a surprised "Uh!" and Doris could see tears welling up in her eyes.[20] In other cases, abductees have reported that the hybrids laugh, seem sad, angry, happy, and so forth—all emotions within the accepted human range.

There is, however, an emotional component of some hybrids that is unacceptable—and out of control. It is as if some hybrids have been improperly socialized and are running loose, doing whatever they please. They have strong sexual drives, but they are not controlled by social constraints. One alien told Allison that the aliens must learn everything, that genetics play almost no role in their personality makeup. He said that although the behavior of the hybrids is, to a large extent, also learned, their human genes affect their emotional reactions and make them less predictable. This unpredictability has been a source of concern to him.

Hybrid emotional problems show up most sharply when they have *personal projects*—especially selected abductees—assigned to them, and when they act independently of aliens.

Personal-Project Hybrids

Some late-stage hybrids have responsibilities that go beyond the normal procedures of the standard abduction scenario. They have *personal projects*, long-term relationships with a human abductee for reproductive purposes. The relationship between the abductee and her personal-project hybrid begins early, when the abductee is a young child, and continues throughout childhood. The abductee is subjected to the normal abduction procedures and then either has private interaction with the hybrid or is escorted by the hybrid during the abduction. They talk and play together and build a friendship.

When the abductee reaches puberty, usually between the ages of thirteen and fifteen, sexual intercourse begins. While other hybrids may have intercourse with the abductee during her abduction lifetime, her personal-project hybrid remains her steadiest reproductive partner. When "Emily" turned fifteen, she began to have intercourse with her personal-project hybrid, and this activity continued once a month for the next six months.[21] "Sally" began sexual activity with her personal-project hybrid at age thirteen. She was puzzled about why he would want to do such a thing. She knew it might lead to pregnancy but her knowledge about sexual matters was extremely limited, and besides, he said it would be all right—nobody would know and he would take care of any pregnancy.[22]

Although sexual activity is primarily for depositing sperm, the late-stage hybrids appear to enjoy it. They often display the human emotions of affection and love toward their selected personal project. During intercourse, they engage in foreplay: They caress, kiss, and so forth. They sometimes talk romantically, professing their love. Abductees often share in the emotional attachment—sometimes profoundly. The "couple" laughs, jokes, and makes small talk. After intercourse, some hybrids even linger for a short time before putting on their clothes and going on to another task. Many abductees experience deep love for their personal-project hybrids during abductions. For some, this can spill over into their "normal" lives and interfere with their social and emotional development.

Both men and women have reported personal-project hybrids. "Rob's" personal hybrid is Janice, with whom he has had several children. The aliens bring him to Janice after the standard procedures are completed and then he interacts with his "family." He usually has intercourse with Janice, although he has been forced to have intercourse with other hybrids as well. He has formed an emotional attachment to the hybrid family that is intensely revived when he sees them.

Indications are that the gray aliens assign the hybrids to specific humans when the abductees and hybrids are young. When they are older, it is a joint decision by the hybrids and the aliens. When Emily was eight years old, her personal-project hybrid gave her a glimpse of how the decisions were made and what they would be doing together in the future. She was on a table having procedures administered to her by a "doctor" (possibly an early-stage hybrid) while having this conversation. She recounted it as if she were an eight-year-old child.

[He] wants me to be his one day. He wants this project. There's something he wants to do. It's a commitment he has to make to his government, and he's telling me he really, really does find me interesting. He really does care. . . . He's going to make me do something else so that I won't be afraid anymore. He said it would be all right. I don't know what they are going to do to me. . . . I don't want some bad thing! He said we don't have to do it for a long time.

He made me see things. I saw a big, big garden, and there's flowers, and there's no bugs and stuff to scare me. There's swans. And I'm older and he's older too. And I have on a pretty dress, a long pretty dress. And he says one day we'll be together when I'm all grown up. "You'll be so pretty, I'll be so proud of you. We'll have such pretty babies. You'll be such a good mother. And you won't have to be afraid. I don't want you to have any stress—nothing for you to worry about." And then they were through. And I looked at him, and the doctor was not happy. He didn't talk, but I knew what they said. It was, "He doesn't choose his own assignments." And he told the doctor that he should tend to medical care and he would worry about the projects. He didn't say anything, they looked it.[23]

For women abductees, a critical criterion for inclusion in the personal-project hybrid program is that she must have normal reproductive function. "Donna" was borderline. When she was fourteen, the aliens found a gynecological dysfunction that threatened her status in the program. Her personal-project hybrid intervened. The hybrids and two gray beings argued about her inclusion as a personal project. The dramatic scene that followed reveals the importance of the personal-project relationship and the interplay between the hybrids and the aliens. Although the aliens are in charge, the hybrids can sometimes assert their will:

He wants me to be reconsidered because I should be in this with him. That we've been together for a very long time, that we have established a working [relationship] and there has been a lot of energy put in here, and that I should be part of this. Their reaction

is that there is something that is wrong. And he doesn't agree with
them. . . . He wants a reconsideration.

What is it a reconsideration of?

I don't really know. He says that I have to be reconsidered to be
working with him and that I need to be with him in this project.
And they said that there is a problem. And I really don't know
what they're talking about. And then I feel like he starts talking
about me as if I was "stock." He starts talking about physical attributes, and that I am in good shape, and muscles are good. I'm
physically fit. I fit, this is not the word, I fit the "criteria." . . . And
their rebuttal is there could be problems. It's not the exterior, it's
the interior. And they agreed that I need to do an examination. He
pushes the issue and tells them they have to tell him more, and
they may be wrong, and he's arguing. He's being very argumenta-
tive. It's a little embarrassing.

How's that?

I've never had anybody stand there and argue at somebody else
about me. . . . But I know I don't want him to go away, that's important.

Do they argue back or does he . . . ?

He's physically displaying his annoyance by stomping every once
in a while and moving around. And they're just standing there very
reserved responding to his outbursts. At one point he actually
makes an audible sound. . . . It's like, "AUGHHHHH!" You know, that
frustration. He does that though when he looks at me. . . . This is
going to sound funny but it's like he's communicating with them in
one way and he's communicating with me in my way. The two of
them walk back toward where one of those little mobile tables
are—mobile cart things—and he turns me around and holds my
shoulders again and looks right at me. Right up in my face.

Does he communicate to you then?

He says that they need to do an exam and that he's not going to
leave me. He's going to stay. That he's going to be with me during
the exam and that it's going to be all right. And that I just need to
relax. It's going to be okay. And that through going through the
exam I'll be able to stay with him. So then he walks me over to
where that table is. And he helps me sit on it, on the end of it, on
the narrow end, because he's a lot bigger than I am. He's taller.
And I'm sitting there, my legs are dangling over the end. He says,
"No matter what happens, remember I'm still with you." Then I lie
down on the table.

Is it sort of a standard exam or is it—?

It's straight gynecological.

They don't do any anything else?

No. Well, he does. He moves my hair and he strokes the side of
my face a couple of times. He's got a hold of my other hand. I ask
him why are they doing this? He said, "Remember, I'm here." . . .

What are they doing down there?

I don't think that they are just in the vagina either. I think they're
probably up in the uterus too. They're checking some sort of a
monitor. I'm going to say that this is like a probe that is going in.
And it has something to do with the walls of the uterus. It's like
they are trying to show him something, and he's not agreeing with
their diagnosis—that it's not all that odd.

. . . When they try to show him something how do they do that?

There is some sort of monitor that they are looking at, and as they
are talking it's showing something on it.

Can you kind of get into their conversation a little bit?

It has something to do with, I don't function normally. That they see this every once in a while and that I don't function as normally or with the ease that they prefer. And there is something about, of course, that with the abnormal functioning it becomes too risky. . . . Detection could occur. I don't know.

So it's detection that's the bottom line?

Yeah. It's too risky. The end agreement is that they would have to monitor the situation. It's like a probation period. And if it ever became too risky, you know, that's it.

Meaning that?

. . . I wouldn't be in the project anymore. But they're going to look at it, and monitor it, and see how it works. He keeps on saying things like, "There have been worse that have done," and he's arguing back to them. That he's seen worse and it's not that bad. And this is a good candidate. . . . This is a "go." This is possible. I get the feeling that they don't really want to do this, but they're going to.

You mean to satisfy him?

Yes. They are giving him the benefit of the doubt. My feeling is, he always takes care of me. And that it shouldn't be too long before we start. . . .

Where is your friend?

Sitting on my right. He's sitting right next to me. Yep, I know what he's doing.

What is he doing?

He's [sexually] exciting me. . . .

He's staring in your eyes?

Yes. It's like he's demonstrating. It's interesting.

So he's doing this sexual arousal business while you are lying there.

Right. As far as I can tell they got what they wanted. They were looking for something. But he didn't let it go all the way to orgasm, at all. . . . And he gets up and walks to the end of the table. . . . They are talking at the end of the table.

They're still debating this?

They're having a good discussion, and the two grays keep on saying it will be monitored. And he finally gives up and agrees to that. It will be monitored.

So he didn't want it monitored?

No, he didn't want it monitored. But he doesn't seem to be winning on that point and is willing to let it go. They're not budging.

So this is where they draw the line?

Right. And the two of them leave. They go out through the door. . . . There I lie and there he is, still being upset.

He's still upset even now although they've left and he's basically won his argument.

Yeah. But he had to give in on some of it.[24]

When "Emily" was fifteen, her personal-project hybrid also had a discussion with her about how the aliens had selected her for the program. Several hybrids abducted her from a wooded area behind her home. Her conscious memory was that she had talked to a deer.

Her clothes were removed, she was placed on a table, and the hybrid told her that he would not harm her.

He keeps telling me he's not and that he'll always take care of me. He's been tracking me for a long time. He already knew where I was, he said that I've been evaluated over the years and he's been studying me and that now that I'm ready to breed, he's decided he wants to be the one to breed with me.

I see. Does he use the word, "breed"?

Mm-hmm. Somebody told him that it wasn't prudent, and he said it's already decided, and the medical tests were favorable. If it looked like I was fertile, that he would bond with me. And people did that sometimes, he said, where he's from, and it's permanent. But the people he's working with think he's making a mistake— that I'm "a resource, not a resort." He made the decision himself.[25]

Once a personal-project hybrid has been assigned to an abductee, he becomes a significant part of her unconscious mind because of the emotional, and human, quality of the experiences. The effects upon the abductee's social and sexual development can be substantial. And most of these effects depend upon the emotional and physical quality of a particular independent abduction experience.

It is their personal relationships with human abductees that allow hybrids to have a semi-independent life beyond the confines of the UFO. Independent hybrid activity constitutes an extremely important part of the abduction phenomenon. Indeed, it is at the very heart of the alien agenda.

10

Independent Hybrid Activity

Independent hybrid activity is a logical outcome of the abduction phenomenon and the Breeding Program, and it has profound implications for the future of human-alien interaction. It involves hybrids who can, for short periods of time, "pass" unnoticed in human society, acting independently and free from the presence and control of the grays.

When I first encountered independent hybrid activity in a regression with Emily, I was highly dubious. The episode involved romantic sexual relations with a handsome human. I had never heard anything like this before and human-looking men making love to women in their bedrooms verged on fantasy fulfillment rather than abduction procedures. I then had little knowledge of adult hybrid behavior and I did not know Emily well enough to trust the possible reality of her narrative.

I have been fooled in the past and I was not anxious to repeat that experience. I told Emily that memories are sometimes not what they seem. I spoke about the pitfalls of false memories, and I tried gently to instill the idea that it was possible that what she had told me was fantasy. Emily was receptive to keeping an open mind about this possibility. Then I talked to the people at the Fund for UFO Research, the organization that had urged her to see me, and told them to be extremely careful with her testimony. I reminded them that confabulation was a common problem, and her entire story could be a rich example of that.

The following year, however, I began to hear other accounts of independent hybrid activity. Eventually, as with other parts of the UFO abduction phenomenon, this evidence became too great to ignore, and I had to concede that independent hybrid activity was a legitimate part of the phenomenon.

How does it happen? Late-stage personal-project hybrids conduct most independent hybrid activity (IHA). Reports suggest that they can exist in human society for about twelve hours. And we find that most IHA takes place between male hybrids and female abductees. (However, this finding may change as researchers uncover more information about IHA.) It appears that most IHA is related exclusively to abductions but usually takes place in a location apart from the normal UFO setting. IHA events occur in a person's home and occasionally in a workplace. Sometimes these abductions take place outdoors, either at night or during the day, in an area where bystanders cannot see the hybrids.

The case of "Deborah," a thirty-one-year-old single woman, provides a good example of independent hybrid activity. She received a phone call from a stranger who told her to come to a "job interview." She arrived at the office, which was sparsely furnished with a few chairs and a desk. And when she sat down, the hybrid activity began immediately and consisted of a strange-looking "interviewer" asking bizarre questions. When the interview was over, she felt strongly that he might have had sexual contact with her. She went home with the knowledge that she had had an "interview" but could not remember details. Days later, she was able to find the building, but it was empty.

The frequency of IHA for most abductees is unknown. It is the exception rather than the "rule," but as investigators uncover more abduction events, more personal-project hybrids and IHA become evident. It is crucial to note that there is little evidence of hybrids being engaged in "normal" human activity—working at a job, living in an apartment, and so forth. When hybrids appear at an abductee's place of work, or even at places like a restaurant or bar, they have come to fulfill the functions of the abduction program. They have not appeared because they are interested in human work and leisure.

When in Public

Late-stage hybrids strive to "pass" for human, but within limits. On board UFOs, one of the reasons that male hybrids are easy to recognize is that they wear nondescript beige or white garments. In public, however, they dress like humans, blend into the general population, and go unnoticed. They usually wear average casual clothes: The males wear jeans or khakis, t-shirts or long-sleeve shirts. Abductees have so far not reported them wearing more formal attire, such as suits, or more casual clothes, such as shorts.

Late-stage hybrids may also dress in military-like clothes such as one-piece jumpsuits that resemble flight suits. Because they look so human, it is easy to mistake them for American military personnel, and many abductees have linked military personnel to their abductions. Over the years, abductees have reported that soldiers are involved with the abductions or that uniformed males, sometimes in military-type surroundings, are present during abduction events.

Hybrids will sometimes abduct people and bring them to abandoned military bases, or even to unused areas of active military bases. Abductees will occasionally see actual armed service personnel in the process of being abducted, still wearing their uniforms. All this, in conjunction with the long-standing and widespread suspicion of a "coverup" by the American government, has led many abductees and researchers to conclude that the government is secretly conspiring with the aliens. Some abductees have even petitioned the Secretary of Health and Human Services to investigate the military's abduction activities.

In fact, there is no evidence that the American government, or any foreign military, is involved with abducting people. Abductees are most likely remembering fragments of IHA during which they were taken to military-like settings. They cannot understand these experiences and place them in proper context because they have not had competent hypnosis or information about IHA was not available to the hypnotist.

It is imperative to gather much more data on IHA. We need to find out why, for example, in public they often travel in unmarked vans or even in helicopters. Sometimes the helicopters are "real"; sometimes the abductee thinks she is seeing a helicopter but is not. Abductees have also described unmarked black helicopters circling their houses. Clearly, most of these are real helicopters. Their proximity to an abductee's house is coincidental and they have nothing to do with abductions.[1] However, some of these helicopters are a part of IHA. To complicate matters, analyses of some helicopter reports reveal that the "helicopters" have no tail assemblies and no rotors, are more circular than tubular, and make no noise. This is a "screen memory" for a UFO.

We need to obtain information on how hybrids react to human society. Occasionally a hybrid will express passing interest in what he sees in public. In one of Susan Steiner's childhood IHA events with her personal-project hybrid, the two of them walked around her neighborhood before going into a UFO. During the walk, he asked her which car belonged to her father, why people had plants in their windows, and what somebody lighting a cigarette was doing. When Susan explained about the cigarette, he laughed and said it was "silly."[2]

Affectionate Hybrid Activity

Some abductees have relationships with independent hybrids that include love, affection, and kindness. Their considerate quality often results in deep bonds with the abductee.

"Emily"

Emily recalls having a romantic and loving relationship with her personal-project hybrid, who talked with her about their life together, the babies they were producing, and sometimes about the abduction program. A close examination of Emily's case reveals that the conversation was usually one-way—on the hybrid's terms. When she asked questions, sometimes he answered and sometimes not. He was the one in charge. He gave the orders and she took them. He rarely asked questions about her family life or work, or about human society and culture.

The main reason for his contact with Emily was reproduction. They had intercourse on most occasions, usually a minimum of two times per event. He would make small talk and say he loved her; he told her he would be back and she would be sad when he left. But to assume that he was insincere would be a mistake. Because he is a late-stage hybrid, there is every reason to believe that he had strong emotional involvement in the relationship, which lasted for years. There are also indications that independent hybrids are not monogamous and have several "projects" simultaneously.

Most of Emily's IHA encounters took place in areas especially chosen by the hybrids. For example, one evening when Emily and her friend Kelly Peterson drove out of a parking structure, they noticed a van tailgating them. After driving a few blocks, Kelly became so annoyed that she jumped out of her car at a red light to reprimand the tailgating driver. When she came back to the car, she was calm. She told Emily that everything was all right and that they were now going to follow another car that had pulled in front of them.

The three automobiles then went to an abandoned airfield that had a VOR (VHF Omnidirectional Range) building. Emily and Kelly got out of the car and familiar personal-project hybrids arrived at the scene. They talked for a short time with two hybrids and then Kelly and Emily went with them into a building for sexual activity. When intercourse began with Kelly and her personal-project hybrid, Emily's hybrid took her into the basement of the VOR building where they talked and had intercourse. The hybrids walked with the women back to their car. Kelly and Emily said goodbye and drove away. They remembered nothing about their experience, but they were two hours late arriving at their homes.

Emily related this event under hypnosis. She said nothing about her memories to her friend Kelly, who also had experienced a lifetime of unusual events. Then, two and one half months after my session with Emily, Kelly decided to look into her unusual experiences. At our first session, I asked her about the tailgating van. She was surprised because she had come to the session with a list of odd things that had happened to her, and this incident was not high on the list. She vaguely remembered being tailgated and wondering why she had gotten home two hours later than planned, but she remembered nothing else. In her hypnotic session, however, she confirmed all the details of the event—from being given instructions by the van's driver to her sexual liaison with a hybrid (she was unaware of Emily's sexual contact in the other building). Kelly also recalled that she had experienced a relationship with her personal-project hybrid over the course of her life.

The two women's accounts diverged only when the hybrids separated them for sexual activity. They also differed on what type of vehicle the personal-project hybrids had arrived in: Emily thought it was a helicopter, and Kelly thought it was an airplane, although it was too dark outside to see the details.

After hypnosis, Emily and Kelly discussed the event and physically retraced their journey. They found the location where the abduction activity had occurred—it was a NASA installation no longer in use. The road into the facility was closed and they could not investigate more closely.

"Donna"

Donna's experiences with IHA began when she was a young child, and by the time she was twenty, she was meeting with her hybrid in public. One such encounter took place in the summer of 1969, while Donna and some friends were on a jetty enjoying the ocean in Maine. When Donna separated from her friends, the hybrid suddenly turned up. He was wearing blue jeans, a jacket, and a t-shirt. His hair came down past his ears. He and Donna hid underneath the jetty and he told her he had seen her in a summer stock play the previous evening.

He said, "I saw you." I asked him what he meant. He said, "I've been watching you. I came to see you." How did he know where I was? He had come, not that week, but earlier to see me perform, and he sat upstairs.

He was in the audience?

Yes. "Why didn't you come see me?" "I couldn't at that time, or the time wasn't right." Some sort of time problem. He's there right now and oh, it feels good. I asked him what about my friends, couldn't I introduce? He says, "No. Don't worry about them."

Do you protest or do you just not worry?

Not worry about it. He's there and that's all I care about. I can't get enough of him. It's like every pore in my body wants to open up and take him.

So you're not thinking how did he get here?

No more. He's here, hey. Oh, I'm lucky to have him here. Can he come stay with me? "I'm sure I could find a way to do it. I don't know how, but I'm sure I could find a way. It's not possible at this time, but we shouldn't think about things like that right now. We should just enjoy being with each other."

You're just sort of crouched down?

. . . No, we're underneath the jetty. We're sitting down leaning back into the nook of the jetty. . . . It's slightly secluded down there. "Where have you been?" "I've been very busy." . . . He has projects. Sometimes they have to do with people and sometimes they have to do with other things. There is something he has to monitor, to try to keep them at acceptable levels. He said that he wants to be with me more than he's often able to. He had been monitoring this area for a while.

So he says that you should enjoy each other while you are together?

Right. I told him that we always enjoy each other when we are together. And he's been a very good friend for a long time. I wish we
could be together more often. Then he kisses me one of the those
kisses—gosh—Oh. I'm getting real embarrassed, because he knows
that I really like it and boy . . . I could turn into a red-hot
poker. . . . You know what? He takes pleasure in seeing just how
far he can push things. He's really enjoying this. It's almost kind of
fun. I start to laugh a little bit. And I tell him, "You're really
having a good time aren't you?" "Uh-huh." "I know exactly what
you're doing." "Uh-huh." "Well, yeah, Donna. Don't think I don't
know you. . . ." He knows that I enjoy it just as much as he
does. . . . I don't like it where we are. I think he senses my discom-
fort. "What are you doing?" "We're going to go elsewhere." . . . He
sits me up real quickly, grabs my hand and says, "Come on." . . .
He climbs back up the jetty but he runs around to the side of the
car that's in the street and squats down, sits down by the tire. . . .
And I'm giggling and laughing. He's just being silly. And he's
smiling and having a good time doing this. It's like he's playing
commando-war. . . . And I'm just giggling and laughing and sitting
in the street by the tire. And he's says, "Come on, you ready?"
"Ready? Where are we going?" "Just run with me." We run across
the street and into this little park thing that's over on the other
side of the street. We're there. . . . I trip as I go past a bush. I trip
and I go flying to the ground. He says, "Some dancer you are,
can't keep your feet under you." And I'm laughing on the ground.
He takes his hand and he shushes me up and he rolls on the
ground too. And we're both kind of laughing and giggling and he's
trying to get me to hush up. And when he does that, the more I'm
laughing. The grass is wet. And he stops laughing. And he asked me
how I've been keeping my body. I said, "It's the same as it always
had been. Just there." He says he has to check. I want to know
what he's going to check for. He's going to check to make sure I've
been keeping it up the right way. I asked him, why now, would he
be interested in my body. What did he think he did, own it? Now

he's the one who's laughing. He said, "In a way." Now I'm going to show him so I'm going to try to get up. He doesn't let me up. I'm pushing. I'm trying to get up. "This is my body, it's not yours." And he said, "Yes, but you let me visit every once in a while." Then he gives me one of those long looks. I can feel myself melting.

He looks into your—

Into my eyes. . . . Yeah, he's straddled over my stomach when I tried to get up and he came very close and looked at me. Then he came even closer and gave me one of those long kisses. You feel your brain exploding and your toes tingling and everything in between absolutely—firecrackers! Oh. It goes into every little nook and cranny in your body. . . . My stomach starts to tighten up. All the muscles in my stomach, my back starts to arch up, my head starts to throw back. And it's just, it just builds on that stare and that look. It just—Ahh. He slides off to my side and is sitting on his hip. And says, "Well I thought you were going somewhere." I just kind of yawn a little bit. Stretch. "No, think I'll stay here." "Did you like that?" "Yes." "Would you like for me to do that again?" "Yes." "Should I do it again?" "Yes." I feel like it comes back over my body. The feeling is like that of almost being crushed. Extreme pressure. . . . It's like he's pushing down as hard as he can. And his hand has come inside my shirt, on my back. He kisses me and then he leans back over to the side. His hand is fondling my body. But he didn't stop kissing me. He asked me if I want to be closer. Should he leave something with me? If he wants to. I feel like I'm floating. . . . I had on pants and I had on a t-shirt and a light jacket. I put on the pants because it started to get chilly at that time. I can feel his hand against my stomach. . . .

His hand is on your stomach and his body would have to be raised?

And my pants are open. . . .

But he's wearing jeans?

Uh-huh. Yeah. You can get around that. . . . [I feel] kind of swept away, kind of floaty and goofy and all of a sudden—"cutchewme!"

All of sudden, what was that?

Oh. Translate "cutchewme." All of a sudden you are wrapped up in the whole act and you're so floaty. It's almost like you were inebriated, but not inebriated. You're not in total contact with your body but with the stimulation inside. The difference between this and normal sex is that a lot of normal sex is external stimulation and this is housed completely from the core and radiates out. Everything is on "absolute"—such a heightened awareness from internal stimulation, but yet you're kind of floating in it. The welling of it is just, it's not even in just waves, it's in a crescendo. It's almost an oscillating crescendo. I can feel it all the way down to the bottoms of my feet and the palms of my hands. Even that is almost electrified. . . . When he turns it on, it's not just the mental stimulation, there is something with this kiss that goes on even beyond that. . . . It feels like I'm going to pass out at any moment if he takes it too far. I'm just gone. . . . And you know when it really got turned on, even higher? When he said about leaving something with me. Then it went from a high level to an explosion. This is totally and absolutely, this is the apex of a kinesthetic experience. . . . He "does his thing" and he stays there for a little bit. He pushes my hair back. I've got very long hair. He pushes my hair back and then he holds my head in his hands, and he looks at me and I get very sleepy. When I, kind of, come to, everything is back on.

Your pants are back on, your shirt is tucked in?

It's pulled over. . . . And when I wake up he's behind me and holding me. He's holding me close.

Is your head on the grass or is it on his lap or—?

It's on his arm. And his leg is up around my body, he's cradling, kind of.

Does he have a normal sexual response? Does he do everything the way you want, you would expect?

No, he's much cooler. He's much more in control. He's very deliberate, and conserves energy. Very targeted. Very focused. It's almost like his interior is highly concentrating on—it's more than the act, but it's like a goal; that he has something that he's aspiring to. Maybe that's a better way to put it. . . . I guess, very biasedly, I'd like to say that he is enjoying it. But it almost becomes, after a certain point, it becomes businesslike. . . .

Does he say anything to you then?

Mostly I'm just making sounds like "hmm." With each sound I make he tends to contract just a little bit around me. It's like a hug and a hold and an embrace. He'll try to be back soon. He has a better chance of being back soon now.

. . . He can come and see you more often now?

I say, "Don't you need to go?" And he said, "No, don't. Just lie here with me for awhile." I say, "I like to hold you. I like to feel you near me." I just get this real feeling of empathy for him, and I just kind of slide around and down on my back and um, say, "Let me hold you."

Does he want that?

He does. He does it, whether he wants it or not, I don't know, but I think that he is enjoying it. I get the feeling that this is the type of thing that he misses. . . . It's a hard question. "If you could come with me would you?"

He asks you that?

He asks, but I also ask him, "If you could stay, would you?" I know it can't be. [He says] something to the effect of, "You must carry me with you, or carry me with you, or have me with you." . . . I tell him that he's like a moonbeam in my life, and that I remember how he feels. He says I should hold that feeling all that time and that he's always with me, [that] I don't always know when he's watching me; he watches me more than I know, and I need to look at the stars, that when he's like this he doesn't want to go back, but he must. . . . "You're part of my purpose but not my work." . . . At that point we sit up. "It will be soon. Keep me in your spirit, in your being. Enjoy where you are, what you're doing." I guess he knows that I am enjoying what I'm doing that summer. . . . And we go and stand pretty much near where I was. He stands behind me and puts his arms around me. He said, "Let's look at the moon together." Then his hands go up to my shoulders. And I turn around and look at him one more time. And he gives me a very gentle kiss, not the other ones. A very gentle kiss. Then he just takes a couple of steps backward. And there's a half-smile on his face. The next thing I know I'm turning around facing the moon.

Do you see him go away?

I guess so. I see him disappear. That way. Up and away.[3]

Years later, Donna became pregnant, and when she was in the hospital after what appeared to be a miscarriage, her hybrid visited her. The miscarriage had occurred under mysterious circumstances. There was no blood or expulsion of fetal remains, and the hybrid indicated to her that it might not have been a miscarriage. He came into her room wearing hospital whites. "Don't worry. Everything is as it should be," he told her. Donna objected, saying that a miscarriage is not the way it should be. He put his hand on her head and she had an overwhelming sense of relief. He then stared into her eyes to see if she was well. He told her that she was "important" and necessary for the fulfillment of his task. He was glad they could continue to work together. She was irritated and asked "Why?" He said it had such extensive ramifications that she could not comprehend completely. And, besides, it gave them an opportunity to be together. They were given a "special existence" together; it was a gift that he can see her so often. He told her that he has a link to her that is not activated with other coexisting projects.[4]

Donna was always happy to see her hybrid, and he said he was always happy to see her. When they were together, they talked about how they were happy to be together, and how they would be together in the future. Donna's sexual relationship with the hybrid slowed after she had a hysterectomy, but he still visits her occasionally. They hug and kiss, and even some sexual activity takes place, but this is now rare.

Abusive Hybrid Activity

The women who have had pleasurable contacts with hybrids are the lucky ones. Other women have experienced ominous and difficult relationships with them. Even the romantic hybrids can suddenly display anger and malice. Intentional cruelty is an important component of hybrid interaction with abductees—especially in sexual situations.

"Emily"

When Emily's marriage was in trouble, she flirted with another man and thought about entering into a sexual relationship with her new admirer. This brought strong and stern warnings from her hybrid, who was usually the romantic type. In reaction to Emily's new love interest, her hybrid was angry and vengeful. During an abduction, he threatened to turn her over to the gray aliens whom she hated, and he even punished her by including her would-be paramour in a *staging* incident. The hybrid "placed" Emily's friend in the hallway near her. When she saw him, she broke away from the hybrid and rushed to her friend, begging him to help her and to try to get her out of there. As she clutched him, she realized it was not her friend, but one of the gray alien "doctors" whom she despised and feared so much. Emily was horrified, but the hybrid laughed.

He said he could do anything he wanted to her and this was just another warning to stay away from her friend.

One could explain this episode as the anguish of a jealous lover, and it might be that. However, it is critical to know that Emily's husband had had a vasectomy and could not deposit sperm. Therefore, a more probable reason for the hybrid's reaction is that he could not allow another man's sperm to intrude upon his private reproductive preserve. During the next several abductions, he forcefully reiterated that Emily should have nothing to do with her friend. Eventually she broke off with her friend and divorced her husband. She has since remarried and moved to another state. It is not known what her relationship with her personal-project hybrid has been since then.

"Deborah"

Other abductees have had experiences with personal-project hybrids that go far beyond anger. Some hybrids demonstrate such cruelty that their "projects" live in fear of being subjected to it again. Deborah's case is a good example of an abusive relationship in which the hybrid rules through fear, intimidation, and punishment. During one abduction, she found herself on the kitchen floor with a familiar hybrid standing near her. She responded as she always did, by adopting the attitude that anything he did to her did not matter.

And he starts dancing around my living room and kitchen. He's twirling around, dancing. The way he's twirling reminds me of what I see at [Grateful] Dead concerts. He looks like he's high on something. . . .

Does he say anything?

He's laughing. And he comes over real close to me and he says, "Look! Look! I'm here. I can come here whenever I want to. You're never, ever going to be safe." . . . He looks at me and he says, "Look what I can do," and I look over to where he's looking. There's like a fire burning in my kitchen. I tell him I don't believe there's a fire there. He says, "Oh, but there is. You feel the heat against your face." . . . He does a sweep with his hands around the kitchen and says, "This is all mine. You think you own this but you don't." He says I can take any of this at a minute's notice. He comes over to me and he says, "I can also fuck you at a minute's notice, and you'll do exactly as I say." And he's right. I feel this fear starting inside of me. Nothing really matters anyway. I tell him he can do whatever he wants because I really don't care. . . . But I should care, I should not want it. But I just don't care.

He comes over and he spreads my legs apart on the floor. He's on his hands and knees in front of me. And he says to me, "I'll remember that you don't care I'm coming." He lifts my shirt and says, "Nice tits." Puts it down. . . . And leans on me and licks my face. And then he pulls me in to the living room. . . . He tells me to look around. He says, "I can destroy your life any time I want, just look at this." He goes and starts dancing on my table. I hear his laughter. He keeps saying, "Remember me!" I put my hands over my ears, like it really matters. And he says, "I can even walk out your front door and no one will know the difference. I'm going to do that right now—I'm walking out your front door." He comes over to me and he says, "I'm one of you. I'm coming back." He starts laughing again. He says, "I'm off. Remember me." Then he laughed, and said, "Maybe I'll go across the street and buy something. They'll never know the difference." That's when I start crying.

What else does he do?

That's all. Then he leaves. . . .

How is he dressed?

Jeans, coat, tennis shoes. His coat is royal blue.

Does he have on an undershirt?

His coat is zipped up. But he actually has blue jeans on. I've never seen them with blue jeans on.

Do you know what kind they are?

I just don't notice it. I feel like I'm not safe in the apartment. He can come any time he wants. . . . I start sobbing. . . .

And where is he?

He went out toward my front door, I'm assuming he did what he said.

Did you hear the door open and close?

No.[5]

Guilt, intimidation, and death are common themes in Deborah's IHA events. The hybrids continually threatened her with death. They pointed weapons at her and held a knife to her throat. She would come back from these events with wounds and bruises on her body, such as a broken collarbone, trauma to her face, a torn Achilles tendon, and a sprained wrist.

Deborah's personal-project hybrid first had intercourse with her when she was seven years old, and the sexual contact continued over the years with him and with other hybrids. He usually did not batter her (other hybrids did that), but in one instance he tried to get her to react emotionally to his activities. She refused, placing herself in a neutral, dissociated state, so that she would not have to contend with the fear and terror of the event. She was sitting on the floor in her home with the angry personal-project hybrid standing next to her.

He slaps me. He hits me. He's never done that before. He pushes me against the wall. . . . I'm feeling empty inside. I don't struggle. He has his hand under my chin. He tells me he can break my neck if he wants to. When I don't respond, he says, "So that doesn't seem to bother you," and he pulls my hair. And he says, "So you like this type of treatment, huh?" And he tells me that nothing is holding me back. I don't struggle. I am not afraid. I tell him I don't care. And he says, "Oh, so you like this huh? Do you want me to do this?" He says, "Just say 'No,' and I'll stop it." I don't say anything. "Just say 'No,' and I'll stop this." I just start imagining that I'm not there. I keep on hearing him yelling. He pushes me to the floor. He's standing over me and I'm lying down. He says, "I'm in total control." And he tells me that I can scoot away if I want and I have full capabilities. So he says, "What do you want?" I tell him I don't care. . . . He says I'm in total control, meaning me. That the grays aren't in control, but he is. So he says, "What do you want?" I tell him I don't care. He still has his clothes on, he's wearing his t-shirt and he squats down on my legs and, and he says, "How come you aren't struggling? I know you don't want this, why aren't you struggling?" He says, "I know you're affected." And I told him it doesn't matter what I want. He gets so angry, he hits me. . . . He hits me with his fist. . . . He hits me full force on my jaw. And he says, "So you like that, huh? After all I've done for you, this is how you treat me? I'm feeling pretty angry. I'll show you what I mean." He stands up, and he starts undressing. He takes off his shirt and it's like I don't try to get away. "You're allowed to go. I'm not stopping you." I just lie there. I'm able to move, so it's not that I am unable to move.

But you're not playing his game.

I don't care. He kneels over me. He says, "You little bitch, you like this type of treatment, huh?"

I'm just looking up. Not looking at him; imagining a lot of other things.

What is he doing?

He's on top of me. He's hurting me. He keeps on yelling at me. "You selfish bitch, all you think about is yourself." While he's doing it. . . . It hurts! . . . Everything inside hurts. . . . My jaw still hurts from when he hit me. . . . I imagine that I'm not there, that I'm back at home. I don't struggle. In a while he's done with me. He just sort of stops. He seems really disgusted with me. He says, "You really liked that, didn't you? Do you want me to do it again?" I don't respond. It seems like I heard him but he wasn't there. And he's squeezing my shoulders. He yells at me, "Didn't you hear me, bitch? Do you want me to do it again?" And he stands up and he tells me to get off the floor, that he wasn't going to satisfy me by doing it.

. . . So he stands up, says he's not going to do it again . . . what does he do next?

Puts on his clothes.[6]

"Laura"

Five hybrids of different stages accosted Laura in her room one night. They did not like the fact that she was using electronic instruments to detect their presence—at least that was the excuse they used. She remembered that they had acted this way in the past, even before she was aware of her abductions.

She was lying next to her husband when the independent hybrid activity began.

There's like five of them coming in from the foot of my bedroom. . . . And they're coming in fast. They're not gray ones. There's one that looks, it looks like it's more gray. But it's still a hybrid that's white. The one looks really close to being human. . . . He's got long hair almost like [my husband] Ed's. . . . I think they came in a clump. I was like on my side. The foot of the bed is down there—I was looking down. I must've turned my head and been looking down, because there's . . . I don't think there's five of them. They came in a cluster, but the one is coming up ahead. He doesn't look happy. He looks mean. . . . God, he's on top of me.

Ed is lying right next to you?

Mm-hmm. There's nothing I can do.

Well, was this guy wearing anything originally?

. . . He's got nothing on him. . . . I'm looking over toward my bedroom door, 'cause three of them are going in, they're going into the kids' room. My kids are going to see this shit.

How do you know?

'Cause they're standing near the door.

The kids are standing in the doorway looking at you?

Yeah.

While he's on top of you?

Yeah. . . . I'm being told this is going to happen to my kids. If I keep this up, it's going to happen to my kids.

If you keep . . . keep this up? Keep what up?

The [detector] and fighting back.

Well, he's on top of you. Is this a full-fledged business, in other words, is this just a demonstration, or does he just—?

I don't know, it's everything. I'm wishing I was dead. I see . . . he gets off of me and there's another one coming over. I can see that first one going over to [my daughter] Janey. Oh, God.

The first one who just got up from you?

Mm-hmm.

What's he doing with Janey?

He's telling me he's going to make her do things if I don't stop.
Oh, damn!

Does Janey react to this or . . . just stand there and absorb it?

She's just real confused. . . .

And what's [the other one] up to?

I can't tell you. I can't. Oh, shit! Oh, God. I'm down alongside my
bed on my knees. I'm doing oral sex on this son of a bitch! . . .
Now, this is what they're gonna make Janey do if I don't stop this.
And probably the other ones. I feel such shame.

. . . Now the other three kids are watching this also?

Mm-hmm.

Does this proceed all the way as well, or is it just a demonstration?

No, no, it proceeds. God!

Does this guy say anything, or is it just the main guy who's
talking, the first guy?

He's not saying anything, but I can sense his anger. He can be so
mean.

What happens when he's finished?

I'm standing up. They're shuffling all the kids back into their room.
The first one is right in my face. He's really angry. I'm not going to
do anything. I don't want to do anything to make them angry
again.

How does he express his anger to you?

It's inside my head—I just know. He said they're going to hurt my kids.[7]

"Beverly"

Beverly's experiences were similar. On one occasion, three hybrids, whom she had encountered before, came into her room, took her out of bed, and began a night of sexual intimidation and terror.

First they made Beverly remember a conversation with a trusted confidante during her adolescence. The confidante had told her not to give her body away unless she was sure, because except for her heart, it was her most precious possession. Then the hybrids told Beverly that they could take her body whenever they wanted and that she was always vulnerable and never safe. One hybrid raped her, and she was forced to perform fellatio upon another. They pinched her, twisted her skin, and hurt her without leaving marks. They pushed an unlit candle into her vagina. They then told her she had caused her children to be abducted.[8]

In a different abduction event, the hybrids put images in Beverly's mind of themselves as her close friends. They then raped her and forced her to perform fellatio with two other hybrids. They hit her, bit her, pinched her, and pulled her hair.[9] On another occasion hybrids made her envision her six-year-old daughter walking into a room ringed with naked hybrids who had erections; she was led to believe that her daughter would be raped by all of them.

During yet another event, the hybrids sat Beverly in a chair, stood around her, and filled her mind with horrendous images. She saw a graveyard with the bodies of people she loves, including her children, who had been hacked to death and were covered with blood. She saw a car almost hitting her child, who was saved at the last moment by an invisible hybrid. Beverly understood that unless she was more cooperative (there was no evidence that she had ever been uncooperative), the hybrid would not save her son. She saw a crucifixion scene with loved ones, including her children, hanging on crosses. Then the hybrids put images of religious figures in her mind and assaulted her.

They do things like, you know, pinch your skin and turn it, just enough that drives the shit out of you but it doesn't bruise. And pull your arms back and neck back or legs, you know, just one on one side and one on the other side and pull your legs apart until you think your muscles are going to tear. Things like that, that hurt and are cruel. And pulling hair and yanking your head back, you know? Things that hurt and nobody can see it.[10]

Hybrid Dysfunction

What are the reasons for this sadistic IHA behavior? It seems possible that some women are selected for abusive relationships. It is also possible that the malevolent behavior of hybrids toward abductees is necessary. Perhaps they need to generate fear, intimidation, guilt, shame, and humiliation to fulfill the objectives of their agenda. An alien seemed to reinforce the hypothesis that sexually violent behavior was part of their program after a particularly violent assault upon Beverly on board a UFO. When it was all over, she asked the alien why he allowed the hybrids to do that to her. He replied, "The expression is necessary." This could mean either that it was a necessary part of the program for all hybrids or that some hybrids must express their sexually aggressive tendencies in this way because they are unable to express them in the controlled society in which they live.[11]

But if the aggressive actions are not necessary procedures, then it is possible that the human genes in the hybrids might be responsible. Because the late-state hybrids are mainly human, they have strong sexual drives but little conscience. It is as if they have human attributes but lack human controls. Even if they do have a conscience, they know that the human victim will immediately forget what has happened to her. The hybrid might assume that there is no lasting effect upon the human and he therefore can do and say anything he pleases with impunity. In addition, abduction reports suggest that the aliens do not have the expertise to "humanize" the hybrids. Without effective controls, the late-stage hybrids are "free" to express their aggressive tendencies.

If hybrids are continually gaining human genes, and thus becoming more human, and if they can exist in human society unnoticed for short periods, then it is possible that in the future they will be able to do so for longer periods of time—or even indefinitely. The implications of this for the future are, at the very least, disturbing. And the mystery deepens. Now we must ask not only what the aliens hope to achieve by their hybridization program, but also whether their intentions are benevolent or hostile.

11

The Nature
of Alien
Intentions

Despite the numerous examples of aggressive and humiliating hybrid behavior, the existence of "benign" independent hybrid activity and the "peaceful" and even polite demeanor of the gray aliens have led some abductees and researchers to conclude that the abduction phenomenon is a positive force. This growing group has launched a crusade to convince the public that the entire alien agenda is benevolent, helpful, and spiritually uplifting. "I see the ET visitors—the so-termed 'alien humanoids'—as friendly and with positive motivations and beneficial effects." So writes Dr. John Hunter Gray (formerly John Salter), professor of Indian Studies at the University of North Dakota, committed social activist, winner of the Martin Luther King award for civil rights work, and an abductee.[1]

Hunter Gray consciously remembered being abducted with his son in 1988. From the fragments he recalled of the event, he knew that kindly extraterrestrials were visiting Earth and that he was personally enhanced by their abduction of him. His view is typical of those of researchers and abductees who believe that aliens are benevolent beings who have come to Earth to help humans on both a personal and a societal level. Since the early 1980s the *Positives* have espoused the belief that humanity is fortunate to have been chosen for this beneficence.

Influential Proponents

In addition to John Hunter Gray, there are several other Positive proponents who have shaped a segment of public opinion about the meaning of abductions and the aliens' ultimate intentions. One of the first to champion the idea that aliens are on Earth for our benefit was University of Wyoming professor of Guidance and Counseling Leo Sprinkle. An early pioneer in abduction research, beginning hypnosis in the mid-1960s, Sprinkle concluded that the simple explanation that beings come to Earth for their own purposes was insufficient.

Eventually Sprinkle developed the rationale that "there are two themes to the ET [extraterrestrial] purpose; 1, ETs are here to rejuvenate planet earth and 2, ETs are here to assist humankind in another stage of evolution." The ETs' method of showing mankind that they are here to help us, he explained, is "through a metamorphosis of human consciousness."[2] The metamorphosis takes place, in part, through the lessons that wise aliens teach humans about cosmic matters. The aliens often communicate these lesson through channeling. In the course of his research, Sprinkle came to realize that he himself is an abductee.

In 1980, Sprinkle held the first of his annual conferences in Laramie, Wyoming, which has become a central meeting place for followers of the Positive point of view. At the conferences, Sprinkle often takes questions from concerned individuals about abductions or sightings and "channels" the meaning of the person's event, directly asking the aliens questions and relating the answers. This total acceptance of the spirituality of the abduction phenomenon has made him popular with many abductees and researchers influenced by New Age thought.

Another proponent of Positive themes is Richard Boylan, a former private practice psychologist in Sacramento, California, and also an abductee. Like Hunter Gray and Sprinkle, Boylan interprets his abduction experiences as profoundly benevolent and beneficial for him. His aliens are environmentally minded creatures who want to raise people's consciousness about Earth's problems and humanity's place in the cosmos. According to Boylan, the "mission" of the aliens "is to communicate to humans the concerns the ETs share—concerns about our violence toward each other and our government's violence toward them; about the ecological destruction and degradation we are visiting upon our earth; about our failure to properly care for and educate each child; about our possession of, and intended use of, nuclear weapons as a way to resolve disputes; and about our becoming more conscious of our heritage and our destiny (which both involve the ETs)."[3]

Boylan believes that the aliens will reveal themselves eventually, and at that time a "conditioned" humanity will not be afraid. When the great event comes, we will welcome the friendly aliens with open arms as we join with them in universal fellowship.

> We look forward as some of the implications of ET-human relationships develop when we finally get to CEIV [Close Encounters of the Fourth Kind—that is, abductions], the open, official, mutually welcomed, meeting of our earth's representatives with the representatives of these other star civilizations, and then we finally have a truly multi-racial world, racial in its true sense of races from other planets since we are only one human race with different colors and bone structures and so forth. . . . If we get rid of our nuclear weapons and our gun-slinging attitude towards solving problems by outdrawing the other guy, then we will be ready for admission into the intergalactic UN, if you will. We can look forward to cultural exchanges or representatives from earth and other civilizations because they have other things to learn from us just as we have other things to learn from them and this may involve the actual exchange of people going to other planets to observe their society and their representatives here walking among us.[4]

To Boylan, the aliens are even more acceptable because they believe in a form of Supreme Being and therefore confirm Judeo-

Christian monotheism: "The ETs, too, realize that there's a Supreme Being or a supreme source of everything. They're not kidded that they are the top of the pile either. They acknowledge a supreme source out there—the fountainhead of all life."[5]

A significant influence on the Positives' belief system has been Massachusetts researcher Joseph Nyman, who began hypnotic regressions of abductees in the late 1980s and added "past lives" to the Positives' vision. When he regressed them to early childhood to recover the first abduction memories, he found he could take some of his subjects back to when they were infants, then back to the womb, and then to a "past life." A few of them "remembered" that they had lived their past lives as aliens. Nyman hypothesized that abductees were taken from the time they were babies because they already had existed as aliens in past lives.

Not only does Nyman find that many abductees think they were aliens in a past life, but he also suggests that some abductees possess an alien's "consciousness," which imbues their present human form. For Nyman, the evidence is "overwhelming" that the aliens impose these dual feelings—human and alien—on the abductees. "It implies the taking up of residence in the human form at birth (or before) of a fully developed intelligence which for a while is aware of both its human and non-human nature and of the pre-arranged monitoring to be conducted throughout life." Abductees and aliens have "melded" together in some way and in a sense abductees and aliens are the same. Abductees live their present lives with a "dual reference," human and alien.[6] This allows the abductee to feel a positive connectiveness to the aliens with a resultant loss of "fear, anxiety, and self-doubt."[7]

Perhaps the most significant spokesperson for the Positive viewpoint is John Mack of Harvard University. As Mack examined the established structure of abductions, he concluded that the aliens' goal was more than administering clinical procedures. Although Mack says the abduction phenomenon is "mixed" and not entirely positive, he believes abductions bring an opportunity for spiritual transformation and heightened consciousness.

Mack has been influenced by psychiatrist Stanislav Grof, who postulated that the human mind could connect with the "collective unconscious," the universe, and all things animate and inanimate, present and past. Similarly, Mack believes that the abduction phenomenon has the potential, like Eastern metaphysical philosophies, to "depict the universe and all its realities as a vast play of consciousness with physical manifestations." The effect of abductions can be "personal growth," which results in "an intense concern for the planet's survival and a powerful ecological consciousness."[8]

In addition, Mack thinks that Western society has cut itself off from "awareness of any higher form of intelligence" in the universe. In his view, the aliens have predicted the destruction of Earth by the encroachment of "technodestructive and fear-driven acquisitiveness," and he suggests that the aliens may be using the hybridization program and visualizations of our self-destruction to bring about the healing of Earth and "the further evolution of consciousness."[9]

Within this framework, Mack began hypnotic regression of abductees in 1990, hoping to "push past" their trauma and unveil the essential goodness of the alien higher consciousness. And like Nyman, he found that a number of abductees whom he hypnotized had lived past lives, sometimes as aliens. Mack concluded that even though most other abduction researchers have not found the past-life-as-alien account, Nyman's "dual reference" was a "fundamental dimension of the consciousness expansion or opening that is an intrinsic aspect of the abduction phenomenon itself."[10]

As a credentialed Harvard faculty member with entree into mainstream intellectual life, Mack became an intellectually courageous and powerful advocate for the abduction phenomenon. Where he deviates from the mainstream is in his belief that the phenomenon transcends conventional ideas about the nature of reality. For Mack, understanding reality requires consciousness expansion that goes beyond traditional science. And such consciousness expansion can only be good for humanity.

A growing number of abductees who are not abduction researchers have also found their experiences spiritually uplifting and transforming. At an abduction conference held at the Massachusetts Institute of Technology, abductee "Susan" explained that the "communication" she receives from "the alien 'guardians' of our planet offers insight and wisdom to a world in need of it. It contains a message of love and support to a planet in need of healing." She also found personal benefit in the experience: "Since my experience, I rejoice in being who I am, with no expectations of how I should be, and complete acceptance of who I am. The changes in me are staggering. My life works as if by magic. . . . Although at one time I thought 'Why me?' now I say 'Thank you for choosing me.'"[11]

Abductee Leah Haley, who related her experiences in her book *Lost Was the Key,* believes that members of the American military— somehow in conjunction with the aliens—abducted her on many occasions and held her in a barrackslike building. Yet despite these clearly negative experiences, her view of the aliens is positive. In her children's book, *Ceto's New Friends,* Haley tells the story of the gray alien Ceto who comes to Earth and meets little Annie and Seth. The three play together, and Ceto invites them on board his UFO. They are happy to go, float up into the object, play various "games," and then are floated back. On the final page, the two happy but weary children look longingly toward the UFO, and the story concludes with Haley writing that "the Spaceship flew away, but Ceto will come back soon to visit his new friends on Earth."[12] Although most abductees have not gone as far as this in "humanizing" and sentimentalizing the aliens, Haley's viewpoint is a logical extension of the desire—perhaps the need—for the aliens to be friendly and helpful.

Taken as a group, the Positives' message is that humans have conducted their affairs in a way that will lead to the degradation of the planet and the end of the human species. Humans have caused poverty, ignorance, and overpopulation, and they risk environmental catastrophe and atomic annihilation. The concerned aliens are "educating" abductees to warn us of what is to come if we do not change our behavior.

The Positives argue that aliens are more fully evolved spiritually than humans, and that they have a heightened awareness of the mysteries of the universe. The aliens recognize the specialness of human life and are also aware of how humankind has erred. They respect the sanctity of human life even more than we do. They care about us and love us. The aliens are the teachers and we are the students. They are the parents and we are the children. They must teach us how to behave. Because they are a benevolent species, they have come to help us find solutions to our problems.

Moreover, the Positives believe that alien guidance is not meant only for society in general. The aliens can help the individual abductee to raise himself spiritually by giving him knowledge of higher realms of existence and the connectedness of all things. They can also aid individual abductees physically by curing various problems that they may have. John Hunter Gray was a recipient of alien largess. His body hair increased, his face and neck narrowed, many wrinkles and blemishes disappeared from his face, and his circulation and blood-clotting improved. He has not been ill since the abduction, and after forty years of smoking, he gave it up with no signs of nicotine withdrawal. He also has had expanded psychic abilities.[13] Hunter Gray is convinced that the aliens treat all people with the same kindness and respect that he received.

A key aspect of the Positive strategy to mold public opinion is to change the vocabulary used to describe aliens and abductions. They have denied the legitimacy of the word *abductee* in favor of the more positively charged *experiencer*. An abductee is a person kidnaped against his will. An experiencer is specially chosen for a very important task. An abductee has unwanted and traumatic medical procedures administered to him. An experiencer is a willing participant in a grand and wonderful plan. An abductee endures reproductive and sexual procedures that are sometimes tantamount to rape. An experiencer helps the aliens create new people for the betterment of aliens and humans alike. Abductees are laboratory animals, but experiencers are united with the aliens to build a better world. To reinforce the phenomenon's harmlessness, the Positives use only neutral or friendly terms to describe abduction events: *visitors* come here for *encounters* with the *experiencers;* the *visitors* are *ETs,* not *aliens.* Using these terms humanizes the aliens and makes them seem friendly and benign. The abduction phenomenon as a whole is "Close Encounters of the Fourth Kind."

Moreover, some Positives aggressively try to discredit researchers who are not in their camp. John Hunter Gray has called abduction researchers who adopt a skeptical or even a neutral stance "gloom and doomers," and he treats them scornfully. He accuses the "gloom and doom" researchers of being either "downright paranoid, motivated by commercial considerations, or ideologically endeavoring to resurrect a new version of the Red Scare."[14] Similarly, Positive Richard Boylan has suggested that mainstream abduction researchers are working together with a "self-serving government elite" and CIA operatives to prevent the "real truth" about alien intentions from coming out. The "gloom and doomers" have made the aliens' plans all the more difficult to carry out, because they play on people's fears.[15]

Both Boylan and Mack de-emphasize the effects of the standard abduction procedures. Boylan believes that gynecological and urological procedures take place only with a very small number of abductees and he rarely focuses on them.[16] And although Mack has found nearly the full range of alien physical, mental, and reproductive procedures, he only mentions them in passing while emphasizing what he finds to be the spiritually uplifting elements. Joe Nyman believes that investigators who find that abductees were victimized have been influenced by the popular media, which have publicized abductees who have been victimized. For Nyman, these investigators have "prejudged" the phenomenon and their abduction work is "superficial," and "incomplete."[17]

The benevolent "spin" that the Positives (both abductees and researchers) put on the abduction phenomenon is puzzling, given the way most people describe their abductions: being unwillingly taken; being subjected to painful physical procedures (sometimes leaving permanent scars); enduring humiliating and abusive sexual episodes, including unwanted sexual intercourse; living with the fear and anxiety of wondering when they will be abducted again.

The Positives acknowledge that some abduction procedures might be painful or traumatic, but they liken the experiences to going to a dentist, where one endures short-term pain for long-term health. They look past fear because the frightened or traumatized abductees fail to understand the aliens' hidden benevolent motivations. Once the "experiencers" grasp the big picture, they will understand that temporary fear and pain are an insignificant price to pay for the enormous rewards they will reap in the future.

Echoes of the Contactees

The Positives, although more sophisticated and complex, echo the "contactee" thought of the 1950s. The contactees were a group of people who spun tales of having continuing contact with benevolent "space brothers" who had come to Earth to prevent humans from blowing up the planet with atomic bombs and upsetting other planets in the process. Contactees were careful to suggest that the aliens believed in a Judeo-Christian god, and some even claimed that Jesus was also a religious figure for them. The contactees followed alien-directed missions to spread the word to stop atomic wars, live together in fellowship, and stamp out communism. Contactee Howard Menger summed it up: "They are friendly people and are by far more advanced spiritually and physically than the people of this planet. At the present time they are observing us. They wish to help us to help ourselves to attain a higher understanding of life and its meaning. . . . They are only here to help you and worship the same Infinite Creator that we do."[18]

At first potentially reasonable, before long the contactee stories become increasingly fanciful. The space brothers gave them short rides in flying saucers—one went from Los Angeles to Kansas City. Howard Menger went to the moon. Eventually, the contactees were flying to Mars, Venus, and the outer planets. Led by "Professor" George Adamski, Daniel Fry, Orfeo Angelucci, Howard Menger, Truman Bethurum, Buck Nelson, and others, the contactees proved to be a terrible embarrassment to legitimate UFO researchers of the period, who had to spend great amounts of time and money combatting them and explain to a confused public that they were charlatans who did not represent legitimate UFO witnesses.[19]

Of the many influences on contactee thought, perhaps the most significant was the 1951 movie *The Day the Earth Stood Still*. The movie portrays humans as warlike and the peaceful alien, Klaatu, as possessing an advanced technology that can end disease for humans. Klaatu has a proto-ecological message: If Earth continues on its aggressive, warlike path, its atomic technology will endanger the community of planets; therefore, the Earthlings must renounce war or the alien will use his robot, Gort, to blow up Earth and end the threat to the planetary confederation's peace.

Although the contactees lost popularity in the 1960s, their legacy is still with us. Devoted followers of the teachings of George Adamski and other contactees still exist in the United States. The modern Swiss contactee Billy Meier has published volumes of philosophical ruminations supposedly derived from aliens who come from the Pleiades constellation. Meier has attracted a large worldwide following and supplies photos, films, and tapes of UFOs, all of dubious origin, in support of his contentions. Dr. Steven Greer has formed an organization that will take a member to a secluded place and signal aliens to come to Earth for private sightings. Greer's claims suggest a special relationship with the extraterrestrials so that they will do his bidding.

The Positive Leo Sprinkle uses the word "contactee" to describe his and other people's experiences. He feels that meditation can cause a UFO sighting, either in the present life or in one or more past lives. He claims direct communication with aliens and can get them to answer his questions virtually on demand.

Using the New Age to Cope

It is extremely difficult for unaware abductees who have not undergone competent hypnosis, or who have had none at all, to come to terms emotionally with their abductions. As a result, they develop coping mechanisms to deal with the continual psychological and physical assault from their experiences. To mitigate their victimization, they transform their lifetime of fear and anxiety into a more psychologically bearable scenario.

These abductees seek reassurance and find organizations and people who share their belief that the aliens are benevolent. Often they become involved with New Age groups that focus on the existence of alternative realities. The abductees learn there is more to life than one can know on a conscious, objective level. When they come in contact with the channeling of aliens or spirit-aliens, they "discover" an explanation for their experiences. In channeling, the entity answers all questions, no matter how grand, esoteric, or trivial. And the channeled messages directly address the rationale behind the abduction experiences: The abductees have been chosen to undertake a mission to help humanity, Earth, the aliens, and the universe. Abductees are not victims—they are important players in a majestic alien plan for the betterment of humanity. Enduring a little fear and pain is a small price to pay for taking part in such an important task.

To circumvent the problems of being taken against their will, living in fear, and being unable to say "no," the New Age abductees believe they have given the aliens "permission" to abduct them, either in a past life or when they were small children. They entered into a verbal contract and, therefore, it is proper, and even legal, for the aliens to abduct them. For New Age Positives, the aliens are humanity's friends. Godlike, they have come from the heavens to help us find our way. Not only do they have superior technology, but their moral sense, desire for peace, spirituality, and ability to love are all far more advanced than ours. Being a part of their cosmic vision is a privilege and an honor.

Often the New Age Positives band together into almost cultlike groups to defend themselves from their detractors—researchers and abductees who have come to different conclusions about the abduction phenomenon. The Positives reinforce one another's feelings and insulate themselves from the terror of their lives; they become angry when "less enlightened" abduction researchers question their interpretation.

For years critics of the UFO phenomenon spuriously claimed that UFO witnesses were forming a "new religion" based on gods from space. This was never true of UFO witnesses who came forward to report their sightings and then went on with their lives. However, abductees and researchers who have accepted New Age teachings share a quasi-religious sentiment in their interpretation of alien intentions. They ascribe benevolent powers to the aliens and have an almost religious fervor in protecting the aliens from wrong-thinking individuals who would treat them more as scientific objects than as miraculous messengers. The Positives simultaneously anthropomorphize and deify the aliens. While the benevolent alien-gods were all-powerful, they have a moral structure not unlike our own. They can destroy us but choose to work for our betterment. In return, they will eventually receive our gratitude and will know that they preserved Earth and the precious life on it, which is intrinsically rewarding to them.

The belief system of the New Age Positives is exceptionally strong because they know the alien-gods exist. After all, they have actually contacted the individual "experiencer," which adds "proof" to their religious belief and drives the "experiencer" to missionary zeal. Each abduction confirms the reality of the phenomenon and strengthens the New Age beliefs. For New Age Positives, the alien-gods are not just a matter of faith—they are a matter of stark fact.

Of course, some New Age abductees have sought assistance from a competent hypnotist, one who is well-versed in the abduction phenomenon. As a result, they remember events that do not seem so positive. Often, the contradiction between belief system and reality is overwhelming, and the abductee breaks off hypnosis, retreating into his protective New Age cocoon.

Rejecting the Importance of Competent Hypnosis

A primary reason for the Positive attitude is that most of these abductees have not undergone competent hypnosis to help them understand what has happened to them. They have only conscious recollections, which are often tainted with screen memories, false memories, fragmented memories, the remnants of imaging and envisioning procedures, and wishful thinking.

In abduction research, memories derived hypnotically under the guidance of a competent hypnotist are more reliable than conscious memories. This is clearly demonstrated by analyzing the abduction "frame"—the first few seconds and the last few seconds of the abduction—which usually takes place in the person's normal environment. *Unaware* abductees (those who have not undergone expert hypnosis) often extrapolate from memory fragments of these periods. For example, an unaware abductee might remember that an alien came close to him or her in bed to "greet" him, when under hypnosis this is revealed to be a staring procedure to subdue the abductee. An unaware abductee will say that he watched aliens in his room, told them that he did not want to be abducted that night, and watched the obliging aliens depart. But under hypnosis, the unaware abductee reveals that the scenario he consciously remembered consists of only the first few seconds of the abduction, when the aliens first appear, and the last few seconds of the abduction, when they leave two hours later. It does not include the actual abduction. The aliens in both cases had originally and falsely appeared to be more reasonable and "human," exhibiting concern for the abductee and honoring his wishes.

Experience with unaware abductees clearly leads to the conclusion that the most serious barrier to competent abduction research is incompetent hypnosis. This problem is compounded by lack of agreed-upon standards for conducting hypnosis on abductees, and by the continuing debate over the meaning of UFO abductions. Without standardized methodology, a hypnotist can use any induction or questioning technique—no matter how experimental, untried, or dubious—to explore abduction accounts. Questionable technique coupled with the hypnotist's lack of knowledge of the abduction phenomenon results in false memories, inserted memories, confabulation, dissociative states, and error.

A second barrier to competent abduction research is the mindset of the hypnotist. Many hypnotists and therapists who work with abductees adhere to New Age philosophies and actively search for confirmational material. During hypnosis, the hypnotist emphasizes material that reinforces his own world view. If both the subject and the hypnotist are involved with New Age beliefs, the material that results from the hypnotic sessions must be viewed skeptically, because their mindset can seriously compromise their ability to discern the facts.

Competent abduction hypnosis is difficult. Each question must be intrinsic to the abductee's narrative and should grow organically from it, without introducing extraneous material. The investigator should critically evaluate each answer in light of the established knowledge of the abduction phenomenon, the abductee's suggestibility and ability to filter out erroneous memories, the internal integrity of the account, and that ineffable but supremely important element—common sense.

When unskilled hypnotists regress an abductee, they fail to situate him in the event's minute-by-minute chronology. Without links to a temporal sequence, the abductee can interpret the events without the facts necessary to guide his thoughts, which leads to confabulation and other memory problems. The inadequate hypnotist and the abductee engage in a mutual confirmational fantasy: the abductee reports the fantasy; the hypnotist assumes that the abductee's narrative is objective reality. And then by asking questions about the details of the pseudo-event, the hypnotist validates its reality.

Research over the years has shown that the aliens are rational. Virtually everything that happens during abductions is, given adequate information, comprehensible and logical. A systematic, rigorous, and skeptical approach to this phenomenon has successfully uncovered its secrets; there is no reason to abandon competent analysis in favor of religious or philosophical belief systems.

Furthermore, mainstream abduction researchers have been unable to uncover anything paranormal, spiritual, religious, or metaphysical about the phenomenon. There is no evidence to support New Age hypnotherapists' contention that once the abductee "pushes past the trauma" of his abduction, he will encounter "spirit guides" or "guardian angels" who will steer him safely through abduction events, protect him in ordinary life, and guide him toward enlightenment. Usually "pushing past the trauma" comes at the expense of rooting the abductee in the reality of what is happening. Thus, the naive hypnotherapist has unwittingly pushed the abductees into unrecognized dissociative states.

Spiritual Assumptions and Validational Questioning

John Mack is a good example of a hypnotist who has relied more on New Age thinking than on an objective approach to hypnosis. Mack's personal study of consciousness transformation and spiritual enlightenment informs and shapes his assumptions and questions during hypnotic regressions. From the beginning of his interest in abductions, he thought the accepted interpretations of the abduction phenomenon—that the beings had their own agenda of physiological exploitation of humans—were inadequate. He also suspected that mainstream abduction researchers were finding the accepted abduction structure because they "pull out of the experiencers what they want to see."[20]

Ignoring the well-documented research about repression, recovered memory, confabulation, false memories, and mistakes that abductees commonly make about visualization procedures, Mack began to delve into the phenomenon from an unconventional perspective. For his hypnotic sessions, he used a combination of traditional hypnosis and modified Grof "breath" work (holotropic breathing), in which the subject regulates the intake and exhaust of oxygen and carbon dioxide. In full-fledged holotropic breathing, people can feel they are experiencing their birth, some can hallucinate quite strongly, and many have powerful emotional reactions. The effect of even modified breath work on hypnosis and on memory formation and retrieval is unknown, but information derived with it must be treated with caution.[21]

In spite of his New Age viewpoint and methodology, Mack found much of the same material that other researchers have uncovered: "These individuals reported being taken against their wills by alien beings, sometimes through the walls of their houses, and subjected to elaborate intrusive procedures which appeared to have a reproductive purpose."[22] But Mack also began to hear more "spiritual" and transformational accounts from abductees who either related conversations with aliens or just "knew." Rather than proceeding with extreme skepticism, he assumed the abductee's veracity and incorporated the information into an idiosyncratic abduction scenario.

Mack is sensitive to charges of "leading" the subject within the hypnotic session. He sincerely says he does "not lead clients in any particular direction so that if information that is relevant to the spiritual or consciousness expanding aspects of the abduction phenomenon emerges during our sessions, it will do so freely and spontaneously and not as a result of specific inquiries of mine."[23] Yet he also sincerely believes that the construction of an abduction scenario depends on the "intermingling or flowing together of the consciousness of the two (or more) people in the room." They "co-creatively" build an experience that they share for the benefit of both.[24]

While Mack does not "lead the witness" in the classic meaning of the phrase, he embraces the "positive" therapeutic technique that leads to mutual confirmational fantasies and easily steers the abductee into dissociative channeled pathways. This technique may be temporarily useful, but it represents the antithesis of the goal of scientific research—to uncover the facts.

Apparently unconcerned with the problems of dissociation and channeling, John Mack accepts "recollections" at face value. For example, one of Mack's subjects, Ed, "remembered" a female being who told the young man that he possessed special gifts and powers and recommended an environmental course of action for him.

> "Listen to the earth, Ed," [the being said]. "You can hear the earth. You can hear the anguish of the spirits. You can hear the wailing cries of the imbalances. It will save you. It will save you. . . . Things are going to happen," she said, but he must "listen to the spirits," even if he is taunted and not feel overwhelmed. "She gave me a flash . . . she opened up that channel and turned up the volume. Some of [the spirits] are crying; some of them are mirthful. She just ran me through the whole thing in a couple of seconds, 'All this you can see, hear, and feel. Other people may think you are crazy.'" The earth itself, the being told him, is enraged at our stupidity, and "the earth's skin is going to swat some bugs off" that do not know how to "work in symbiotic harmony" with it.

Instead of treating this "dialogue" with extreme skepticism, Mack asks the validational question that confirms the fantasy and calls for more information: "I asked Ed how this swatting off was going to happen."[25] By posing this question, he unknowingly joins with the subject in a mutual confirmational fantasy that assumes the authenticity of the information and adds import to it.

There are many examples of validational questioning in Mack's published research, which make the information upon which he bases his theories exceptionally suspect. But despite his methodology, Mack's Positive stance is appealing to many people, and his methodology is typical of the researchers who have found abductions to be positive. The Positive outlook, however, does not only emanate from methodological inadequacies. There are procedures that aliens perform within the abduction phenomenon that also generate Positive feelings—but in unexpected ways.

Alien Affirmation of the Positive Viewpoint

Some abductees think that aliens are benevolent as a direct result of abduction procedures. The aliens can be civil, caring, and even kindly. They can ensure that the abductees will not feel pain during invasive procedures. They can sometimes cure ailments. They can be appreciative. They do reaffirm that the abductee is a "special" person. For women, the Mindscan procedure, with its elicitation of romantic and sexual feelings, can encourage them to feel love and affection for the aliens. When these women think of aliens, they do so with a vague yearning, a sense of emotional emptiness, as if recalling a haunting memory of a long-lost lover.

Abductees have spent their lives entangled in the abduction phenomenon, and the aliens sometimes use this fact for their own purposes. They often tell abductees that they are part of the alien "family," and they frequently tell children that the aliens are their "parents." Abductees often feel a sense of loss when their hybrid offspring are taken away, reinforcing the idea that they have an emotional interest elsewhere, not on Earth. For these abductees, the aliens must be benevolent. The two species are working together to create a better world. The Positive interpretation is a natural outcome of these close links and active collaboration.

Are the Positives Correct?

It is premature to assume that the Positives are completely wrong about alien intentions. It is possible that the aliens will, in the end, help humankind and the world. Their intervention in the rush of human events might be a positive step toward solving the problems of disease, the environment, and war. However, at this time the evidence of benevolent intentions is, at best, ambiguous. One thing is certain: Most abductees say the phenomenon has had a devastating effect on their personal lives. Many have phobias, scars, bruises, and physical problems, especially gynecological and urological dysfunction. Many live in fear that it will happen again and feel guilty that they cannot protect their children.

The debate over alien intentions again brings up the question of what is believable in abduction research. Hypnosis, consciously recalled memories, false memories—is there a way of separating the "signal from the noise"? Uncovering the reality of abduction events is difficult but feasible. Methodological rigor has developed a core of solid information, confirmed by hundreds of abductees, and it has enabled investigators to understand the abduction phenomenon. Alien intentions, an area that could not be addressed from an evidentiary standpoint in the past, depends on the aliens' ultimate goals. Their intentions are linked to the end of their program and can be narrowed down to three possibilities: Their actions are mutually beneficial to both the aliens and humans; they are beneficial to the aliens and intentionally harmful to humans; or they are beneficial to the aliens who simply do not care what human consequences their actions might have.

Is there any way to discern what the outcome will be? Our present state of knowledge has finally allowed us to understand what most probably will happen in the future when the aliens' goals and intentions will be made evident. We do not yet have all the pieces to the puzzle but the outlines are well-defined and the picture is clearly recognizable. It is not a picture that I enjoy looking at.

12

Life As We
Know It?

The aliens continually refer to the future. They say it will be better for humans and aliens. When they impregnate women, they say the women are "carrying the future." They refer to the "children of the future." They talk about a "change" coming—a difficult change but an inevitable one. What we are seeing in the abduction phenomenon is apparently a *process*. Everything that has happened to the abductees and all the aliens' activities are part of a process leading to a predetermined goal for the future. That process has been continuing for the entire twentieth century, and at some point in the near future it will end and the goal will be achieved.

Contrary to the optimistic predictions of the Positives, I do not like what I see for the future. And the more information I gather about the abduction phenomenon, the more ominous the picture looks. When the end comes—and it will come—what will happen to humanity?

I have had an aversion to addressing this question, preferring to ignore it. In a sense, it is easier and more comforting to listen to people's abduction accounts, try to make sense of what is happening, and not confront the implications for the future of what they are saying. The accounts are so extraordinary that it is easy to get lost in the minutiae of alien procedures and avoid taking a "step back" to gain perspective on where all this is leading. But in spite of my reluctance, it must be done.

The aliens have brought to Earth a highly efficient program of human physiological exploitation. The breeding and hybridization programs have intruded upon our world and taken control of abductees' lives. The aliens have explained to the abductees that these programs are needed to "salvage" the future. They have focused their communication with the abductees on the need to save the environment, on the need to prevent or at least cope with mass destruction, and on the benefits of The Change, which is the way some of them refer to the culminating event in their plans for the future. But just who will benefit from The Change?

Saving the Environment

A puzzling aspect of the abduction phenomenon is the environmental concern that aliens and hybrids display. They say that pollution and other problems are destroying the environment and that humans have been doing Earth a disservice. If they are concerned with Earth's environment, there must be a reason. The Positives believe the aliens' environmental message. However, the conclusion that an environmental "cleanup" is uppermost in the aliens' minds is subject to question.

It is significant that the aliens almost never say or do anything to help the environment; they only lament its desecration. For example, they showed Pam Martin scenes of devastation to cities and wildlife, which made her aware of human responsibility for the problem.

I get the feeling that there's communication going on now.

What's he saying to you?

I don't know if it's something about getting past it. Like avoiding it. I don't know why they're showing it to me. I can get this off the five o'clock news. I already know this. . . . He says that this, had to avoid this, or this could be avoided, or this has to be avoided, or something like that. . . . I don't know, I just get the feeling like they think we're really stupid. Like there's something wrong with us. I get the feeling like, when he conveys that to me, that he's looking at all of us like a group. . . . It's like they're not blaming us, but like, they're holding us responsible. . . . I keep getting the feeling like we're supposed to fix this as a group. He doesn't seem to understand how it works around here.[1]

Lucy Sanders also received a strong message suggesting Earth was in danger and humans were the problem.

Now they have a screen in front of me. They're telling me something about the future. "What must be known for the future." I see a bomb going off. I see a crack in the world. There's lava coming out. I'm looking at it from above the world, and a big crack in the world. The world is turned and a crack came in it. And black clouds everywhere and bad wind. And people on the ground dead. I see dead bodies everywhere. "This cannot happen. This will not happen. This shall not happen. This must not happen. Only you can do something about it. Only you can do something about it. . . . You must stop it. It is coming. We are coming. You must stop it. You must stop the destruction. Your good is our good."[2]

Kathleen Morrison's personal-project hybrid told her humans did not understand that their actions had effects beyond themselves. Although humans were a "hindrance" to the planet, he did not suggest corrective action. During this exchange, Kathleen was looking at the stars from a UFO's window while her hybrid embraced her.

It is gorgeous up here. Reinforces how tiny we are, how tiny our concept is. In less than a blink of an eye, we are born and die. We have many opportunities to screw things up in that time though [laughs]. . . . I'm in the full throttles of an embrace and this is wonderful. I love feeling his arms around me. This might sound funny but he almost talks like he has a love affair with the Earth.

How do you mean?

That it's one of the most beautiful places he's seen. That it has such an opportunity for peace and tranquility. And that man is very short-sighted into his own personal needs. It is kind of like he [the human] doesn't have the big picture. And in fact, we don't realize it but we don't only affect ourselves. And even when he's saying things like that. . . . It's almost as if he's massaging my brain with every word. I think maybe that can be also a part of his love of things. . . . It's like the human population is at a crucial stage of, we're becoming a hindrance to the planet rather than helping the planet. There's an importance of enlightenment. And I interject someplace in here, "We're not all like that. We're not all that way." My question is, "If I was that way, would I be here?" And he asks like, "What do you think? Do you think we would invest our time with someone who would not make a difference?" And that kind of takes me back. It's a left-handed compliment because he used the plural "we invest" rather than "he invests in me." I realize it's meant as a compliment but . . . and he can tell there's a change in me, in my energy. I don't know, I guess I stiffen a little bit.[3]

If the aliens are genuinely concerned with the fate of our planet, then it must be because they have some stake in it. Telling selected abductees that the environment is threatened is useless. The majority of them will not even remember the conversation, and most abductees are neither environmental nor political activists. Moreover, concern for the environment appears to be relatively new on the aliens' agenda. Researchers can date the abduction phenomenon directly to the late 1920s, and family stories suggest its origin in the 1890s. Were the aliens concerned about the environment when they began their Breeding Program at the turn of the century? If so, we have found no evidence suggesting this. It is most likely that the stratagem of environmental concern developed well after the Breeding Program was in place.

Seen in this context, researchers must treat statements about the aliens' environmental concerns with utmost skepticism. It is entirely possible that they are using these pronouncements to justify the Breeding Program. They may also be using them to lend morality to their activities. If they can instill in abductees the idea that the human race will destroy itself and they are here to prevent that, then it becomes easier for them to defend their actions and to solicit help from the abductees. Almost as important, the environmental message paints the aliens as benevolent, which fits in nicely with what many humans so desperately want them to be.

Is it not possible that the aliens are concerned about the environment because they want a clean Earth for themselves? The fact that humans live on a sullied planet does not seem important to them, but that *they* might have to live on a despoiled planet may be intolerable.

Preventing Destruction

Images of mass destruction are extremely common during abductions—much more so than environmental images. Virtually every abductee has had to watch scenes of destruction. Tidal waves, floods, earthquakes, atomic bombs, and wars and their aftermaths abound. Devastated cities lie in rubble. Dead people are everywhere. Injured and dying men, women, and children cry out for help to the surviving abductee. Abductees are led to believe that this is going to happen, that it need not happen, and that humans have caused it.

The aliens sometimes suggest a way to avoid destruction—themselves. They are working to avert this unhappy scenario. Their Breeding Program is the hope of the future and will lead to peace and contentment. They can bring about a happy ending to the horror. Patti Layne had this experience:

And they said that they needed some parts, some things from me and that it would help everyone on the planet. They said that there are going to be some bad things that are going to happen. . . . They gave me some pretty vivid images. . . . And I sat on the chair and they put this scope on my head. . . . They said that there are going to be some bad things that are going to happen. They told me terrible things would happen to the earth and that it would just blow up, and cities would crumble and mountains would fall and the sun would be black. And they said that it's bad because people can't stop being greedy and that they were doing something to help us, and I don't know how. I couldn't make the connection how putting something into my stomach would help us.[4]

For Terry Matthews, the catastrophic scene ended with happy hybrids strolling in a peaceful setting. First the aliens directed her attention to a screen on which she saw a large explosion:

It looks like a mushroom cloud from the top. That's what it looked like.

Is it earth, or some other planet?

I don't know, I could just see the bomb. Just the explosion. . . . It was real brilliant and puffs of white cloud and I know it wasn't in my head. It was up on the screen.

What else do you see up there as you sit there?

For a minute I thought I saw armies and crashed planes. Armies, like foot soldiers marching forward and I saw a crashed plane and then I saw a field with nothing growing in it, not even weeds, just bare. Just saw a little girl with puffy cheeks . . . standing next to a wall. She looks very poor. Looking very angry and lonely. It was just a flash image though, it was very fast. These images aren't very long.

Do you hear any sound with them?

I don't think so. Although with the explosion at the beginning, I almost felt the vibration of it even though it was just an image. It startled me though so it might have been just my adrenaline. I don't know, but I don't hear any sound. I feel like I hear a gray talking in his . . . you know, not talking. Thinking. Kind of like voiceover.

What is the gray sort of thinking, or can you get a sense of that?

Yeah, but it sounds hokey. Like, "This is going to happen." That's not the words. "Inevitable," that's the word I hear. That's the way it translates. And I feel like I'm watching propaganda. . . . I feel like it's, like when you're a kid and they threaten, "You better be good or Santa Claus won't bring you anything," you know? That's the feel of it. But I don't know what they want from me. I don't know why they want me to see this.

What's the next image you see up there?

It was real fast. The first one was like as far as the eye could see, it was barren and dead, you know? Not dead people, just dead earth, I guess. Dead soil. No trees, no buildings and then all of a sudden I started to see pretty fields, flowers and . . . hybrids.

What are the hybrids doing?

[The scene] looks happy.

The hybrids are happy?

Well, contented or . . . I feel a nice day.

. . . What are they doing?

Walking, everybody's moving kind of slowly and peacefully, even the children. Looks like an [laughs] alien greeting card. That's what it looks like. It's propaganda, I know it is. . . . Just like it's a garden of some kind. . . . It reminds me of . . . the way they're walking in pairs very slowly . . . like they're having a leisurely Sunday afternoon, you know? Like it's perfect or something. . . . It's like a very huge garden that goes on and on and on.[5]

During Allison Reed's five-day abduction, she witnessed many scenes of devastation. The aliens told her that during a future period of human strife, they will intercede and save us from ourselves.[6]

Roxanne's Zeigler's experience ended with optimism. She saw army people in uniforms and then there was an explosion.

And then [I see] a bomb going off. It's like a mushroom. It's kind of, like everything's like turning black and white. And the color is all gone. It's like sheer desolation. And a raging fire—trees burned, and . . . animals running. People with like black, blistered skin . . . kind of nothingness, just smoldering. And everything's all quiet and still black and white. The sun is coming out, and a vague whiteness is like covering the land. There's like . . . something I've heard before.

What's that?

It's like, "All's well that ends well." It's like there's this voice coming out of the sky, and this brightness envelops the earth. And the darkness is going away, and the desolation is going away. And the grass is growing. And there's some butterflies that are coming out. And the flowers are growing. And, it's like luminous beings. It's almost like angelic figures around and all in light. And the people are moving around and doing all kinds of things. And people are smiling again. Everybody looks healthy and strong. And children are playing games outside. The animals look content. And the forest is green. There are ships, lots of ships. And all these people are coming out of the ships. It's like people are greeting each other, and they're kind of like, okay, back to business, so to speak, you know. There are a lot of ships arriving, and people are coming out from the ships, almost as if some of them had been here before. It's like they've been away a while, but it's like they're coming home.

When they come out of the ships, how do they look? Do they
look just like normal people?

They're not wearing the same clothes that we wear. They're coming
out with like this luminous cloth. . . . But, they're all different
colors, like all different races. They're taking these beings to, and
it's like they're showing them around. . . . It's like there's no fear of
them or anything. I get the feeling, though, that these—the ones
that are still, still look alien—they still can't live here. I guess they
can stay for short periods of time, then they have to at least go to
their ships or something. But, there are parts of them that are with
us because they have all these other people that are a mixture.
Things won't go back the way they were—things will be better.
There will be a lot different technology, and people can utilize
their gifts. People will learn to get along better, at least these
people have. There is more respect for the earth and all that's
living. And, there is more love and acceptance . . . more opportunity to realize good potential. The screen is fading. . . . This person
who [is] standing beside me seems to be saying that, you know,
"Don't worry, it won't be so bad as it looks. We just had to test
your emotions." There will be changes, and it won't be so bad.
They are not causing the changes to take place on the earth, but
something's coming. He says that we need them. They have to
make people like them that can survive in our society. We need
what they have to offer. In other words, we might have an awful
time trying to recover, and their being here will make things easier
for us—not to be afraid.

Now, he says something is coming. Does he say what's coming, or
not?

. . . He says it'll be made clear as times goes by. He says what they
are doing is necessary. It has to be done, and they're not trying to
hurt us in any way. But, some of the things may hurt—they try to
take away the pain. They try to make the memories go . . . because
the memories give us trouble here with the people, and it's not
time yet. But eventually all will be all right. It'll all become clear.[7]

The Change and the Role of Abductees

If these accounts of salvation are true, then the aliens' message is clear: After the catastrophe, whatever it is, takes place, the late-stage hybrids and perhaps the aliens themselves will engage in a general integration into human society. As one hybrid told Claudia Negrón, "Soon all life will be changed. People will be different."[8] Presumably, we will all live in peace and harmony. The environment will be healthy and there will be no more war or conflict.

Like the environmental message, the salvation message may have a subliminal purpose—a reassuring communication to be used before or during The Change. This suggests that abductees—the aliens rarely mention nonabductees—might have a more active role in the future program of integration. These plans are revealed in a variety of ways.

Calming

One of the abductees' responsibilities in the future will be to calm people. They seem to be in training for this role. The aliens often have them calm other abductees during an abduction. For example, while Kay Summers was waiting with a group of abductees for a UFO, the hybrids made her calm the victims and try to keep them from crying.[9] The aliens told Susan Steiner to get off her table and calm her friend Linda, who was lying on a table next to her.[10] Pam Martin calmed her neighbor on board the UFO while he was lying on a table. She put her hands on his shoulder and forehead and tried to keep him from being so scared.[11] The aliens led Kathleen Morrison to believe that when the time was right, she would act as a calming agent between people. She would, in her recollection:

make people feel good . . . communicating knowledge . . . bridging communications between people . . . creating a sense of community and wholeness, oneness. And this is going to sound strange because I don't only think it's people, I think it's also supposed to be ideas too. It's supposed to be to communicate how similar things are that look dissimilar.[12]

It is important to remember that the aliens are adept at calming people, and do so during every abduction. Teaching abductees how to calm people seems pointless if the aliens are present. That suggests that they might want the abductees to do it in the future without their presence.

Helping

The aliens sometimes require the abductees to help them with tasks. Carla Enders helped persuade a recalcitrant woman to breast-feed a hybrid baby.[13] The aliens directed Kay Summers to put a machine underneath the midsection of a woman lying on a table; when she accomplished her task, they were pleased with her performance.[14] Terry Matthews helped obtain sperm from four men lying on tables. She held her hands in a certain position on their genitals while an alien stared into the men's eyes.[15] Pam Martin also helped obtain sperm. With an alien at her side, she floated through a window into a neighbor's home, and at the alien's direction, masturbated a sleeping man (also an abductee) who had been "switched off."[16]

During some of these helping procedures, the abductee wears special clothes—often a skin-tight blue uniform. Wearing the garb and helping the aliens can lead the abductees to have intense feelings of guilt and shame. But that is clearly not the aliens' intent. Rather, it would appear, again, that they are grooming the abductees for some future role.

Rescuing

The aliens seem interested in rescue. From time to time, they will evoke the desire in an abductee to rescue someone. For example, Christine Kennedy observed a "town" inhabited by hybrids that was threatened by a flood. She knew the hybrid babies there would die if they were not rescued, and she felt sorrow at the prospect and guilt that she could not save them.[17] Charles Petrie received the idea through a visualization that a colony of aliens was living at the bottom of the sea and that their cable lifeline was not functioning properly. He envisioned himself diving with others to fix the cable and rescue the aliens.[18]

In Allison Reed's envisioned scene of devastation, she rescued a baby amid the explosions, smoke, rubble, charred bodies, and wounded survivors reaching out to her. Unknown people chased her as she ran with the baby down a path to a white light and was finally safe. After that vision, she felt safe with the aliens and glad that she was part of their program. The aliens told her, "It's in the future."[19]

Facilitating

Some abductees indicate that they themselves will smooth the way for The Change. They do not know specifically what they will do, but they think they will know when the time comes. The aliens told Pam Martin that when the world changes, they will call upon her to help people adapt to the new reality.

They're telling me things of the future. . . .

What are they telling you?

I can't tell if they're putting me on or what. This sounds really nuts. It's like they're explaining things to me, preparing me for a time when I'll have a lot of responsibility. But I don't have to worry about anything, it's like they'll be there to guide me, to tell me what to do.

What context? How do they mean that? . . .

Well, it has something to do with teaching other people things. . . .

They tell me people will be listening to me. I think I'm thinking with two minds because I'm thinking then and I'm thinking now. At the time I was listening to them, going along with it. Right now I'm thinking this is really nuts.

What else did they say you're going to wind up doing?

. . . Just that they're preparing me. But they don't say preparing me for what. . . .

So . . . you're teaching people things and they're going to listen and all that?

Yeah.

What will you be teaching people?

About the new life, after the world changes. Helping people adapt. And right now they're preparing me to accept the unacceptable.

Okay. What do they mean by "after the world changes"? Do they explain what kind of change? Do they give you a sense of that?

Well, the world won't be like we're accustomed to it. They'll be here.[20]

Other abductees feel that they will have specific roles to perform to facilitate the onset of The Change when the time comes. During a Mindscan procedure with an insectlike alien, Reshma Kamal was told that she was "one of them." When she protested and said she was *not* one of them, the insectlike alien told her "a plan is going to take place and I would be in it that way." She was shown images in which she acted as a traffic director to help move panicked and distraught crowds of people through the streets to a central location. Those who were nonabductees would be confused and frightened, the alien explained, but she would not be. She was "part of the plan."[21]

Facilitating The Change may explain why abductees feel infused with mysterious knowledge. For years many of them have been saying that the aliens have given them knowledge but that they cannot bring it to mind. Hypnosis rarely works to recover this knowledge. The aliens tell the abductees that the memories will be recovered when "it is time."

In typical fashion they told Steve Thompson, an apartment house maintenance supervisor, something he knew was important but would not be able to remember because "it is not yet time to know."[22] Patti Layne's knowledge was linked to a possible implant. She was told she would learn later what it was about:

He started saying something to me, but I can't tell you what it is.

You can't remember, you mean?

I can't remember it. It's like it's a secret, but I can't remember what it is. Something to do with what he put in me. He said it would be there, something about in time this will serve a purpose. It will tell you what to do when it's time . . .

Do you know what this means?

It seemed to make sense at the moment, but it doesn't now. It kind of left me with the feeling that it was extremely important, some grand plan.[23]

Carla Enders was eight years old when an alien told her something was impossible for her to bring to mind. Recalling the experience as an eight-year-old, she had trouble verbalizing the mechanism of telepathy and what an alien was telling her:

Like it's just not real. Like how can it [the alien] be talking to me in my head? And I can't really understand what it's saying to me in my head. Like another language or something. Like maybe, it's putting things in my head, and later I'll hear it. I don't know, like a recording or something. But that I can't understand it right now.

It's like it's storing something in my head, whatever it's saying to me. Like it's almost saying to me, that I won't understand what it's saying to me. Like it's telling me I won't understand it. It's not time for me to understand it. But someday I'll understand it. But it's still in my head. Whatever it is. Whatever he said, is in my head.

It's in your head at the time when you're eight years old?

Yes.

She then visualized images of aliens dying. They were on the ground outside and lying on the floor in various rooms. She thought that other abductees in the room with her were seeing the same thing.[24]

Allison Reed was told that there would be many changes in the future and she would know what to do.

He's talking about the future. There's going to be a lot of changes. And there's going to be a lot of unsettling and turmoil. . . . I'm to understand that it's my cooperation with them is—I'm going to know what to do. I have a safety valve. I don't get it, I don't know what's going to happen, and he's not being specific. There's just something, my sense is on a global scale. In the future, I don't know how far. It may not even be, something, he's just letting me know that there's going to be something, and it's going to be horrible, but that I'll know what to do. And that I'll just know, they've been teaching me. He doesn't use the word programming, but that's how I can describe it. They've been programming me—whatever it is, something's going to happen and I needn't worry because I have the information though I don't know I have the information and I'm going to know what to do and that all of what they do to me has something to do with preparing me, as well as themselves, for whatever this is that's going to happen. . . . Something is going to happen; it's going to be catastrophic. It's in the future, whatever that means, and I'm going to know what to do and that information's coming to me from my experiences.[25]

The unsettling conclusion is, of course, that abductees are "trained" and "prepared" for later events and it is in this context that the puzzling primary experiences of *staging* and *testing* can be understood. Some of these procedures may be part of the training program that abductees begin as small children. In the staging procedure, abductees are required to participate in a "theatrical" production which is a combination of envisioning and playacting. Susan Steiner witnessed another woman abductee scream and run around the room out of control. Suddenly the panicked woman ran into a wall and was accidentally stabbed by a sharp instrument protruding from it. She fell to the floor bleeding. Susan was told to go to her and try to help. Distraught, Susan went to the unfortunate woman and when she bent down she realized that the woman was actually a gray alien. The entire affair had been staged.

In testing procedures, abductees are required to operate special devices that indicate that they have received specialized knowledge in operating the equipment, or they are required to perform seemingly impossible mental tasks like viewing something through the eyes of an alien. The aliens must have a reason for inculcating these specialized skills and that reason could very well be for future tasks.

Alterations of Abductees

Feeling infused with knowledge may be related to the common belief among abductees that the aliens have physiologically altered them and their children. Beginning with the "first generation" of abductees, the aliens have continued to abduct their progeny, which indicates that the descendant abductees have certain desirable qualities.

Abductees feel something was done to them that facilitates the abduction process, and this "something" will be "switched on" in the future when the aliens need it. Many abductees think their implants keep them in the abduction "pipeline," and that they may govern their behavior in the future. Abductees also feel that the aliens have effected some sort of neural manipulation that makes them different. For example, it is common for abductees to feel increased "psychic" abilities—they "know" what people are thinking. These alleged abilities peak a short time after an abduction event and then dissipate. Sometimes the increased abilities are so intense that they frighten the abductees.

It is not unusual for abductee parents to say that their children have been "altered." Children sometimes say that even though they were born from their mother's womb, they "know" they do not belong in their family. Some abductees can point to so many significant differences between them and their siblings, parents, and other relatives that one can easily see how they would question their genetic link.

The evidence for physiological alteration of abductees is purely anecdotal, and we have been unable to identify those procedures that result unequivocally in permanent changes. The aliens are characteristically silent on this issue, although they have told abductees that their hybrid babies are more intelligent than normal children and have a somewhat accelerated growth. On some occasions the aliens tell the pregnant woman that her normal human fetus has been "changed." Pam Martin's human fetus was removed and then replaced in her uterus. The aliens explained to her that "he'll know things that he won't be able to explain to other people."[26] Is this true of all children who have been abducted?

Perhaps the Roper Poll provides a clue. The Social/Political Actives, a group the Roper organization included in the survey, answered positively in far greater numbers than other groups to *all* questions on the poll, indicating that there might be a larger number of abductees in this group. According to the Roper Organization, these people are "influential Americans." They are the "trend *setters* rather than the trend *followers*" [italics theirs].[27] They are wealthier and better educated than most Americans, and presumably above average in intelligence. If indeed there are more abductees in this group than in other groups in society, then there may be a subtle alteration taking place, which does not necessarily show up in individual abductees but is manifested in statistics for large groups. That could suggest that the aliens are somehow altering humans to facilitate their agenda. But at this point there is not enough information to confirm that frightening thought.

After the Change

The aliens sometimes describe the future after The Change.
Courtney Walsh saw what she called a "propaganda film" on a
screen about the route to happiness in the future. It began with the
removal of a fetus from an abductee.

It seems like a screen, but I don't know if it really is. And there's a
picture of an embryo, and it's implanted, it's growing, and then it's
getting harvested out again. It feels like a propaganda film, like,
"Isn't this good." I get the feeling there's some beings there that
want me to watch it. But I'm not really watching it, I have my
head in my hands. I'm not really watching it that closely. It's like I
hear them saying, "Do you think she watched it?" "Yes, she
watched it." "Well, she wasn't really paying attention." "No, it
doesn't matter, it already took."

When you look at this film, and you see them removing the fetus,
what do they do with it then?

Put it in a little jar. And they move it to a bigger jar, and then they
move it to an incubator that's as big as a baby. And it has tubes
going into it. And we're watching it, and there are beings taking
care of them. But it's like all so rosy and cheery, and the female
beings are stroking the babies, and talking to the babies, it's just
really happy. And there's a picture of a toddler—baby toddler
girl—and you just get the feeling like, "Aren't these fine children?
Aren't these good, strong, fine children?"

Do they show them older than that?

It's just so stupid. It almost seems like they show a couple of these
toddlers, and they're smiling, and in behind them files [walks] like
several aliens, and it's just so stupid. Their hands are on the kids,
or each other, and behind them are older adult humans, and they
have their hands on each other and everybody's happy. It's really

stupid, I know. It's just really dumb. And everybody's smiling and they're all dressed in white and they're standing there and you feel like, "Together we're going to achieve" something. Something about "completion, or happiness." I don't even know if this is real. It's just so stupid. It's obviously fake. Even to me at the time. This is trash.[28]

Kathleen Morrison also observed a harmonious scene with humans, aliens, and hybrids together in an outdoor setting in the future.

He's showing me some real wonderful pictures. I think this is the way things are supposed to be with us together.

With you and the big guy, or aliens and humans?

It's a mixture of aliens and humans. It's all different types of aliens though, all different colors of humans. It's on a craggy landscape with rocks. It's smooth underfoot. It elicits a feeling of euphoria.

What is everybody doing?

Talking. Walking between groups of people and talking. It seems an odd place to have a gathering.

What else is he showing you, if anything?

Embracing between hybrids and humans. Interspecies.

Interspecies?

Embracing. It's almost like the grays looking at this as their, the feeling I'm getting is like of a wedding, everybody's so happy. [Kathleen added later that the women's abdomens seem to be very full, rounded.] And that this is good and enjoyable. I don't see any little hybrids or little children. It's not territorial. There's not a jealousy. There's the biblical statement that's coming to mind. . . . It

sounds like, "And they looked upon their work and it was
good." . . . The grays are having like a matriarchal/patriarchal way
of feeling toward what's occurring.

There are grays in this scene?

There are no little grays, there's only the hierarchy [taller]
grays. . . . They're intermingled in there and they are fostering this
and everybody's happy with this.[29]

Claudia Negrón was taken into a room filled with containers of
gestating fetuses, and an alien told her that some of the fetuses were
hers.

Oh, my God! Do I have some of these babies in here? Maybe
some of them are mine.

Is that what he sort of indicates to you?

Uh-huh, that's what he's indicating.

How do you feel about that?

It feels so strange. I feel good. They are not from this world, but
they are going to be in this world.

Is that sort of what he says?

That's what he is saying. The two species are merging and becoming better. To build a better world. That seems to be what they
are really concerned with. Other things too. They have something
else in mind; that's what they are telling me. . . . These are going to
be special people. They are here for a special reason. But he won't
tell me what the reason is. I want to know too much, I want to
know a lot. . . . When the time comes, they will show me. The time
is not now. He says that sometimes they let us keep the children
and sometimes they don't. It's all on how they want things to be.[30]

Allison Reed saw a similar media presentation of what life might be like with the hybrids. She and other abductees were brought into a room with a large screenlike device, and she observed a beautiful park scene with people having picnics and playing ball. Her extraordinary recollection is a profoundly disturbing description of the aliens' plans for a perfect future.

I see on this screen, sunshine, happy, good things. Good things. Things are good. Everything about this is good. Everything about it is good.

What kind of an image are you looking at?

It varies. There's flowers, there's gardens, there's families, there's families interacting. I don't know. I can't tell. I can't tell.

Can't tell what?

They want us to see this and tell the "thems" from the "us's" and you can't tell. You can't pull out in these family settings like, we have a park and there's a couple families, you know? And there's ball-playing and they're doing some like sparklers and games. I can't tell if there's a family of "thems" or if there's "thems" intertwined within the established families. If they're the same, I cannot, I cannot [tell the difference].

Is this the point of it? That you can't tell?

It's like a challenge. "Find for me our creations. Find for me, pull them out of this picture." And I can't.

You mean that's what the point of the picture is?

There are hybrids there, there are people—I can't even call them hybrids anymore—there are people there that were not brought about through a normal human evolution and here we are. They

were brought about in the process of many years of experimenta-
tion. "Find where they are. You can't tell the difference." *I* can't
tell the difference. . . .

When you say playing ball, in the ball-playing scene are they just
throwing the ball around? Are they playing baseball or something?

It's like a beach ball.

Oh, I see. . . . Do they give you any clues or hints as to who's who
or what's what?

I kind of feel like that's the point. That's the point, you can't
tell. . . . This is like a mental test and everybody get your pencils
out, number one, you know? Where are the hybrids? You have
thirty seconds to answer this question. I don't know. Number two,
you know? . . . Do you see a hybrid family? No. They don't use
that word, far from it—our "creation," almost like they want me to
find their created million-dollar family. And I can't. That's the way
it comes across.

You lost me there for a second. It's like within the family you can't
tell, and between families you can't tell.

Exactly. They try to narrow it down a little bit. Can you find a
single family that has one and there'll be an overall picture. . . .
There's some over there and they're playing like with the ball, and
there's some over here playing games. I almost see like blankets
squared off and families. . . .

Is there any sound in this film, or media display, whatever it is?

It's like a background sound of—like some laughter, like laughter
but it's very dull. It's like almost off-in-a-distance-type sound.
They're all white. Everybody's Caucasian, there's no Spanish,
Black, Oriental.

How are they dressed? Are they dressed for winter, for summer?

Spring. Everyone's dressed. Men have pants on. Some have shorts. You know, springy. It's very pleasant, very nice. I don't know what the point is here but I can't pick out what they're asking me to. . . . It's very, it's kind of scary. I find it scary. But I don't even know if this is real. I mean, they could *all* be them or could all be us and I could be looking for nothing. But I feel it's important enough for my opinion that in this scene there are hybrids and I think the point of it is, I think they've achieved their goal. They've mastered the splicing and dicing, test-tubing, and they can fit in now. You can't tell them apart. They're proud of that. . . .

Do you get a sense of for what purpose this might be—that this is being achieved?

No, not right now. What happens now is that the film kind of stops and it's all in color. And what I'm looking at is, like I said, there's like a blanket here and families and kids. There's a whole bunch of blankets, it's all scattered, and families doing things. I think each blanket represents an individual family, that's their picnic area. Like everything kind of stops. Now there's down here maybe it's about one, two, three, well, between a third and fourth blanket area I'll say, there's a man standing there. Everything's in color, it stops. And he's originally facing this way. He turns his head and looks at me and he's like black and white and that's one. And then it starts over there, down a little bit. There's this little girl in a little pink dress. She's got hair about down to here, dark hair. And the same thing happens to her. The whole picture's still but you can see her head turn, look at me and stop and it's black and white. Now she's in black and white. And they do this with a couple people and they're the ones that I missed and couldn't tell the difference.

Do they look any different when you see them? Can you suddenly realize, "Oh yeah, that's one," or you still wouldn't know?

There's only one way to tell and that is that energy field, that energy field around them but unless you can see it, you'll never know.

An energy field around them.

But you know, the man, the woman, the family he's with—they didn't turn black and white. And his kids didn't turn black and white. Only him. My feeling is she, of course, is not of them.

You mean, the wife?

Right. But I don't know if the two kids are just not considered one of them because . . . they don't consider the offspring of this hybrid and this woman to be worthy of the black and white. They're us. . . . Maybe because she wasn't a hybrid, I don't know. But the children, his offspring, are not considered hybrid though they come from hybrid stock. So anyway, everything just goes. The black and white color disappears and everything just goes to everybody playing. That's when I hear the thing about the energy field.

That it's the energy field that distinguishes them?

But I can't see it. I can't see it on anybody. But there's going to be a few people that can see it and will know. This is crazy. The ones that can see it or can distinguish . . . those who can see the energy field and can know the difference and would have an uprising about it, then would be subsequently terminated. So there's a power thing. I don't feel experiment. I kind of feel this is not only going genetically and for that purpose, I feel there's a political power or motivation as well in the underlying scheme of things. . . . They all look so happy. They're healthier. You know, this is almost like a running commercial or a program, as though I'm an investor and they have this program and they want me to invest in it and they're showing me the beginning to the projected end. It's what I feel like.

A prospectus or something.

Um-hum. They're healthier. They don't know everything in this. They don't say it that way but there's things to be worked on. They just put it that way. That these people are healthier, the black and white ones. That they've not mastered everything, they're close to it. It's kind of like an all-around superior model.[31]

Allison then saw her own family standing in the park. She, her husband, and her two children were about seven to nine years older. They blended into the scene with the other families and everything was perfect.

A late-stage hybrid was exceptionally blunt with Reshma Kamal during a long conversation about what the aliens were planning to do. He provided another chilling glimpse into the future.

And he's saying to me that, "You know how you have memories?" And I'm saying like, "What do you mean, memories?" He's saying, "You know how you remember your father, your mother, your sister, the birthday parties?" I think he's giving me an example and I'm saying yes. And he goes, "Someday people who are like you will not have those memories either. They'll be like me." Like him meaning. And I'm saying, "What do you mean by that?" He's saying, "Don't you understand that?" I said no, or rather, I don't say no, I just shake my head. And then again he tells me to listen. He says, "There will only be one purpose for you. You won't have memories like you do now." I'm asking him like, "You mean *me?*" He goes, "No. The people who will come after you." I don't know what he means by that. He's asking me, "Are you understanding?" I'm shaking my head like I don't. I'm asking him, "They're not going to take me away, are they?" And he's saying, "They don't need to take you away. They will come." I don't know what he means by this. Again I ask him what are they doing. . . . He looks down and he looks up at me again and he lifts his arm up. He saying like, "Do you see this?" And I say, "What? Your arm?" He goes, "Never mind." I said, "No, tell me. Tell me. What are [the aliens] doing?" And he's saying all they're interested in, that no matter what happens at all, is that they control.[32]

The Alien Agenda

All the evidence seems to suggest that integration into human society is the aliens' ultimate goal. And all their efforts and activities appear to be geared toward complete control of the humans on Earth. Indeed, the abductees are already living with the burden of alien visitation and manipulation.

It is now possible to discern at least four specific programs that the aliens have put into effect to achieve their goal:

1. *The Abduction Program.* The aliens initially selected human victims around the world and instituted procedures to take these humans and their progeny from their environments without detection.
2. *The Breeding Program.* The aliens collect human sperm and eggs, genetically alter the fertilized embryo, incubate fetuses in human hosts, and make humans mentally and physically interact with the offspring for proper hybrid development.
3. *The Hybridization Program.* The aliens refine the hybrids by continual alteration and breeding with humans over the generations to become more human while retaining crucial alien characteristics. Perhaps humans are also altered over time and acquire alien characteristics.
4. *The Integration Program.* The aliens prepare the abductees for future events. Eventually, the hybrids or the aliens themselves integrate into human society and assume control.

The aliens have suggested that the time is not far off when their programs will end and they will have achieved their goal. Many abductees feel that "something is going to happen" soon and that the aliens have their goal within sight. Claudia Negrón was told that time is short:

One of them is talking to me.

What is he saying?

He's saying that I am helping them and that I should feel proud of that. They're happy with me, and that I'm helping them a lot. They say they need to do this, they have to do this, and that I should be happy I'm a part of this. They can't tell exactly what it is right now, but they will later. At another time they'll tell me.

They'll tell you what it is?

They'll tell me what it is, and they'll show me. They'll take me there and show me, but right now they can't. It's almost complete but not yet. There is more they have to do. . . .

So he says that it's almost complete, but not quite, and they still have some things to do? . . .

Well, I understand that he's talking about the future and that he's talking about them—their race. They have to be so secret about it. It has to be that way, otherwise it would never work.[33]

Pam Martin was led to believe that the alien agenda had three stages—gradual, accelerated, and sudden. The aliens indicated to her that they are now in the accelerated stage and she felt that "all this is going to 'go down' sooner than what people think."[34] An alien told Jason Howard that it would happen around 1999.[35] The aliens are generally vague about dates, but most imply that The Change will come, as they told Claudia Negrón in 1997 when she directly asked, "Soon. Very soon."[36] The indications are that this could mean from within the next five years to within the next two generations.

It is disturbing that the aliens and hybrids seem primarily concerned with the Earth, not with human beings; they do not comment on the preservation of life or the value of humanity or human institutions. They say they want to make a better world, but they never talk about partnership with humans, peaceful coexistence, equality. Reshma Kamal was told that after The Change, there will be only one form of government: The insectlike aliens will be in complete control. There will be no necessity to continue national governments. There will be "one system" and "one goal."

As if to reaffirm their plan, when aliens talk about the future, they do not say what most abductees and researchers want them to say: "Soon we will be gone. Our program is at an end. Thank you for your help. Once we leave no one will be sure we were ever here." This is *never* stated. The future for the aliens and hybrids is always a future on Earth where they will be integrated with humans. They offer no other possibility.

There is yet another very disturbing aspect to the aliens' view of the future. When they refer to the "humans," they are talking about abductees. The future of, and with, nonabductees is rarely the subject of much conversation. They told Reshma Kamal that nonabductees will be kept as a small breeding population in case the hybridization program has unforeseen problems. Allison Reed was led to believe that nonabductees are expendable. The evidence seems to suggest that the future will be played out primarily with aliens, hybrids, and abductees. The nonabductees will have an inferior role, if any at all. The new order will be insectlike aliens in control, followed by other aliens, hybrids, abductees, and, finally, nonabductees.

What Can Be Done?

The secrecy surrounding the abduction phenomenon shows that the aliens have instituted an elaborate effort to prevent their detection. Detection, therefore, may be where they are the most vulnerable. If so, then perhaps we still have the opportunity to intervene. Yet so far, all our attempts at intervention and prevention have been ineffective. Experiments to interfere in abductions by using video cameras and other electronic equipment have, by and large, failed to stop them, although they have sometimes decreased their recurrence.

Moreover, in recent years abductees have reported a marked increase in the frequency of their abductions. Perhaps this is an artifact of society's increasing awareness of the phenomena. Whatever the case, curtailing abductions—and their consequences—does not seem feasible at present. The program's longevity, the aliens' comments about its being close to completion, and society's disbelief in its existence—all suggest that its denouement will come before the public understands the gravity of the situation.

I have no illusions about making the standard plea to the scientific community to take a serious look at this phenomenon. UFO researchers have been asking for this assistance since the late 1940s to no avail. It is clear that unless there is a dramatic, irrefutable, public event, the scientific community is probably not going to research the UFO phenomenon—regardless of how important this subject is. And even if scientists now decide to conduct serious research, it may very well be too late.

13

Accepting the Unacceptable

I have spent nearly all of my life in an academic setting, and I have always believed in the primacy of reason and logic. Studying the abduction phenomenon has made me seem, to my colleagues and many lifelong friends, illogical and out of touch with "reality." Now I am in the extremely uncomfortable position of reinforcing their opinion, not only because I have found the abduction phenomenon to be "real," but also because I have become somewhat apocalyptic in view of its purpose. I have come to the conclusion that human civilization may be in for a rapid, and perhaps disastrous, change not of our design and I am all the more uncomfortable because the reason for this change is the *least* acceptable to society—alien integration.

My conclusion that alien integration will soon bring about dramatic social change bears no relationship to other more familiar apocalyptic visions. It has no religious underpinning like the Second Coming, no technological basis like nuclear holocaust or environmental tampering. Any of these rationales would give it at least a minimal standard of credibility. I am aware of my conclusion's superficial similarities to cultural constructs like science fiction or millennialism, but the evidence does not warrant this link. I have not derived my conclusion from human thought or endeavor in any way, save through the conduit of memory. My conclusion is based on my knowledge of activities beyond our control, conveyed through narratives told by victims of its advance guard—accounts that society sees as irrefutable evidence of mental derangement.

There are those in society who might "admit of the possibility" that the abduction phenomenon exists, but most are not in a position to influence scientific or public opinion. In the vacuum of an acceptable scientific paradigm, the media have picked up the subject as a guaranteed way to generate revenue, and although at times treated fairly, it has become just another tabloid topic, competing with other bizarre and extraordinary events that seize the public's attention.

Our encounters with the abduction phenomenon have often come through the haze of confabulation, channeling, and unreliable memories reported by inexperienced or incompetent researchers. When competent research reveals the phenomenon, the revelation is so fantastic that it is intellectually and emotionally impossible to embrace. It smacks so much of cultural fantasy and psychogenesis that the barriers to acceptance of its reality seem unsurmountable.

Yet, I am persuaded that the abduction phenomenon is real. And as a result, the intellectual safety net with which I operated for so many years is now gone. I am as vulnerable as the abductees themselves. I should "know better," but I embrace as real a scenario that is both embarrassing and difficult to defend. In spite of that, I must go where the evidence leads me. I have come to view the alien abduction phenomenon and its purpose as an asteroid hurtling toward Earth—discovered too late for intervention. We can track its progress and yet be utterly incapable of preventing the collision.

As much as I want to be optimistic, I find little to fuel hope for the future. In a way, I wish I could be like the Positive researchers, existing in a naive but happy dreamland, awaiting the coming of the Benevolent Ones who will engulf us all in love and protection. The Positives' beliefs, shrouded in their own form of spirituality, must be guided by a utopian vision that is lacking in mine.

The challenge of understanding UFO sightings that occupied so much of my time and attention when I first began my research is now a distant memory. Then I treated the phenomenon as a giant puzzle, not realizing that the completed picture would be far more distressing than the optimism and excitement I felt in the act of putting it together. As the pieces fell into place, an unease began to take hold of me. I realized early on that the UFO phenomenon was the only physical occurrence that we have ever encountered that actively dictates the terms upon which it could be studied. I did not understand that our inability to study the phenomenon was part of a calculated program to hide its activities and purpose.

The flood of information coming from the abduction phenomenon caused me to have epiphanic shock, much like the abductees go through when they realize what has been happening to them. Now I have insight into alien actions and motivations. The mysteries of UFOs "chasing" cars, disappearing, leaving marks on people's bodies, and so forth—all are routine elements of abduction activity. What researchers were hearing from those who had these experiences or even sighted low-level UFOs were merely fragments of memories, often distorted and always incomplete. With competent hypnosis, what I have heard from countless people who have been abducted and taken aboard UFOs were complex, matching, detailed accounts all leading to unavoidably distressing conclusions.

When I first heard of certain alien procedures, they sounded irrational and illogical, but as I learned about alien goals, they have proven to be the opposite. Everything the aliens do is logical, rational, and goal-oriented. With the use of superior technology, both physical and biological, they are engaging in the systematic and clandestine physiological exploitation, and perhaps alteration, of human beings for the purposes of passing on their genetic capabilities to progeny who will integrate into the human society and, without doubt, control it. Their agenda is self-centered, not human-centered, as would be expected from a program that stresses reproduction. In the end it is possible that it will be of some benefit to us, but if we survive as a species, the price for this charity will be relinquishment of the freedom to dictate our own destiny and, most likely, our personal freedom as well.

Through competent research, many of the abduction phenomenon's challenges have been met, many of its mysteries solved. And one of its aspects has emerged with crystal clarity. The aliens have fooled us. They lulled us into an attitude of disbelief, and hence complacency, at the very beginning of our awareness of their presence. Thus, we were unable to understand the dimensions of the threat they pose and act to intervene. Now it may be too late. My own complacency is long gone, replaced by a sense of profound apprehension and even dread. We know what their behavior means, and now it is imperative to ask what the consequences of that behavior will be for future generations of human society. Perhaps, the answer to that question will not be found until they have completed their agenda, but I do not think that we will have to wait very long.

It has taken us more than fifty years, but we have finally learned why the UFOs are here. We now know the alarming dimensions of the alien agenda and its goals. I could never have imagined it would turn out this way. I desperately wish it not to be true. I do not think about the future with much hope. When I was a child, I had a future with much hope. When I was a child, I had a future to look forward to. Now I fear for the future of my own children.

If you think that you may have been involved with the abduction phenomenon, I would like to hear about your experiences. Please write to:

> Dr. David M. Jacobs
> Department of History
> Temple University
> Philadelphia, PA 19122

> Or: Djacobs@VM.Temple.edu

All communication will be confidential. Time permitting, all correspondence will be answered.

Acknowledgments

Writing this book has been both an individual and a collaborative effort. My editor at Simon & Schuster, Fred Hills, demonstrated his courage by encouraging me to write this book originally. He and his colleague Burton Beals were continually supportive and extraordinarily helpful in editing and putting the manuscript into its final form. Once the reader understands how strange the material is, one can understand how open-minded and intellectually honest Hills and Beals are. They embody the true meaning of professionalism. Assistant editor Hilary Black also graciously provided editorial help.

My agent, Meredith Bernstein, provided faith and understanding in the travails that inevitably overtook me. I am very fortunate to have her as an advocate on my behalf.

John and Nancy Dodge not only transcribed most of the abductee tapes for my research but helped immeasurably by creating a database of abduction activity. Carolyn Longo and Wendy Henson helped with transcribing tapes and answering my mail. Wendy Roda not only transcribed tapes but provided critical analyses for the manuscript. Dr. K. D. Manning, Dr. Roy Steinhouse, Corkie Joyen, Katherine Beauchemin, Jerome Clark, Dr. Michael Swords, and Carol Rainey supplied valuable comments in the book's early stages.

Budd Hopkins, my friend and "partner in crime," provided his usual insight, wise counsel, and invaluable support for my efforts in this book. He has helped me maintain my equilibrium in a world of fact, fantasy, and frustration.

Since the mid-1960s, my wife, Irene, has relinquished part of her life for my research. Not only did she provide the most meticulous editing of the book, but she did it several times as the manuscript developed. This, in addition to coping with my embarrassing obsession for all these years, is duty above and beyond. Mere appreciation is not enough.

Finally, without the abductees this book could not have been written. Their bravery, perseverance, and humanity in the face of the overwhelming nature of the phenomenon fills me with admiration and awe. I hope this book does justice to their lives.

Notes

Chapter 1: Recognizing the Signal

1. For a discussion of an early apocalyptic group, see Leon Festinger, Henry Riecken, and Stanley Schachter, *When Prophecy Fails* (New York: Harper Torchbooks, 1964). See also James R. Lewis, ed., *The Gods Have Landed: New Religions from Other Worlds* (Albany: State University of New York Press, 1995).
2. David M. Jacobs, *The UFO Controversy in America* (Bloomington: Indiana University Press, 1975).
3. John Fuller, *The Interrupted Journey* (New York: Dial Press, 1966).
4. Ray Fowler, *The Andreasson Affair* (Englewood Cliffs, N.J.: Prentice-Hall, 1979).
5. Budd Hopkins, *Missing Time* (New York: Marek, 1981).
6. David M. Jacobs, *Secret Life: Firsthand Accounts of UFO Abductions* (New York: Simon & Schuster, 1992).
7. Budd Hopkins, *Intruders: The Incredible Visitations at Copley Woods* (New York: Random House, 1987).
8. Karla Turner, "Alien Abductions in the Gingerbread House," *UFO Universe*, Spring 1993. See also Leah Haley, *Lost Was the Key* (Tuscaloosa, Ala.: Greenleaf Publications, 1993).

9. John E. Mack, *Abduction: Human Encounters with Aliens* (New York: Scribners, 1994).

10. Budd Hopkins, *Witnessed: The True Story of the Brooklyn Bridge UFO Abductions* (New York: Pocket Books, 1996). See also Thomas J. Bullard's excellent analysis of themes in published abduction accounts to 1987, *UFO Abductions: The Measure of a Mystery* (Mount Rainier, Md.: The Fund for UFO Research, 1987).

Chapter 2: "I Know This Sounds Crazy, But . . ."

1. Training a video camera and recorder on an abductee every night has produced limited results. Some abductees report a dramatic decrease in abductions. Most report that the frequency of abductions tends to decrease only a bit. So far, no abductions have been videotaped. Rather, tapes reveal people getting up and inexplicably turning off the VCR, or unusual power outages during which the camera turns off, or the camera simply goes off mysteriously. See Jacobs, *Secret Life*, pp. 258–60.

2. The names of the abductees have been changed. In sexual experiences, they were assigned additional pseudonyms.

Chapter 3: Shadows of the Mind

1. For a short discussion of some of my hypnosis techniques, see David M. Jacobs and Budd Hopkins, "Suggested Techniques for Hypnosis and Therapy of Abductees," *Journal of UFO Studies*, New Series, vol. 4, 1992, pp. 138–51. A revised version of this article is available to qualified therapists and researchers. For an excellent survey of abduction critiques, see Stuart Appelle, "The Abduction Experience: A Critical Evaluation of Theory and Evidence," *Journal of UFO Studies*, vol. 6, 1995/1996, pp. 29–79.

2. For an overview of memory, see Daniel L. Schacter, *Searching for Memory* (New York: Basic Books, 1996).

3. Lawrence Wright, *Remembering Satan* (New York: Vintage Books, 1995). Ingram was falsely accused by his daughters of sexually abusing them. He knew that his daughters did not lie, so he felt that he must be guilty and that he must have repressed the memories himself. With that conviction, he "remembered" his abusive actions and eventually confessed. When he remembered a sexual abuse event that had been concocted by a psychol-

ogist, he realized too late that his memories of criminal activity were false, along with those of his daughter.

4. Michael D. Yapko, *Suggestions of Abuse* (New York: Simon & Schuster, 1994), p. 93.

5. Elizabeth Loftus and Katherine Graham, *The Myth of Repressed Memory* (New York: St. Martin's Press, 1994), p. 66.

6. Loftus and Graham, p. 165.

7. I investigated forty-nine of these abductions within seven days of occurrence.

8. Jack Thernstrom, session 7, October 10, 1990. Incident: 1968, age twelve.

9. "Julie." Incident in 1959.

10. Janet Morgan, session 12, March 16, 1989. Incident: May 19, 1988, age thirty-three.

11. Lily Martinson, session 1, December 8, 1989. Incident: 1970, age twenty.

12. Raymond Fowler, *The Andreasson Affair* (Englewood Cliffs, N.J.: Prentice-Hall, 1979).

13. For further information about hypnosis and abductions, see Thomas E. Bullard, *The Sympathetic Ear: Investigators as Variables in UFO Reports* (Mount Rainier, Md.: The Fund for UFO Research, 1995), and Thomas E. Bullard, "Hypnosis and UFO Abductions: A Troubled Relationship," *Journal of UFO Studies*, vol. 1, 1989, pp. 1–58.

14. Dissociative fantasies take place when the mind mistakes its own internally generated thoughts as coming from outside sources.

15. John E. Mack, *Abduction: Human Encounters with Aliens* (New York: Scribners, 1994), p. 171.

16. Mack, p. 173.

17. Edith Fiore, *Encounters: A Psychologist Reveals Case Studies of Abductions by Extraterrestrials* (New York: Doubleday, 1989), pp. 235–36.

18. Fiore, p. 333.

19. Fiore, p. 260.

20. Mack, p. 382.

21. Mack, p. 23.

22. Mack, p. 31.

23. Fiore, pp. 333–34.

24. Yapko, pp. 42–61.

25. John Fuller, *The Interrupted Journey* (New York: The Dial Press, 1966), pp. 122–23.

26. Fuller, p. 198.

Chapter 4: What They Do

1. Barbara Archer, session 6, June 27, 1988. Incident: March 1988, age twenty-one.
2. Lucy Sanders, session 6, February 12, 1992. Incident: 1987, age thirty.
3. Laura Mills, session 2, June 7, 1991. Incident: 1981, age thirty-three.
4. Belinda Simpson, session 2, April 25, 1989. Incident: January 1989, age thirty-seven.
5. Lydia Goldman, session 9, July 6, 1992. Incident: March–April, 1992, age sixty.
6. Claudia Negrón, session 7, December 8, 1995. Incident: spring 1983, age forty-one.
7. Claudia Negrón, session 7, December 8, 1995: Incident: spring 1983, age forty-one.
8. Kathleen Morrison, session 15, May 4, 1995. Incident: April 20, 1985, age forty-five.
9. Joel Samuelson, session 2, June 2, 1993. Incident: 1992, age thirty-five.
10. Carla Enders, session 5, July 28, 1993. Incident: May 1993, age thirty-eight.
11. Terry Matthews, session 22, November 8, 1996. Incident: 1974, age twenty-four.
12. Budd Hopkins, "Invisibility and the UFO Abduction Phenomenon" (*1993 MUFON Symposium Proceedings,* Seguin, Tex.: Mutual UFO Network, 1993), pp. 182–201.
13. Gloria Kane, session 1, July 15, 1988. Incident: 1960, age seventeen.
14. Christine Kennedy, session 23, March 29, 1993. Incident: March 2, 1993, age thirty-one.
15. Allison Reed, session 4, August 30, 1993. Incident: August 19, 1993, age twenty-nine.
16. Courtney Walsh, session 2, May 23, 1993. Incident: summer 1992, age twenty-two.
17. Jack Thernstrom, session 4, March 9, 1990. Incident: 1969 or 1970, age thirteen or fourteen.
18. Reshma Kamal, session 5, March 18, 1996. Incident: February 27, 1996.
19. Allison Reed, session 13, January 11, 1994. Incident: December 22, 1993, age thirty.

Chapter 5: What They Are

1. Michelle Peters, session 8, June 30, 1993. Incident: June 23, 1993, age thirty-one.
2. Kathleen Morrison, session 21, October 23, 1995. Incident: summer 1971, age twenty-one.
3. Susan Steiner, session 9, January 10, 1996. Incident: September 1995, age forty-three.
4. Reshma Kamal, session 2, August 8, 1995. Incident: October 1993, age thirty-three.
5. Allison Reed, session 25, July 6, 1994. Incident: October 1986, age twenty-two. Of the 700 episodes that I have investigated, seven have occurred when the person was either drunk or had taken cocaine, marijuana, or LSD. Allison's five-day case was one of these. She and her husband, Jerry, were living in a small house in Florida with their ten-month-old baby, Brian. It was a Sunday evening and the baby was asleep. They decided to have some cocaine together. She and her husband went out onto the deck where she noticed a light in the sky that was getting brighter. The next thing the two consciously remembered was watching television together the following Friday. They thought that their cocaine had been bad and they had been in a mental "fog" from Sunday to Friday. But they noticed that the baby was fine, with a clean, dry diaper. None of them was hungry or thirsty. They did not have to urinate or relieve their bowels. Everything was as it had been Sunday evening. None of the food in the house had been eaten. Under hypnosis her testimony took eight three-hour sessions of recollections from episode to episode during the abduction.
6. Diane Henderson, session 4, July 14, 1994. Incident: summer 1974, age fifteen.
7. Pam Martin, session 4, October 28, 1994. Incident: 1962, age eighteen.
8. Susan Steiner, session 5, October 9, 1995. Incident: September 30, 1995, age forty-three.

Chapter 6: Why They Are Secret

1. James Lipp, in United States Air Force, "Unidentified Aerial Objects: Project 'Sign,'" February 1949, pp. 32–35.

2. Donald E. Keyhoe, *The Flying Saucers Are Real* (New York: Gold Medal Books, 1950), p. 174.

3. Keyhoe, p. 128.

4. Quoted in Donald E. Keyhoe, *Flying Saucers From Outer Space* (New York: Henry Holt, 1953), p. 217.

5. Aimé Michel, *The Truth About Flying Saucers* (New York: Criterion Books, 1956), p. 225.

6. Michel, p. 224.

7. Aimé Michel, *Flying Saucers and the Straight Line Mystery* (New York: Criterion Books, 1958), p. 230. See also Aimé Michel, "The Problem of Non-Contact," *Flying Saucer Review*, Special Issue, October–November 1966, pp. 67–70.

8. Michel, pp. 224–226.

9. See, for example, Trevor James, "The Case for Contact," *Flying Saucer Review*, vol. 7, no. 6, November–December 1961, pp. 6–8.

10. Dr. Olavo Fontes, cited in Jim and Coral Lorenzen, *Flying Saucers Startling Evidence of Invasion from Outer Space* (New York: Signet, 1966 [1962]), p. 198. See also Jim and Coral Lorenzen, *Flying Saucer Occupants* (New York: Signet, 1967), p. 207.

11. Richard Hall, Ted Bloecher, and Isabel Davis, *UFOs: A New Look* (Washington: National Investigations Committee on Aerial Phenomena, 1969), p. 5.

12. Jacques Vallee, *The Invisible College* (New York: Dutton, 1975), p. 208.

13. Vallee, pp. 2, 194–202.

14. See, for example, Ann Druffel and D. Scott Rogo, *The Tujunga Canyon Contacts* (New York: Prentice-Hall, 1980).

15. J. Allen Hynek, "The Case Against E.T.," *MUFON 1983 UFO Symposium Proceedings* (Seguin, Tex.: Mutual UFO Network, 1983), pp. 118–26.

16. Frank B. Salisbury, *The Utah UFO Display: A Biologist's Report* (Old Greenwich, Conn.: Devin Adair, 1974), pp. 194–95.

17. John E. Mack, *Abduction: Human Encounters with Aliens* (New York: Knopf, 1994), p. 421.

18. This notion contradicts the astronomical community's familiar lament that Earth is only an insignificant planet, circulating around a nondescript sun, in an average galaxy.

19. Reshma Kamal, session 9, January 24, 1997. Incident: November 19, 1996, age thirty-six.

20. Lucy Sanders, session 6, February 12, 1992. Incident: 1987, age thirty.
21. Claudia Negrón, session 6, September 12, 1995. Incident: 1949, age eight.

Chapter 7: Infiltration

1. "Hidden Memories: Are You an Abductee?" *OMNI* December 1987, p. 55. Pamela Weintraub, "True Confessions," *OMNI,* February 1989, pp. 18, 127. Don Berliner, Dr. Bruce Maccabee, and Rob Swiatek, *The OMNI Abduction Questionnaires: Final Results* (Washington: The Fund For UFO Research, 1989).
2. The Roper Poll results were published in *Unusual Personal Experiences: An Analysis of the Data from Three Major Surveys Conducted by the Roper Organization* (Las Vegas: Bigelow Holding Corporation, 1992).

Chapter 8: The Hybrid Species—Children

1. Allison Reed, session 23, June 7, 1994. Incident: October 1986, age twenty-two.
2. Reshma Kamal, session 7, October 14, 1996. Incident: October 28, 1996, age thirty-five. If the gray aliens are products of early hybridization experiments with humans, it would explain their apparently nonfunctional and perhaps vestigial nose ridges, mouth slits, and earholes.
3. Kathleen Morrison, session 14, April 17, 1995. Incident: December 29, 1994, age forty-six.
4. Allison Reed, session 14, February 2, 1994. Incident: January 29, 1994, age thirty.
5. Susan Steiner, session 6, October 23, 1995. Incident: 1985, age thirty-two.
6. Diane Henderson, session 4, July 14, 1994. Incident: summer 1974, age fifteen.
7. Sarah Stevenson, session 4, October 17, 1974. Incident: 1987, age thirty-seven.
8. Roxanne Zeigler, session 4, July 25, 1994. Incident: June 28, 1994, age forty-nine.
9. Claudia Negrón, session 2, April 3, 1995. Incident: 1946, age five.
10. Susan Steiner, session 4, September 18, 1995. Incident: October 1977, age twenty-five.

11. Kathleen Morrison, session 12, February 23, 1995. Incident: April 1956, age seven.
12. Doris Reilly, session 3, January 17, 1994. Incident: 1965, age ten.
13. Carla Enders, session 2, July 20, 1993. Incident: 1965, age ten.
14. Susan Steiner, session 5, October 9, 1995. Incident: September 30, 1995, age forty-three.
15. Carla Enders, session 3, July 21, 1993. Incident: 1966, age eleven.

Chapter 9: The Hybrid Species—Adolescents and Adults

1. Susan Steiner, session 3, September 1, 1995. Incident: May 1995, age forty-six.
2. Kathleen Morrison, session 19, July 26, 1995. Incident: 1957, age eight.
3. Christine Kennedy, session 23, May 13, 1994. Incident: April 1994, age thirty-one.
4. Allison Reed, session 10, November 29, 1993. Incident: November 22, 1993, age twenty-nine.
5. Allison Reed, session 25, May 6, 1994. Incident: October 1986, age twenty-three.
6. Susan Steiner, session 4, September 18, 1995. Incident: October 1977, age twenty-five.
7. Reshma Kamal, session 5, March 18, 1996. Incident: February 27, 1996, age thirty-five.
8. Allison Reed, session 30, January 11, 1995. Incident: December 1994, age thirty-one.
9. Kathleen Morrison, session 11, February 6, 1995. Incident: January 4, 1995, age forty-five.
10. Allison Reed, session 13, January 11, 1994. Incident: December 22, 1994, age thirty.
11. I have changed the abductees' pseudonyms for certain sexual episodes so that they will be protected.
12. "Beverly." Incident: 1994.
13. "Paula," session July 27, 1996. Incident: June 18, 1996. The lesion was biopsied and the laboratory report read, in part, "The blood clot is partially covered by squamous lining and seems to represent a thrombus occurring in a vein or hemangioma."

14. Stan Garcia, session 2, May 31, 1989. Incident: December 31, 1987, age thirty.

15. Terry Matthews, session 4, January 9, 1995. Incident: August 24, 1994, age forty-six. Kathleen Morrison, session 7, June 9, 1994. Incident: April 1994, age forty-four. Terry Matthews, session 12, October 20, 1995. Incident: September 1995, age forty-seven.

16. Susan Steiner, session 10, February 23, 1996. Incident: February 17, 1996, age forty-three. Allison Reed, session 10, November 29, 1993. Incident: November 22, 1993, age twenty-nine. Allison Reed, session 14, February 2, 1994. Incident: January 29, 1994, age thirty.

17. Allison Reed, session 20, April 29, 1994. Incident: October 1986, age twenty-three.

18. Reshma Kamal, session 5, March 18, 1996. Incident: February 27, 1996, age thirty-five.

19. Allison Reed, session 23, April 29, 1994. Incident: October 1986, age twenty-three.

20. Doris Reilly, session 4, February 21, 1994. Incident: fall 1960, age five.

21. "Emily," session, August 3, 1993. Incidents: February 1977; March 1977.

22. "Sally," session, January 10, 1996. Incident: 1965.

23. "Emily," session, May 11, 1993. Incident: June 1970.

24. "Donna," session, July 26, 1995. Incident: 1963.

25. "Emily," session, April 2, 1993. Incident: September 1977.

Chapter 10: Independent Hybrid Activity

1. One woman videotaped some unmarked helicopters flying around her house and eventually followed them. They landed at a nearby air base, even though the base commander had initially told her that there were none there. He later admitted the existence of helicopters at the base. That same woman also had independent hybrid activity during which the hybrids arrived in helicopters.

2. Susan Steiner, session 9, January 10, 1996. Incident: June 1965, age thirteen.

3. "Donna," session, June 1995. Incident: August 1969.

4. "Donna," session, December 1995. Incident: February 12, 1982.

5. "Deborah," session, February 1994. Incident: February 6, 1994.

6. "Deborah," session, July 1995. Incident: July 20, 1995.

7. "Laura," session, May 1994. Incident: February 1993.

8. "Beverly," session, February 1994. Incident: February 16, 1994.

9. "Beverly," session, May 1994. Incident: May 3, 1994.

10. "Beverly," session, July 1994. Incident: July 22, 1994.

11. "Beverly," session, July 1996, Incident: June 1996.

Chapter 11: The Nature of Alien Intentions

1. John Salter (John Hunter Gray), "No Intelligent Life Is Alien to Me," Internet Web Site: UFO Directory and Forum, 1995, p. 1.

2. Leo Sprinkle, Lecture, Project Awareness UFO Conference, Gulf Breeze, Fla., May 1994.

3. Richard Boylan, *Close Extraterrestrial Encounters: Positive Experiences with Mysterious Visitors* (Tigard, Ore.: Wildflower Press, 1994), p. 156.

4. Richard Boylan, Lecture, Project Awareness UFO Conference, Gulf Breeze, Fla., May 1994.

5. Ibid.

6. Joseph Nyman, "The Familiar Entity and Dual Reference in the Latent Encounter," *MUFON Journal*, March 1989, pp. 10–12. See also Joseph Nyman, "The Latent Encounter Experience—A Composite Model," *MUFON UFO Journal*, June 1988, pp. 10–12.

7. Joe Nyman, "Forward [sic] to 'Abductees Anonymous,'" Internet Web Site: Abductees Anonymous, 1996, p. 4. Nyman has been ambivalent about whether his abductees actually were aliens in another life, although he believes that their accounts are not confabulated. See Joseph Nyman, "Dual Reference in the UFO Encounter," in Andrea Pritchard, David E. Pritchard, John E. Mack, Pam Kasey, and Claudia Yapp, eds., *Alien Discussions: Proceedings of the Abduction Study Conference Held at MIT* (Cambridge, Mass.: North Cambridge Press, 1994), pp. 142–48.

8. John Mack, "Foreword," in David M. Jacobs, *Secret Life: Firsthand Accounts of UFO Abductions* (New York: Simon & Schuster, 1992), p. 12.

9. Mack, "Foreword," pp. 12–13.

10. Pritchard et al., eds., p. 146.

11. "Ecology Awareness—Susan," in Pritchard et al., eds., p. 152.

12. Leah Haley, *Ceto's New Friends* (Tuscaloosa, Ala.: Greenleaf Publications, 1994).

13. John Salter (John Hunter Gray), "An Account of the Salter UFO Encoun-

ters of March, 1988: Their Background, Development, and Ramifications," privately published, 1992, pp. 14–15.

14. Salter, "Account," p. 21.
15. Richard Boyland, Lecture, Gulf Breeze, 1994. See also Richard Boylan, *Close Extraterrestrial Encounters*, p. 18.
16. Richard Boyland, Lecture, Gulf Breeze, 1994.
17. Nyman, "Forward" [sic], p. 2.
18. Howard Menger, narrative for the record album *The Song From Saturn*, ca. 1961.
19. See David M. Jacobs, *The UFO Controversy in America* (Bloomington: Indiana University Press, 1975).
20. Interview with John Mack, in C. D. B. Bryan, *Close Encounters of the Fourth Kind: Alien Abductions, UFOs, and the Conference at M. I. T.* (New York: Alfred A. Knopf, 1995), p. 271.
21. John E. Mack, *Abduction: Human Encounters with Aliens* (New York: Charles Scribner's Sons, 1994), p. 390. See also John Mack, "Helping Abductees," *International UFO Reporter*, July/August 1992, pp. 10–15, 20.
22. Mack, *Abduction*, p. 19.
23. Mack, *Abduction*, p. 46.
24. Mack, *Abduction*, p. 391. Experienced researchers have found that an interactive dynamic will always exist between abductee and researcher, but it is of the utmost importance that the researcher separate his own viewpoint from the abductee's testimony. Any analysis of the testimony must take into account the analyst's and the subject's preconceptions. For Mack, this is not a major concern. The interactive dynamic is an important therapeutic tool. The intertwining of the two personalities—abductee and investigator—often creates a fictional account that Mack finds desirable and therapeutically meaningful.
25. Mack, *Abduction*, p. 61.

Chapter 12: Life as We Know It?

1. Pam Martin, session 2, September 26, 1994. Incident: July 1984, age fifty.
2. Lucy Sanders, session 12, January 23, 1995. Incident: January 1995, age thirty-eight.
3. Kathleen Morrison, session 21, October 23, 1995. Incident: summer 1971, age twenty-one.

4. Patti Layne, session 3, August 5, 1987. Incident: September 1979, age sixteen.

5. Terry Matthews, session 8, March 24, 1995. Incident: November 4, 1988, age forty.

6. Allison Reed, session 23, June 7, 1994. Incident: October 1986, age twenty.

7. Roxanne Zeigler, session 4, July 25, 1984. Incident: June 24, 1995, age forty-nine.

8. Claudia Negrón, session 9, March 1, 1996. Incident: February 26, 1996, age fifty-four.

9. Kay Summers, session 7, December 13, 1993. Incident: December 5, 1993, age twenty-nine.

10. Susan Steiner, session 5, October 9, 1995. Incident: September 30, 1995, age forty-three.

11. Pam Martin, session 3, October 12, 1994. Incident: August 2, 1994, age fifty.

12. Kathleen Morrison, session 13, April 3, 1995. Incident: spring 1992, age forty-two.

13. Carla Enders, session 4, July 27, 1993. Incident: early 1993, age thirty-eight.

14. Kay Summers, session 1, August 3, 1993. Incident: July 1993, age twenty-eight.

15. Terry Matthews, session 13, November 17, 1995. Incident: August 5, 1995, age forty-six.

16. Pam Martin, session 11, May 2, 1995. Incident: December 23, 1994, age fifty-one.

17. Christine Kennedy, session 8, July 8, 1992. Incident: March 1991, age thirty.

18. Charles Petrie, session 12, February 26, 1991. Incident: 1986, age thirty-four.

19. Allison Reed, session 5, September 20, 1993. Incident: September 3, 1993, age twenty-nine.

20. Pam Martin, session 15, September 26, 1995. Incident: 1975, age thirty-one.

21. Reshma Kamal, session 7, October 28, 1996. Incident: October 14, 1996, age thirty-six.

22. Steve Thompson, session 2, October 8, 1989. Incident: 1969, age nineteen.

23. Patti Layne, session 19, January 16, 1989. Incident: summer 1979, age sixteen.

24. Carla Enders, session 6, July 28, 1993. Incident: October–November 1963, age eight.

25. Allison Reed, session 5, September 20, 1993. Incident: September 9, 1993, age twenty-nine.

26. Pam Martin, session 25, December 13, 1996. Incident: January 1970, age twenty-six.

27. Brad Hopkins, David M. Jacobs, and Ron Westrum, *Unusual Personal Experiences: An Analysis of the Data from Three National Surveys Conducted by the Roper Organization* (Las Vegas: Bigelow Holding Corporation, 1992), p. 24.

28. Courtney Walsh, session 5, June 17, 1993. Incident: June 12, 1993, age twenty-two.

29. Kathleen Morrison, session 20, August 9, 1995. Incident: August 1, 1995, age forty-five.

30. Claudia Negrón, session 3, April 27, 1995. Incident: early summer 1994, age fifty-two.

31. Allison Reed, session 16, March 4, 1994. Incident: February 21, 1994, age thirty.

32. Reshma Kamal, session 5, March 18, 1996. Incident: February 27, 1996, age thirty-five.

33. Claudia Negrón, session 3, April 7, 1995. Incident: early summer 1994; age fifty-two.

34. Pam Martin, session 3, October 12, 1994. Incident: August 7, 1994; age fifty.

35. Jason Howard, session 6, April 20, 1988. Incident: 1976, age seventeen.

36. Claudia Negrón, session 17, February 7, 1997. Incident: January 28, 1997, age fifty-five.

Index

About the Author

David M. Jacobs lives with his wife, Irene, and two children, Evan and Alexander, in a suburb of Philadelphia. He is associate professor of history at Temple University in Philadelphia. He has been a UFO researcher since the mid-1960s and is the author of numerous articles, papers, and presentations on the UFO and abduction phenomena. His previous books include *The UFO Controversy in America* (Indiana University Press, 1975) and *Secret Life: First-hand Accounts of UFO Abductions* (Simon & Schuster, 1992). He is considered the world's foremost academic scholar on the UFO and abduction phenomenon, and he teaches the only regular curriculum course on the subject in the United States.